BMW Airhead Twins
THE COMPLETE STORY

Other Titles in the Crowood MotoClassics series

AJS and Matchless Post-War Singles and Twins	Matthew Vale
BMW GS	Phil West
Classic TT Racers	Greg Pullen
Douglas	Mick Walker
Ducati Desmodue	Greg Pullen
Francis-Barnett	Arthur Gent
Greeves	Colin Sparrow
Hinckley Triumphs	David Clarke
Honda V4	Greg Pullen
Moto Guzzi	Greg Pullen
Norton Commando	Matthew Vale
Royal Enfield	Mick Walker
Rudge Whitworth	Bryan Reynolds
Triumph 650 and 750 Twins	Matthew Vale
Triumph Pre-Unit Twins	Matthew Vale
Velocette Production Motorcycles	Mick Walker
Velocette – The Racing Story	Mick Walker
Vincent	David Wright
Yamaha Factory and Production Road-Racing Two Strokes	Colin MacKellar

BMW Airhead Twins

THE COMPLETE STORY

PHIL WEST

THE CROWOOD PRESS

First published in 2020 by
The Crowood Press Ltd
Ramsbury, Marlborough
Wiltshire SN8 2HR

enquiries@crowood.com

www.crowood.com

© Phil West 2020

All rights reserved. No part of this publication may be reproduced or transmitted in any form or by any means, electronic or mechanical, including photocopy, recording, or any information storage and retrieval system, without permission in writing from the publishers.

British Library Cataloguing-in-Publication Data
A catalogue record for this book is available from the British Library.

ISBN 978 1 78500 695 1

Typeset and designed by D & N Publishing, Baydon, Wiltshire

Printed and bound in India by Parksons Graphics

CONTENTS

	Preface	6
	Introduction	7
CHAPTER 1	IN THE BEGINNING: THE BIRTH OF BMW	11
CHAPTER 2	1920–1930: THE MOVE INTO MOTORCYCLES	19
CHAPTER 3	1930–1940: BMW TAKES ON THE WORLD	47
CHAPTER 4	1940–1949: WAR TAKES ITS TOLL	76
CHAPTER 5	1950s: FROM BOOM TO BUST	87
CHAPTER 6	1960s: FROM BOOM TO BERLIN	106
CHAPTER 7	1970s: FROM SPANDAU TO SUPERBIKES	122
CHAPTER 8	1980s: AN AGE OF ADVENTURE	144
CHAPTER 9	1990s: THE END OF THE AIRHEADS?	173
CHAPTER 10	EPILOGUE	184
APPENDIX	AIRHEAD PRODUCTION NUMBERS	205
	Index	206

PREFACE

Say 'BMW motorcycle' and most motorcycle fans will automatically think 'airhead boxer twin'. The distinctive air-cooled, horizontally opposed, twin-cylinder engine layout has been so intrinsically linked with the legendary German marque that, for most of BMW's history, no other manufacturer has even attempted to use it.

And what a history that is. From powering the very first BMW motorcycle in the 1920s to style icons, racing and record-breakers in the 1930s; from wartime workhorses to a new generation of luxury tourers in the 1950s and 60s; and from the first faired superbike in the 1970s to the creation of the original 'adventure bike' in the 1980s, BMW's versatile airhead boxer was at the heart of them all. Consistently proving itself over the years, the engine became so beloved that, when BMW tried to replace it in the 1980s, a huge backlash ensued. It was quickly reinstated.

The backbone of the Bavarian marque was eventually 'killed off' in the 1990s, due mostly to environmental and regulatory demands, but its new oil-cooled replacement was deliberately as close to the original in terms of style and versatility as it could be. Even then it was not quite the end of the airhead. The iconic twin lives on today not just as a revered classic but also as a style icon that often forms the basis of numerous customs and specials. BMW regularly revisits the boxer back catalogue for its fashionable new retros and is currently developing an all-new air-cooled boxer twin, intended to be a big-bore cruiser rival to Harley-Davidson's equally legendary V-twins.

The BMW airhead story is certainly a biggie, then, spanning nearly a century and touching almost every type of motorcyclist. It has proved to be a demanding one to tell, and the writing of this book would not have been possible without the assistance of BMW itself, particularly BMW UK and BMW Motorrad's extensive archive in Munich. To them I give my thanks. Thanks are due too to my long-suffering and ever-patient wife, Sarah, who is my rock, and to my boys, Tom and Olly, not forgetting Sarah's Dylan, who are my inspiration. They all helped make the writing of this a pleasure. I hope I have done it justice and that you enjoy it, too.

Phil West, motorcycle journalist, editor and author

INTRODUCTION

No type of vehicle is more defined and characterized by its engine than a motorcycle. Comprising, according to popular folklore, of 'two wheels, an engine and not a lot else', a motorcycle's powerplant is not just its motive force, it also plays a major role in defining its image and character. It is its beating heart. The motorcycle owner is more than likely to know whether his or her engine is two- or four-stroke, its number of cylinders and their layout, and will probably even be familiar with the valve train, final drive system and state of tune. All those elements together give that 'beating heart' its character, create its appeal and encourage its fans and following. In comparison, how many car drivers would know much about the configuration of their four-wheeler's motor?

Where would Harley-Davidson be without its signature air-cooled, push-rod, 'potato-potato' 45-degree V-twins, which have been the American marque's staple since before the war? How about Ducati, legendary manufacturer of Italian exotica, which has been defined by its devotion to the Desmodromically-driven, 90-degree 'L-twin' since the early 1970s?

There are many more examples: historic British marque Triumph, although it has a recent tradition of in-line triples, is identified most with its classic, parallel twin, first created for the 1936 Speed Twin 500 and finding its ultimate expression in the iconic 1959 T120 R Bonneville. One of the Hinckley marque's latest new bikes is a modern take on that Speed Twin.

Moto Guzzi, the 'grand dame' of Italian motorcycling, has been inextricably and uniquely linked with its characteristic engine layout – the transversely mounted 90-degree V-twin complete with shaft drive – ever since the 1967 V7. Today, thoroughly evolved versions of that motor, in both small (750cc) and big block (now 1400cc) forms, continue to characterize the marque.

But the one motorcycle maker that is more closely associated with one particular type of motor than any other is BMW, with its boxer twin. Although periodically using other types of engine, such as singles, straight fours and, today, parallel twins, transverse fours and even straight sixes, the German manufacturer has relied on one type of engine – the flat, opposed-piston twin – for longer and over a wider range of models than any other manufacturer. (The possible exception is Harley-Davidson, with its Vees, although Harley did not adopt its signature V-twin until 1909, six years after the firm's foundation, whereas BMW motorcycles were boxer twins from the outset.)

The boxer twin layout was not actually a BMW invention. It dates back much further, to 1896, when German engineer Karl Benz pencilled a new four-stroke engine. His flat horizontally opposed twin-cylinder engine involved two pistons that reach top dead centre and bottom dead centre at the same time. The piston action was likened to two prize fighters trading blows, which is where the term 'boxer' engine was born. As a power unit it also had the advantages of being tightly packaged, robust and versatile.

It was not until 1920 that the newly reorganized aero engine company, BMW, became associated with the type. One of the company's leading engineers, Martin Stolle, had a British 500cc flat twin motorcycle, with the cylinders positioned fore and aft. This intrigued BMW designer Max Friz, who then designed his own version of the unit to be used primarily for aviation and as a static generator engine. This engine, designated the M2B15, was also sold to a number of up-and-coming German motorcycle manufacturers. Despite the inherent overheating problem of the fore/aft cylinder arrangement, it was such a success that BMW began to produce its own motorcycle using the engine, marketed under the Helios brand.

It was what happened next that truly set BMW motorcycles, and what became its signature boxer engine, on the road to success.

■ INTRODUCTION

FROM BARTER TO BMW – THE ORIGINS OF THE BOXER

The original idea for a horizontally opposed 'boxer' engine was first patented by German engineer Karl Benz in 1896 but it was a Briton, Joseph F. Barter, who first fitted it to a motorcycle. After fitting a single-cylinder motor to a bicycle in about 1902–1904 and finding it unsatisfactory, he tried a flat twin boxer instead, mounting a 200cc engine in line with the frame and quite high up. He used chain drive to a counter shaft with a clutch then connected to the rear wheel by a belt.

Barter's Light Motors Ltd put the 'Fairy' into production in 1905 but the company folded in 1907, and the rights to the motorcycle and engine were sold to Douglas Engineering. Douglas modified the Fairy by increasing capacity to 350cc. In 1911, the engine was moved lower in the frame and later gained mechanically operated valves. There were two models: a 350cc producing 2¾hp and a 544cc producing 4hp.

During the First World War, Douglas provided around 70,000 motorcycles to the military and at the end of hostilities many remained in Europe. In Germany, a 500cc Douglas found its way into the hands of Martin Stolle, works foreman at BMW, and this was the model that inspired BMW's chief engineer Max Friz. According to an alternative history, it was a British ABC design from 1919, which had a 400cc transversely mounted, chain-driven boxer twin, that had been sold to BMW. However, this has been flatly denied by the Bavarians…

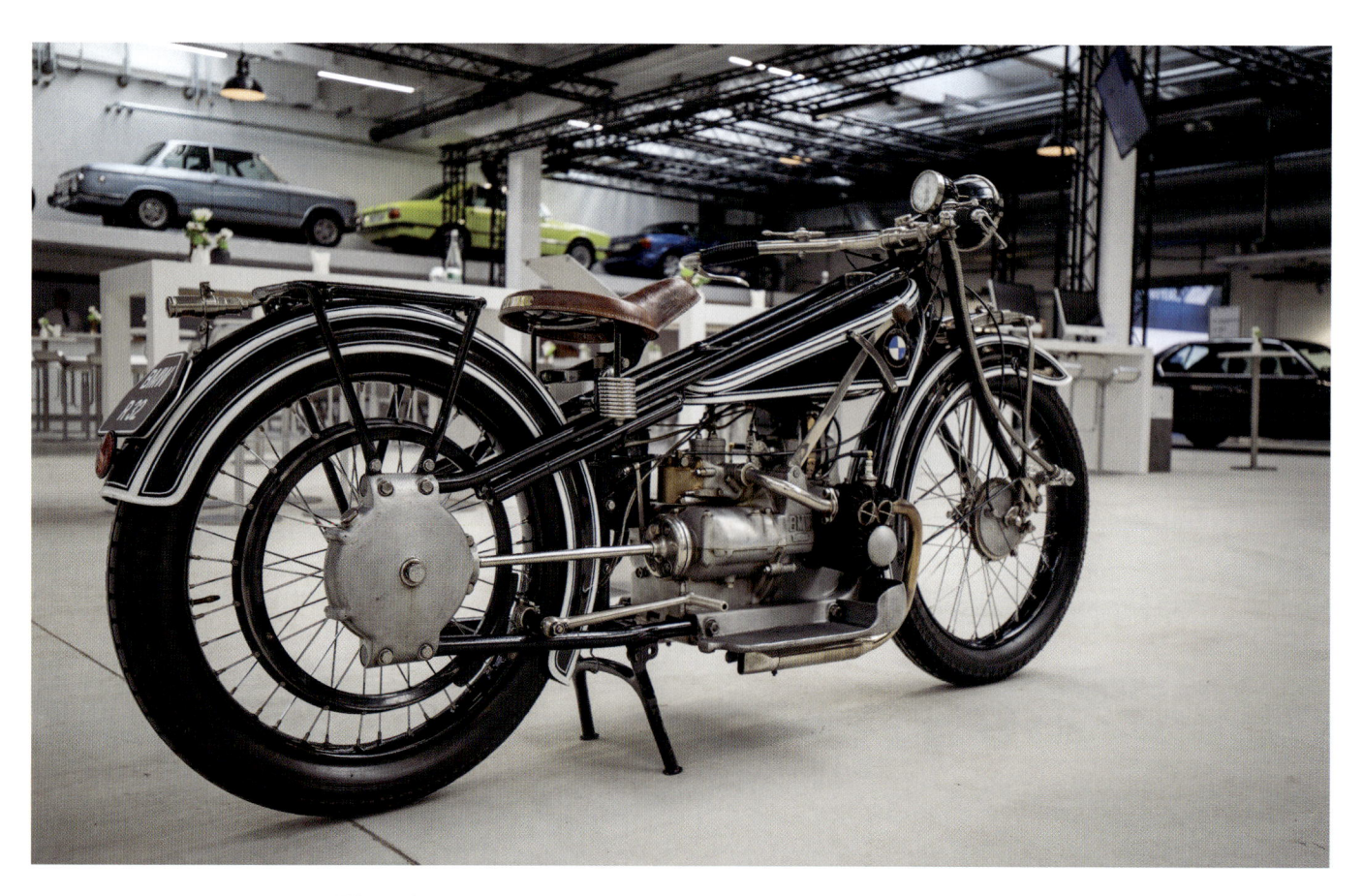

The original 'airhead', an R32 at the BMW Museum in Munich.

INTRODUCTION

Friz was a man of ingenuity. He soon realized that the overheating problem could be solved simply by turning the M2B15 engine through 90 degrees, so that the cylinders ran across the width of the frame. In this layout, both cylinders would be exposed to the passing air. The simple repositioning also allowed the use of a shaft final drive system, as the crankshaft now lined up with the gearbox, friction clutch and driveshaft. This proved to be a superior (direct and clean) method of delivering driving torque to the rear wheel in comparison with the usual chain and sprocket system. The crankshaft and three-speed gearbox of the revised 500cc M2B15 engine benefited further by being contained within their own cast cases, unlike the separate engine and gearbox pre-unit powerplants of many European motorcycle manufacturers.

Designated as the M2B33, the revised engine was the first true BMW boxer powerplant and would power the first Friz-designed BMW motorcycle, the 1923 R32. It was quite simply a revelation, so much so the Bavarian marque stuck with the distinctive engine layout for decades of successors. BMW did build smaller singles from time to time as a cheaper alternative to the larger, more luxurious twins. However, by the outbreak of the Second World War, and particularly as the German firm grew in the 1950s and 60s as a specialist manufacturer of luxury, large-capacity touring motorcycles, the words 'BMW' and 'boxer' became synonymous.

Of course, it took other great machines after the R32 to cement that identity – and there were plenty. There was the pre-war (1937) Kompressor, which became the first foreign winner of the Senior TT and also set a land speed record. There was the wartime R75, which was arguably the best military motorcycle of all and went on to be blatantly copied both in Russia and the USA. At the beginning of the 1950s came the 500cc R51, while the end of the decade saw the introduction of the sporty 600cc R69. The end of the 1960s was the era of the all-new /5 series, which was followed in the 70s by not just the R90S but also the revolutionary, aerodynamically faired R100RS. Then in the early 1980s came the truly ground-breaking R80G/S, the world's first adventure bike.

All of these machines – and many more – were air-cooled, opposed-piston flat twins. As such, they were instrumental in creating the BMW boxer legend. The story of those bikes, of the creation of BMW, of its inspired designs, and of all of the different air-cooled boxers, right up to their ultimate replacement in the 1990s, is one that has it all: revolutionary designers, heroic racers, wartime conquests, adversity and triumph, innovation and glory – and, of course, brilliant BMW bikes. Loads of them. No wonder they retain such a strong and devoted following to this day.

The TT-winning supercharged BMW Kompressor.

The 1960 R69S, one of the most revered BMW boxers of all.

The iconic 1973 R90S (and rider in period gear!).

The 1980 R80G/S, the boxer that saved BMW and created the 'adventure' class.

CHAPTER ONE

IN THE BEGINNING: THE BIRTH OF BMW

*The original **BMW** roundel logo. Today it is one of the world's most recognized brands.*

To appreciate fully the history and culture of BMW motorcycles and thus the origins and philosophy surrounding the company's use of the airhead boxer twin, it is useful to have an understanding of the origins of BMW itself. At its inception, the company was about anything but bikes.

The Bayerische Motoren Werke (or, in English, Bavarian Motor Works) is now primarily known for cars such as the X5 or 3 series, with motorcycles a comparatively minor, although still important, sideline. It now includes the historic British Mini brand as well as Rolls-Royce. As recently as 2018, the company built in excess of 2,500,000 vehicles, in plants in countries as diverse as Brazil, Egypt, India, South Africa, the USA and, of course, Germany. BMW motorcycle production for the same period, meanwhile, was around 150,000 globally, with the vast majority of those built in Germany at the Spandau Factory in Berlin. (The exception is BMW's recent, entry-level G310 single-cylinder family of machines, which are made in association with TVS in Chennai, India.)

BMW's origins, however, at the beginning of the twentieth century, were very different, with the 'motoren' in the name applying more to aircraft engines than to any other type.

Although the company's official history dates its founding to 7 March 1916, the story of BMW's origin is less clear-cut. For example, the company did not officially adopt the BMW name until a year after its formation. To add to the confusion, the BMW name was then transferred to a different company in 1922. Essentially, however, the birth of BMW is the story of two fledgling aero companies in the 'Wild West' aviation days of the First World War. One specialized in planes while the other focused on engines, and the two were eventually merged to become one.

BMW motorcycles came about as a result of the post-First World War Treaty of Versailles in 1919, which forbade German aircraft production for five years. (Another, later, by-product was the formation of Messerschmitt in the 1930s from the remnants of one of the old aero firms, which later became responsible for the Bf 109 and Me 262 of the Second World War.) Looking to save the company after the ban on aircraft production, BMW began to supply proprietory engines to other motorcycle manufacturers, and made the move into producing its own motorcycles in 1923. Perhaps this history helps to explain why, today, motorcycles remain such an important part of the BMW identity. The subsequent move into car manufacture came only in 1928, after BMW purchased the Automobilwerk Eisenach car company.

BMW's modern headquarters and museum in Munich.

The early twentieth century was an exciting, dynamic and pioneering time for the development of aviation, with daring, ambitious young men being inspired by the record-breaking feats of the Wright Brothers in 1903 and Louis Blériot in 1909. It was a fascinating period characterized by the rapid emergence (and often just as swift disappearance) of new aircraft companies. In Germany, one of the very first of these was the Aeroplanbau Otto-Alberti workshop near Munich, founded in 1910 by Gustav Otto, the son of Nikolaus Otto, who had defined the principle of the four-stroke internal combustion engine in the 1860s. Renamed Gustav Otto Flugmaschinenfabrik in 1911, this company began aircraft manufacture specializing in the 'pusher' propelled aircraft then used by the Royal Bavarian Flying Corps.

Flugwerk Deutschland was another of those early aviation companies, founded in 1912 to manufacture aircraft and aero engines. Although headquartered near Aachen, it also had a branch in Munich at a former bicycle factory, managed by Joseph Wirth and a young aero engine designer by the name of Karl Friedrich Rapp. As was common in those days, Flugwerk ceased operations in 1913. Rapp, along with Viennese investor, Julius Auspitzer, purchased the remnants and founded a new company, Rapp Motorenwerke, to continue engine and aircraft production at the Munich site. It was Rapp Motorenwerke that became the core business from which BMW would later emerge.

Rapp's proximity to Otto was crucial – indeed, one of the reasons for Rapp launching his business was because he had a contract with Otto to supply four-cylinder Type II aero engines. With the onset of war in 1914 the demands for that engine, and for other types, increased, and Rapp was able to expand his business rapidly. However, this growth would also, ultimately, prove to be the cause of Rapp's demise, in turn leading to the creation of BMW.

One of the newer engines demanded by the war ministry was the Austrian Austro-Daimler V12. In early 1916, Viennese Franz Josef Popp, who worked for the Austro-Hungarian government, was looking for a sub-contractor to help manufacture the V12. Although he was sceptical about Rapp's own abilities in terms of design and production, he recognized that his company had good facilities and a talented workforce. Rapp Motorenwerke was awarded the contract, with the proviso that Austro-Daimler would delegate an officer to Munich to oversee quality control. That man was Popp himself.

A disciplinarian with an obsessive eye for detail, Popp quickly became increasingly involved in the running of the entire company at Rapp Motorenwerke. Rapid expansion led to a need for capital investment, which came from central government, along with state control. Karl Rapp, meanwhile, had become distracted in trying to gain recognition for his new six-cylinder engine, basically a Type II four-cylinder unit with two extra cylinders crudely grafted on. The clumsy design was not a success. The unevenly spaced cylinders and asymmetrical crank resulted in an inordinate degree of vibration, so much so that the Prussian ministry, despite its

IN THE BEGINNING: THE BIRTH OF BMW

GUSTAV OTTO – LAYING BMW'S FOUNDATIONS IN FLIGHT

Gustav Otto was key to the creation of what would become BMW.

The son of Nikolaus Otto, the inventor of the four-stroke internal combustion engine, Gustav Otto was a leading pioneer in the German aircraft and aero engine industry in the early 1900s. He was to be integral to the formation of what would become BMW.

After first founding the Aeroplanbau Otto-Alberti workshop, Otto designed, in 1910, a biplane which created a sensation. Several companies later, in 1913, after selling 47 aircraft to the Bavarian Army, Otto opened the Otto-Flugzeugwerke factory. He chose Munich for its location, in order to be close to the German government's military procurement process.

Despite Otto's success, however, wartime stresses led to financial problems (and his own medical issues), which ultimately led to his forced resignation. In February 1916, his assets were taken over and reorganized to become Bayerische Flugzeugwerke, which was owned by engineering company MAN and a consortium of banks. The new company, known as BFW for short, and later the site and shell into which BMW was moved, was officially registered on 7 March 1916 – the date is recorded today by BMW's corporate history as marking its foundation.

Following the First World War, Otto began a new move into automobile manufacture with the Starnberger Automobilwerke, but continued to suffer health and personal issues. He was divorced in 1924 and his ex-wife died in mysterious circumstances in 1925. Tragically, Otto committed suicide in 1926, at the age of just 43.

The original Otto-Flugzeugwerke factory.

■ IN THE BEGINNING: THE BIRTH OF BMW

KARL FRIEDRICH RAPP – BMW'S 'INDIRECT' FOUNDER

Karl Rapp. BMW was formed out of Rapp Motorenwerke.

Karl Friedrich Rapp was a German aero engine designer and engineer who went on to found Rapp Motorenwerke in Munich in October 1913. This was the company that went on to be re-formed as BMW. As such, although he was ousted from the company before it was renamed, Rapp is acknowledged today as an 'indirect' founder of BMW.

Rapp was born in 1882 in Ehingen, but little is known of his childhood. He trained as an engineer, being employed first by the Züst automotive company from 1908, before joining Daimler in 1911. He left Daimler in 1912, to head a branch of Flugwerke Deutschland near Munich.

After the liquidation of Flugwerke in 1913, Rapp and an Austrian investor named Julius Auspitzer bought the assets and set up Rapp Motorenwerke on the same site, with the intention to build and sell aircraft and automotive engines. With a contract to build the Otto Type II engine, expansion was rapid. By 1915, Rapp Motorenwerke employed 370 workers and was one of the key Bavarian companies contributing to the German war effort. However, many of Rapp's own designs were flawed and unsuccessful.

After the securing of a contract to build the Austro-Daimler V12 for the Austrian government, Rapp was joined by Franz Josef Popp, who was tasked to supervise the order on behalf of the Austrian war ministry. Rapp's design for a six-cylinder Type III engine had been rejected, so Popp employed designer Max Friz to come up with a new design, which was duly accepted. Rapp resigned shortly after, in spring 1916, leading to the reorganization of the company under Popp. It was renamed Bayerische Motoren Werke (BMW) GmbH the following year.

After leaving the eponymously named company, Rapp became chief engineer and head of the aero engine department of the L.A. Riedlinger Machine Factory, where he was employed until October 1923. In the 1930s Rapp moved to Switzerland, where he ran a small observatory. He died in Locarno in 1962.

desperate need for a high-performance six-cylinder Type III engine, refused to approve it.

At this point, Popp took matters into his own hands. First, he hired a young former Daimler engineer named Max Friz, who came armed with his own idea for a powerful, high-altitude aero engine – in other words, just what the Prussian war ministry were after. In the years to come, it was Friz who would become the designer of BMW's world-beating first motorcycle, the R32 of 1923.

Second, with government officials losing patience with Rapp and his flawed six-cylinder, Popp took his opportunity to make a radical change when a team of inspectors travelled to Bavaria. Their aim was to turn the Rapp works away from producing its own engines and towards manufacturing Daimler or Benz designs under licence, along with being a repair depot. According to BMW legend, Popp used the inspectors' lunchbreak to present Friz's plans for a new high-altitude, six-cylinder engine. The inspecting team were so impressed that they went on to place an order for 600 units – before a single prototype had been produced. In short, the Friz engine turned Rapp Motorenwerke into an essential contributor to the war effort virtually overnight and so changed the direction of the whole company.

However, it also signalled the end for Karl Rapp. The price of the lucrative contract was the removal of Rapp from control and a re-formation of the company. In April the following year it was renamed Bayerische Motoren Werke GmbH, and the first incarnation of BMW was born.

BMW's first product, naturally enough, was the Type III engine, which quickly became renowned for good fuel economy and, in Type IIIa form, for high-altitude performance. The resulting orders for the engine from the German military contributed to further rapid expansion. An increased requirement for capital investment and the

FRANZ-JOSEF POPP – BMW'S EARLY GUIDING FORCE

Franz-Josef Popp was one of the key men responsible for the founding of BMW, and its first general director, from 1922 to 1942.

Born in Vienna in 1886, he gained a degree in engineering in 1909 and at the beginning of the First World War joined the Austro-Hungarian and Royal Aviation Troops, where he oversaw aircraft engine production, latterly at the Austro-Daimler works. Identifying insufficient production capacity for its own new 12-cylinder aircraft engine, Austro-Daimler tasked Popp with finding a suitable manufacturer. The contract was awarded to Rapp Motorenwerke in Bavaria in 1916, and Popp was despatched to Munich to oversee production. Concerned about poor standards, he began to take on the role of Rapp factory manager and, aware that Rapp required a quality designer, hired Max Friz.

Following the failure of Karl Rapp's Type III design and the success of Max Friz's version, it was decided that Rapp should be removed from control of his eponymous company. Popp was installed as managing director and the company was reorganized, to be renamed as Bayerische Motoren Werke GmbH in April 1917. Following BMW's conversion into the public limited stock company BMW AG, in November 1918, Popp became chairman of the board and general director.

In the aftermath of the First World War, he attempted to diversify BMW's products and was instrumental in assisting Camillo Castiglioni in the creation of the new BMW AG in 1922. Following this, under Popp's management, BMW began to expand into motorcycles and motorized transport, including, from 1928, cars.

During the 1930s, BMW became Nazi Germany's leading aircraft engine manufacturer and, in 1933, Popp himself joined the Nazi Party, although he maintained he did so purely to prevent his removal as general director. Wartime tensions and disputes led to his removal in 1942 and, despite attempting to rejoin BMW after the war, he was unsuccessful. He died in Stuttgart in 1954.

Franz Josef Popp was a crucial force behind BMW right through its early years.

---

financial difficulties that came with it also led to BMW being floated as a public limited company: BMW AG was founded on 13 August 1918, taking over all the assets, workforce and orders from BMW GmbH. The private company was wound up on 12 November 1918. The share capital of the new BMW AG amounted to 12 million reichsmarks and was bought by three groups of investors. One third of the shares was taken up in equal parts by two banks, another third was acquired by Nuremberg industrialist Fritz Neumeyer, and the final third was taken up by Viennese financier Camillo Castiglioni, who would later be instrumental in the re-direction of BMW.

The biggest difficulty for original BMW came with the end of the First World War. Under the terms of the Treaty of Versailles in 1919, all German companies were banned from aircraft production. BMW was forced to turn to farm equipment, household items and railway brakes, and, as was the case for much of the post-war German economy, times were hard. Railway brakes were the most lucrative area of manufacture, being sub-contracted from railway company Knorr-Bemse, but BMW was still barely profitable and most of its aircraft skills, patents and facilities, remained unused. By 1920, most of BMW, including Castiglioni's shares, had been absorbed by Knorr-Bemse.

BMW was not the only former German aero company facing troubled times. Despite initial success, Gustav Otto's pioneering Flugmaschinenfabrik also quickly ran into difficulties, particularly after the onset of war. In 1916, financial pressures led to the company being taken over by a consortium of banks and reorganized as Bayerische Flugzeugwerke AG, or BFW, on 7 March of that year – incidentally, the same date that is considered to mark the birth of the BMW company, for reasons that will become shortly clear…

Max Friz designed the first Type III engine before moving into motorcycles.

BELOW: **Production of the 500th Type IIIa aero engine in 1918. This was the engine that launched BMW to success.**

THE ORIGINS OF THE BMW ROUNDEL

Today, BMW's blue and white roundel logo is one of the world's most recognized and revered commercial symbols, but its origins are not generally well known.

The name Bayerische Motoren Werke was first registered in July 1917 by Franz Josef Popp, who was keen to distance the new aero engine company from the old Rapp Motorenwerke. The first trademark, however, was not registered until 5 October of that year. It was an evolution of the old Rapp logo, featuring the same circular design, but one key difference was the insertion of the letters 'BMW' into the top section of the outer ring. The inner section was divided into quadrants in blue and white, inspired by the colours of the Bavarian Free State, but in reverse order – it was illegal in Germany at that time to use national symbols in commercial trademarks.

Contrary to popular folklore, the logo was not in any way originally intended to represent an aircraft engine or propeller. That association comes from a 1929 advertisement, which featured aircraft with the image of the roundel in the rotating propellers. The advertisement was created following BMW's successful acquisition of a licence to manufacture the American Pratt & Whitney radial aircraft engine. It was a significant development for BMW, which came at a time when the business world was about to enter the Great Depression.

The concept of the spinning propeller was given further exposure in an article written by Willhelm Farrenkopf, published in 1942 in a BMW journal. This also featured an image of an aircraft with a spinning roundel and the folklore was born.

In the original design of the roundel, the lettering and outline were in gold, but by the time the first BMW motorcycle, the R32, was released, in 1923, it had changed slightly. The letters were still in gold but the font was bolder and the letters were closer together. This was the style that was submitted to the German Register of Trade Marks in 1933, although a variety of versions were still used. Proportions changed, the shade of blue varied and the lettering could be in gold, white or silver, with serif or sans serif fonts in different sizes, with little rhyme or reason.

By the 1950s, there was a more concerted effort to standardize the roundel, with white lettering that became silver when used on cars and motorcycles. In the 1960s the serif font was replaced by sans serif, and this was being used on all motorcycles by 1966. A slightly bolder font was adopted subsequently and this has remained as the standard.

The company briefly flirted with an additional variant in the early 1970s and 80s, conceived to identify its high-performance 'M' cars. This comprised the standard BMW roundel but with the BMW Motorsport 'rainbow' colours surrounding it. In 1997, BMW moved to depicting the roundel in 3D when used in the printed form, giving it a bolder look. Today the BMW roundel is ranked in the top ten of the world's most recognized commercial logos and is an iconic symbol in its own right.

The new BMW logo was based on that of Rapp Motorenwerke, with the addition of the colours of Bavaria.

1916 1923 1936
1954 1970s-1980s Current

Over the years, the BMW roundel has continually evolved.

■ IN THE BEGINNING: THE BIRTH OF BMW

FIRST SOARING SUCCESS – THE BMW TYPE III, IIIA AND IV AERO ENGINES

The first product of the newly formed Bayerischen Motoren Werke, or BMW, in 1917, was the Type III engine designed by Max Friz, which had also been dubbed 'BBE'. It was water-cooled, and laid out in an in-line six-cylinder configuration, which guaranteed optimum balance and therefore little vibration. Registered on 20 May 1917, it was quickly a success, but an even bigger breakthrough came later that year when Friz integrated a simple throttle butterfly into the 'high-altitude carburettor', which enabled the engine to develop its full power high above the ground. This was the reason why the engine, now known as the Type IIIa, gained unique superiority in air combat.

In 1918, the engine was used to power a BFW biplane to an altitude of 5,000 metres in just 29 minutes. It was an impressive feat that led to strong demand for BMW engines from the German military, in turn leading to the rapid expansion of BMW. Later, a Type IIIa was also used to power a Junkers F.13 passenger aircraft, which, with eight people on board, reached an altitude of 6750 metres, a record for a passenger aircraft. The following year, on 17 June 1919 – just before the terms of the Treaty of Versailles prohibited the German manufacture of aircraft engines – a successor to the Type IIIa, the Type IV, was used to set a new world altitude record. The plane was a DFW-F37/III, piloted by BMW test pilot Franz-Zeno Diemer, and took 89 minutes to reach 9760 metres (32,013ft). It was BMW's first official world record.

ABOVE: **The setting of a world altitude record in 1918 fuelled BMW's first successes.**

Franz-Zeno Diemer before setting his world altitude record in 1919.

CHAPTER TWO

1920–1930: THE MOVE INTO MOTORCYCLES

At the start of the 1920s, BMW was in virtual disarray. Banned from aero engine manufacture, its facilities were under-utilized and it was barely solvent. It was also, technically, not even the same company it would soon become following a takeover, merger and renaming. That came in 1922 and led directly to BMW's emergence as a motorcycle manufacturer, with the pioneering, radical – and, crucially, boxer-twin-powered – Max Friz-designed R32 in 1923. Before then, however, a number of crucial developments took place.

THE 'BAYERN ENGINE'

The signing of the Treaty of Versailles in June 1919 was an event that not only fundamentally re-shaped Europe, and particularly Germany, but also indirectly created a new future for BMW. Banned from manufacturing military aircraft and engines, the company whose only First World War product was the Type IIIa aero engine was suddenly forced to find alternative work. At first, BMW tried to sell cut-down aero engines to the marine and industrial sector, but there were not enough orders to keep the company going. In the end, BMW owed its survival to Knorr-Bremse, a railway brake manufacturing firm that was looking for contracts in Bavaria.

Although it was now profitable, BMW's aero engine patents, aluminium foundry and other aero facilities remained idle – so much so that, in 1920, major shareholder Camillo Castiglioni decided to sell his BMW shares to the chairman of Knorr-Bremse. Still seeking alternative work for its facilities, BMW general director Popp asked works foreman Martin Stolle to come up with a small proprietary engine for use as a generator. Stolle had a British Douglas motorcycle powered by a longitudinal boxer twin engine. Engineer Max Friz suggested 'reverse-engineering' the engine and the result was the M2B15, a portable, 494cc air-cooled boxer twin that produced 8.5bhp at 3,400rpm. It quickly came to the attention of some of Germany's fledgling motorcycle manufacturers and soon became known as the 'Bayern engine'.

Heller, Biso, Corona and Victoria are some of the earliest recorded motorcycle manufacturers who used the Bayern engine to power their motorcycles. However, while it proved reliable as a generator, installing it in a motorcycle chassis, with the two cylinders running in-line with the length of the frame, tended to restrict the cooling effect of the air passing over the rear cylinder. Despite some overheating problems, the engine was such a success that BMW eventually decided to use it to produce its own motorcycle. The first BMW-powered motorcycle was born under the manufacturing name of Helios, a brand inherited in the company merger. (Around the same time, incidentally, BMW also developed and manufactured a small motorized bicycle powered by a Kurier two-stroke engine and called 'Flink'. This proved unsuccessful.)

THE BIRTH OF BMW

Towards the end of 1921, financier Camillo Castiglioni, who had earlier sold his shares in BMW AG, became significant in the story again. With engine specialists BMW becoming more and more subsumed into Knorr-Bremse, and Helios owner Bayerische Flugzeugwerke similarly struggling on, Castiglioni made a bid for BFW. By early 1922, with the assistance of BMW's Franz Popp, he had convinced owners MAN to sell up. Then, with the Munich manufacturing facility of BFW's former Otto works in his pocket, the Helios motorcycle that came with it and the ban on aero engines about to be lifted, Castiglioni did another audacious deal: on

■ 1920–1930: THE MOVE INTO MOTORCYCLES

THE FIRST BMW BOXER – THE M2B15

In 1921, Max Friz asked to borrow a British Douglas motorcycle owned by one of his foreman, Martin Stolle. His idea was to 'reverse-engineer' a new BMW light industrial engine from the bike. The resultant motor was the M2B15, a side-valve 494cc air-cooled longitudinal boxer twin that produced 8½hp at 3,400rpm. Adopted for a number of German motorcycles, including Victoria and the Helios, it became the inspiration for BMW's first complete motorcycle, the 1923 R32.

When Camillo Castiglioni bought the premises and manufacturing machinery of BFW, negotiated a separate deal for the engineering know-how and BMW brand and merged them together under the BMW name, one of the by-products was the formerly BFW-owned Helios motorcycle division, which used the BMW-built M2B15 engine. It was almost inevitable that a BMW-built and -branded motorcycle would follow.

ABOVE: **BMW's proprietory M2B15 engine paved the way for the company's move into motorcycles.**

German motorcycle manufacturer Victoria was among the first to use the BMW engine.

1920–1930: THE MOVE INTO MOTORCYCLES

Helios also used the BMW engine; it was subsequently absorbed by the Bavarian company as part of its reorganization.

Financier Camillo Castiglioni played a key part in BMW's re-organization.

21

■ 1920–1930: THE MOVE INTO MOTORCYCLES

CAMILLO CASTIGLIONI – THE MONEY MAN WHO CREATED MODERN BMW

Camillo Castiglioni was fundamental to the creation of the modern BMW.

Financier and banker Camillo Castiglioni was the wealthiest man in Central Europe during the First World War. He was also particularly significant in the early days of European aviation and in the formation of BMW.

He was born on 22 October 1879, the son of a rubber merchant, in Trieste, now in Italy but then part of Austro-Hungary. As a young man, he trained as a lawyer and quickly became an expert in international finance. He was also passionate about flying. Around 1901, along with Viktor Silberer and Franz Hinterstoissera, he helped found the Viennese aero club and quickly recognized the tremendous financial potential of an aviation industry. In 1914 he purchased German aircraft company Hansa, then acquired a majority holding in Austro-Daimler and was influential in the granting of a licence agreement to Rapp. In 1918, at Castiglioni's insistence, the Viennese Wiener Bankverein acquired the majority of the new BMW AG's share capital.

After selling his own BMW shares in 1920, in 1922 Castiglioni purchased all BMW's equipment relating to engine construction, the associated know-how and the rights to the name 'Bayerische Motoren Werke AG'. The Bayerische Flugzeugwerke was renamed BMW AG and the new company continued production at the BFW plant, with BMW moving into motorcycles.

Castiglioni was also one of the voices that urged BMW to purchase the Eisenach Automobilwerke in 1928 and so move into car production. Due to financial difficulties in 1929 he was obliged to surrender his holding of BMW shares to a consortium of banks. He retired to Switzerland, then Milan, where he set up a private bank and once again amassed a considerable fortune. He died in 1957.

20 May 1922, he bought the BMW name, logo and engine-building business (but not its premises) from Knorr-Bremse for 75 million reichsmarks.

With the deal done, Bayerische Flugzeugwerke was merged with BMW and the factory and headquarters were established at the old BFW premises. The new concern was renamed BMW and retained BFW's incorporation date of 7 March 1916. In short, the current BMW was born. To this day, the original establishment of BFW is recorded in the company's official history as the birth date of BMW. BMW's headquarters have been at the same address ever since.

BMW'S FIRST MOTORCYCLE

The newly incorporated and revitalized BMW moved quickly. First, later that year, an expanded factory – BMW's first – was built on the old Otto site. Second, following Victoria's switch to another engine supplier, and having

A new, expanded factory was built on the old Otto-Flugzeugwerke site.

acquired both Helios and the M2B15 engine, BMW decided to make its own major move into motorcycle manufacturing. The new chief engineer and designer Max Friz was in full support.

Friz was assigned by BMW's general director Popp to assess the Helios and propose a development plan. The Helios had never been particularly successful and had been criticized particularly for its poor suspension, so he quickly decided that the best thing to do was to scrap it and start again. With a new brief to create a machine that would not just be worthy of the BMW name but would also create a solid platform for future models, Friz and colleagues Rudolf Schleicher and Franz Bieber set to work.

The result, the R32, was released in 1923 and unveiled at the Berlin Motor Show in September of that year. It was the first true BMW motorcycle with the original, transversely mounted, air-cooled BMW boxer twin engine and was, quite simply, a revelation. Friz's master stroke had been to rotate the configuration of the previous MB215 twin through 90 degrees. The two cylinders, instead of pointing fore and aft, as with the Helios and preceding Douglas, now stuck out on each side, creating the BMW boxer twin layout that is so synonymous with the brand today.

■ 1920–1930: THE MOVE INTO MOTORCYCLES

ABOVE: **The Friz-designed R32 became BMW's first motorcycle in 1923.**

Max Friz's **M2B33** engine set the template for all future **BMW** boxers.

1920–1930: THE MOVE INTO MOTORCYCLES

The R32 proved instantly popular for its handling, quality and style.

BELOW: The transverse-mounted boxer enabled the use of shaft drive.

25

■ 1920–1930: THE MOVE INTO MOTORCYCLES

ABOVE: **The handsome styling and black/white livery of the R32 also became BMW staples.**

More than 3,100 R32s were built in just three years.

26

1920–1930: THE MOVE INTO MOTORCYCLES

1923–26 R32

Engine		Rear suspension	Rigid
Type	BMW air-cooled boxer twin	Tyres	26-3in cross-ply
Internal code	M2B33	Wheels	Wire spoke, steel rim
Block material	Cast iron	Rim width	2.5in
Head material	Cast iron		
Bore and stroke	68 × 68mm	*Brakes*	
Capacity	494cc	Type	Front 150mm drum, rear block
Valves	Side-valve, 2 valves per cylinder		
Compression ratio	5.0:1	*Dimensions*	
Carburettor	1 × BMW Spezial 22mm	Wheelbase	54.3in 1380mm
Max. power (DIN)	8.5bhp @ 3,200rpm	Overall length	82.7in 2100mm
Max. torque	N/A	Overall width	31.5in 800mm
Fuel capacity	3.07gall (14ltr)	Overall height	37.4in 950mm
		Unladen weight	268lb 122kg
Transmission			
Gearbox	3-speed, manual	*Performance*	
Clutch	Single dry plate	Top speed	59mph 95km/h
Final drive	Shaft	0–60mph	N/A
Chassis		Price	RM 2,200
Frame	Tubular steel twin loop		
Front suspension	Twin cantilever spring	No. built	3,090

This reorientation had two immediate advantages. First, it significantly improved cooling of the air-cooled unit. With the previous in-line arrangement, the rear cylinder in particular could overheat because of its being hidden from the airflow. The new transverse configuration meant that both cylinders were equally exposed to the air. The second benefit was that, because the crank and gearbox shafts had also been turned through 90 degrees, the desired Cardon-style shaft drive system was far more easily arranged. Friz then also redesigned the engine cases so that the crankshaft and three-speed gearbox were all lined up and included. It was a 'unit' design, unlike the separate engine and gearbox 'pre-unit' designs that many motorcycle manufacturers used right up to the 1960s. In addition, at a time when many motorcycles still used 'total-loss' lubrication systems, the new BMW engine featured a recirculating wet sump, again something that was not commonly used on motorcycles until the 1970s and the arrival of the Japanese.

Designated the M2B33, the result was the first purpose-built BMW motorcycle engine, which established the idea of the air-cooled, transverse boxer twin with shaft drive and was the basis of the first Friz-designed BMW motorcycle. However, although the boxer engine layout and shaft drive set the template for the majority of BMW motorcycles to follow, there was much more to the R32 than just the configuration of its motor.

The R32 also delivered very secure handling, partly due to the low centre of gravity created by the engine layout. It was easy to work on and it rapidly gained a reputation for reliability. Another reason for its success was its beautifully crafted aesthetics. Last but by no means least, disappointed by the inadequacies of the Helios and inspired by his background in aircraft, Friz also placed great emphasis on quality and durability, aspects that would become traditionally associated with BMW's boxer twin motorcycles over the years to come. From the outset, the R32 was a premium product, with a price to match. At 2200 reichsmarks in 1923 the R32 was significantly more expensive than most rivals.

The R32, however, proved a sensation, selling so successfully (3,100 in just three years) that it was able to secure the future of the whole BMW company.

27

■ 1920–1930: THE MOVE INTO MOTORCYCLES

THE FIRST OF MANY: THE 1923 BMW R32

In December 1922, barely five weeks after being given the go-ahead, BMW chief designer Max Friz completed the design of the revolutionary R32. The finished machine, with its distinctive, transversely mounted, air-cooled, shaft-driven boxer twin powerplant, went on public display in September the following year.

Like many brilliant motorcycling ideas – like, for example, BMW's own mould-breaking R80G/S in 1980 – the core idea of the R32 was incredibly simple and based on using as many existing components as possible.

Friz's brainwave was the reorientation of the boxer twin engine. BMW already had experience of this configuration, in its production of the M2B15 motor that was used, longitudinally, in the Helios. However, Friz wanted the new motorcycle to be shaft-driven, so that it would be less vulnerable to the dirt, sand and mud that were common on the poor roads and tracks of the day. The solution was to turn the boxer twin in the frame and make the engine and transmission in one unit. The added advantages were that the cooling of both cylinders would be improved and equalized, and that the machine would be easier to service. BMW motorcycles would quickly become associated with durability and ruggedness. This association began with the R32, and the unusual adoption of a wet-sump lubrication system that recycled the oil. The BMW tradition for boxer engines and overland touring motorcycles was born.

ABOVE: **Designed as a whole from the outset, the R32 was truly innovative.**

A striking profile and black livery became BMW staples up to the 1960s.

28

1920–1930: THE MOVE INTO MOTORCYCLES

Much of the rest of the R32 was relatively conventional: the new engine was housed in a welded, tubular steel duplex loop frame with a leaf-sprung front fork. Its performance was not particularly outstanding either – the 494cc side-valve unit produced 8.5bhp and was good for about 60mph. However, the combination of elements, helped by the low centre of gravity, delivered class-leading, sure-footed handling. The R32's durability and reliability impressed from the outset and, with an emphasis on quality and a finish that would be familiar to modern BMW owners, it was immediately identified as a quality, premium machine that few rivals could match.

The R32 was unveiled at the Berlin Motor Show on 28 September 1923. It was a date that marked the beginning of BMW as a motorcycle manufacturer, and established a template for generations of BMW motorcycles – an air-cooled boxer twin with cylinders mounted horizontally to the direction of travel and with an integral manual gearbox with shaft drive. And it has stood the test of time, with BMW working on the latest version – an all-new, 1800cc cruiser unit – today

RIGHT: **The engine's 'unit' construction, including the gearbox, was years ahead of competition.**

BELOW LEFT: **The hand gearchange, typical of the era, meant footboards not footpegs.**

BELOW RIGHT: **The R32 also redefined quality, although the lights in those days were extras.**

29

■ 1920–1930: THE MOVE INTO MOTORCYCLES

THE FATHER OF THE BMW BOXER – MAX FRIZ

German engine designer Max Friz was crucial to the new BMW company's success, initially in the aero industry then, in the 1920s, with its move into motorcycling. He designed not only BMW's most successful engine of the First World War era, but also its first complete motorcycle, the 1923 R32. As such, he is considered the father of the BMW air-cooled boxer.

Born on 1 October 1883, and originally from Urach, the young engineer was apprenticed to the Kuhn steam engine company in Cannstatt in 1898. In 1902, he enrolled at the Royal Building Trade School in Stuttgart-Esslingen, then, in 1906, he joined Daimler. In 1912–13, he designed the first practical German aircraft engines and also worked on the design of the engine for the Mercedes racing car that won the 1914 French Grand Prix.

Frustrated that chief engineer Paul Daimler was ignoring his suggestions on engine development, specifically for an over-sized, high-compression engine that Daimler was committed to supercharging, at the end of 1916 Friz applied to work at Rapp Motorenwerke. Initially, Karl Rapp considered turning him down, but before Franz Josef Popp intervened, aware Rapp lacked an able designer.

Designer Max Friz was the creator of the familiar BMW boxer engine layout.

Soon after staring work on 2 January 1917, Friz designed a new high-altitude aero engine with an innovative carburettor that was superior to any other German design. It would gain world renown as the Type IIIa. The success of the engine led to the exceptionally fast growth of the renamed Bayerische Motoren Werke GmbH. When the company was reformed in 1922, Friz was named the first chief engineer and design director of BMW AG. He was instrumental in the design of both BMW's first motorcycle engine, the M2B15 in 1921, and its first complete motorcycle, the R32, in 1923.

In 1937, with BMW's continued growth into automobiles, Friz succeeded Leo C. Grass as General Manager of Flugmotorenfabrik Eisenach GmbH, overseeing BMW's automobile engine design and development.

Friz retired in 1945 and was awarded an honorary degree from the Munich College of Advanced Technology in 1954. He died on 9 June 1966.

DEVELOPING AND UPDATING THE R SERIES

Significantly, BMW did not rest on its laurels. Friz's R32 was progressively improved throughout the 1920s, with the R37, then R42 and R52 of 1926–1928, to the R11 and R16 of 1929, with their pressed-steel frames.

The first of these came quickly. Motorcycle racing was hugely popular in the 1920s and many racers loved the R32, despite its modest 8.5bhp power output. Inspired by this, a racing version was quickly developed. In 1924, BMW engineer and keen racer Rudolf Schleicher developed an overhead-valve boxer engine, complete with lightweight aluminium cylinder heads and higher compression. After he had ridden his prototype to victory in the prestigious ADAC Winter Rally of that year, the prototype engine was officially developed into the M2B36 engine in 1925 and incorporated into the BMW R37 production model. This motorcycle shared the chassis of the R32 but made double the power – 16bhp. It was enough to propel it to an impressive collection of motorsport victories. In 1925 alone, more than 80 racing events were won by riders on R37s.

As BMW's motorcycle model range expanded, so its racing activities on two wheels grew increasingly diverse. Ernst Henne won the German championship in 1926 and the Targa Florio in 1928. In fact, up to 1929, *all* German championships in the 500cc class were won by BMW.

Throughout the rest of the decade, BMW would offer its standard tourers in side-valve form, with its more sporting and expensive variants using the overhead-valve version of the

1920–1930: THE MOVE INTO MOTORCYCLES

The 1924 ohv R37 became popular with racers.

boxer twin. In this way the R32, after three years in production, was the first to be updated, into the 1926 R42. Distinguished by detachable, lighter, aluminium cylinder heads that were now finned to assist with cooling, it produced 12bhp thanks to an uprated carburettor. With an updated chassis and a cheaper price tag than the original R32, the R42 was an instant sales success. More than 6,500 machines were produced in just two years and the model remained in production until it was replaced in 1928 by the R52. The R42 was also notable for having a drum front brake, and a contracting friction band on the driveshaft to help retard the rear, in place of the old block and pulley rear brake. Its new frame, which cradled the engine lower and further back, had improved weight distribution and enabled straight front frame down tubes to be used. (Electric lighting, incidentally, was still regarded as an 'extra' and would not be standardized until 1928.)

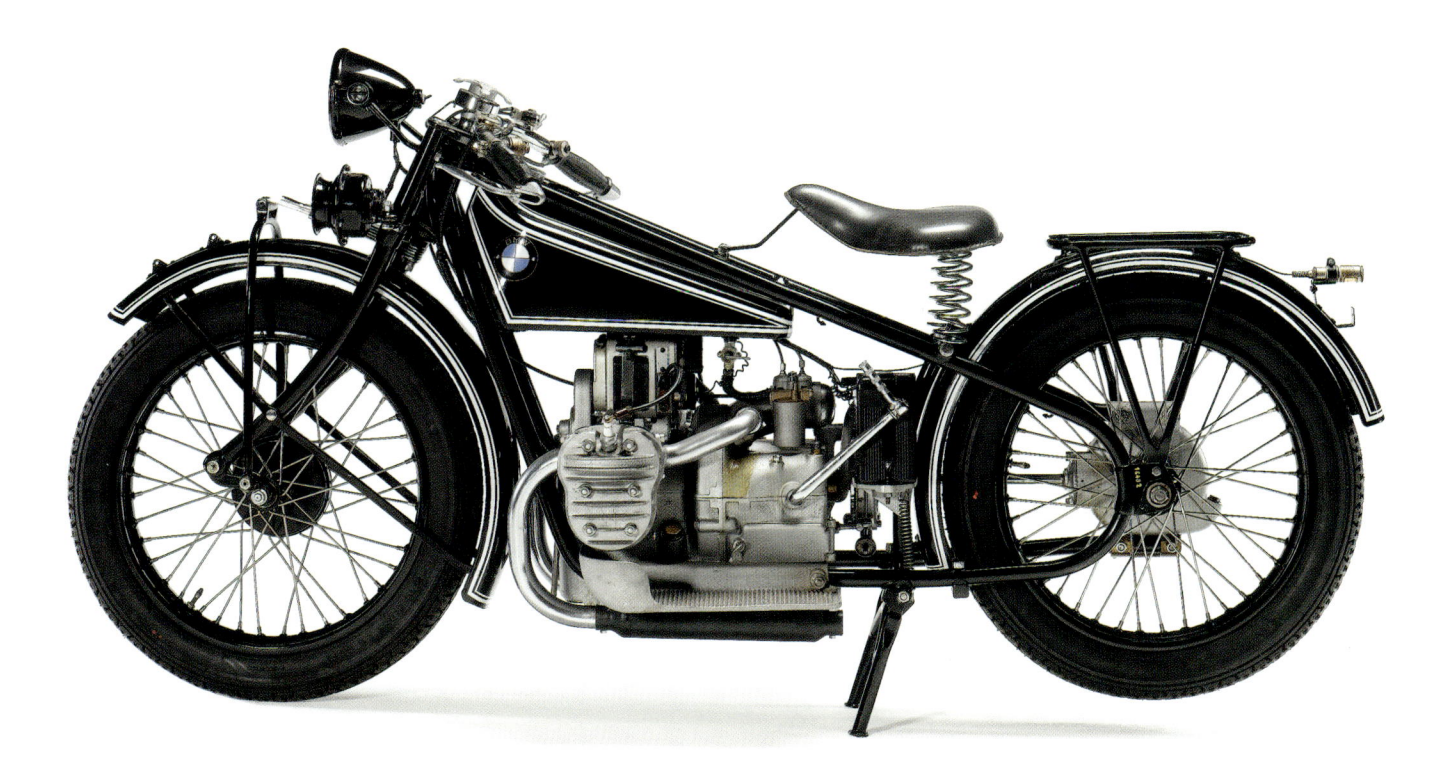

The first update to the R32 was with the R42 in 1926.

31

Later versions of the R42 had uprated brakes and lighting.

The ohv R37 was updated into the pricey R47 in 1927.

BMW's first 750s comprised the side-valve R52 and the ohv R63.

With 24bhp, the R63 was the sportiest BMW until the end of the 1920s.

■ 1920–1930: THE MOVE INTO MOTORCYCLES

With electric lights and uprated gearchange, the R63 was also the most refined model of the time.

1929's side-valve R11 and the ohv R16 (pictured here) featured new pressed-steel frames.

1920–1930: THE MOVE INTO MOTORCYCLES

When the sporty, overhead-valve R37 was also succeeded the following year, in 1927, it became the R47. This bike had the same chassis as the R42 but produced 18bhp, was capable of 68mph and was considerably more expensive.

In 1928, BMW brought out the final development of this first of the R series with revised engines and leaf-spring front suspension, and also, for the first time, offered 750cc versions. The short-stroke (68mm), 486cc, side-valve tourer was called the R52, produced 12bhp and replaced the R42. The sportier, ohv R57 produced 18bhp and replaced the R47. A longer-stroke (78mm) version of the side-valve displaced 745cc, was called the R62 and produced 18bhp, making it one of the fastest machines of its day.

Finally, there was a longer-stroke 745cc version of the sporty ohv-powered model, called, slightly confusingly, the R63. With an output of 24bhp and a top speed of over

THE NEED FOR SPEED

Along with a huge surge in interest in motorcycle racing, the 1920s were also characterized by a seemingly relentless quest to raise the world land speed record, both on four wheels and two. While the automobile land speed record was repeatedly contested by the likes of Malcolm Campbell and Henry Seagrove, who had achieved 231mph by the end of the decade, on two wheels it was people such as Bert le Vack battling on Brough Superiors. By 1929, the motorcyclists had raised that particular bar to 129mph.

When BMW decided to challenge for the record, they turned to a special, supercharged version of the 745cc ohv version of the boxer twin, dubbed the WR750. On 19 September 1929, BMW factory rider Ernst Henne was recorded at 134.6mph on a section of the new autobahn north of Munich. It was the first of six world land speed records that Henne would secure for BMW over the next eight years, topping out at 173.6mph in 1937.

BMW rider Ernst Henne achieves yet another victory on his R47 in 1926.

■ 1920–1930: THE MOVE INTO MOTORCYCLES

120km/h, this remained the sportiest BMW model until the end of the 1920s. These latest versions had electric lights as standard, a new gear lever that connected directly to the gearbox and also a new kick-starter at its rear. They were the most refined of all the first R series.

BMW was not quite done with the 1920s just yet. The Bavarian marque's second-generation boxer appeared in 1929, when the soldered, tubular steel frames of the early models gave way to all-new, pressed-steel versions, which gave the R11 and R16 models that used them a somewhat stylized, Art Deco appearance. It is no coincidence that the pressed-steel frames came shortly after BMW's move into car production a year earlier. The steel-pressing equipment and skills now available to BMW's motorcycle engineers gave them new possibilities and a pressed-steel frame, they decided, was both more rigid and cheaper to produce than one made from welded steel tubes.

Developed specifically for use with a sidecar, the R11 was the base model, with the R16 being a sportier version with twin carburettors that helped increase output to 33bhp. Both were quickly seen as typifying the 'German school' of motorcycle design – they were robust, stylistically quirky and above all practical. In the years that followed, frame design – like suspension-system design – was in a state of constant evolution, with the aim of providing a sportier ride, more comfort and improved safety.

BMW had come a long way in the 1920s, from producing its very first motorcycle, in 1923, to a state of continual development, with a series of landmark models, a number of speed records and more than a little race success. And alongside all this, it also came up with its first single-cylinder model, the 250cc R39 of 1925.

All told, this continued period of success went hand in hand with ever-increasing production figures. Between the first full year of production in 1924 and 1929, the number of units BMW delivered to customers rose from 1,640 to 5,680. A motorcycling dynasty was born.

BMW CARS

On top of its core business of aircraft engines, followed by its successful transition into motorcycles from 1923, BMW made its next diversification, this time into cars. In 1929 BMW took over Fahrzeugfabrik Eisenach, a metal fabricator whose facilities would be key for BMW's expansion. (It also

BMW first moved into cars by producing British Austin 7s in 1929.

1920–1930: THE MOVE INTO MOTORCYCLES

A BMW dealership in Berlin in 1929 selling cars and bikes.

made British Austin Sevens under licence.) Over time, these cars were developed and re-engineered, first into six-cylinder luxury vehicles and then, from 1936, into the BMW 328 sports car. As such, aero engines, motorcycles and cars would remain BMW's key products up to the Second World War.

Following the war and the fall of the Eisenach plant into Soviet hands, car production moved to Bavaria in 1952, commencing with the 501 luxury saloon. Sales were too low to be profitable, so BMW supplemented this with building Isettas under licence.

Throughout the austerity years of the 1950s, sales of luxury cars were slow, and at the same time the profit margins on BMW's micros cars were minimal. Both factors contributed to BMW finding itself on the verge of bankruptcy by the end of the decade, and the whole company almost being sold to Daimler-Benz. At the last minute, following a historic shareholders' meeting, shareholder and financier Herbert Quandt decided to take a controlling interest and quickly changed the direction of the company. Quandt's investment, along with the success of BMW's new 700 small car (which was powered, incidentally, by a modified motorcycle air-cooled boxer twin) set BMW on a new course to success in the 1960s and beyond.

KEY MODELS

1925–26 R37

BMW's second boxer was effectively a racing version of the R32, with new aluminium cylinder heads (a world first) and an overhead-valve system replacing the R32's side-valves. This improved airflow and enabled higher compression and a doubling of the power output. This 'alternative' ohv sports boxer approach would continue with BMW's updated models throughout the 1920s. The R37's chassis was virtually identical to that of the R32, but gained a flat spring front wheel rocker, drum brake to the front and rear brake wedge block. Despite having no lights, horn, speedometer or pillion seat, it cost 700 reichsmarks more than the R32. The year 1925 also saw the introduction of BMW's first single-cylinder machine, the 250cc R39.

The 1925 BMW R37 was a popular racing machine.

1925–26 R37

Engine
Type	BMW air-cooled boxer twin
Internal code	M 2 B 36
Block material	Cast iron
Head material	Aluminium
Bore and stroke	68 × 68mm
Capacity	494cc
Valves	ohv, 2 valves per cylinder
Compression ratio	6.2:1
Carburettor	1 × BMW Spezial 26mm
Max. power (DIN)	16bhp @ 4,000rpm
Max. torque	N/A
Fuel capacity	3.07gall (14ltr)

Transmission
Gearbox	3-speed, manual
Clutch	Single dry plate
Final drive	Shaft

Chassis
Frame	Tubular steel twin loop
Front suspension	Twin cantilever spring
Rear suspension	Rigid
Tyres	26-3in cross-ply
Wheels	Wire spoke, steel rim
Rim width	2.5in

Brakes
Type	Front 150mm drum, rear block

Dimensions
Wheelbase	54.3in 1380mm
Overall length	82.7in 2100mm
Overall width	31.5in 800mm
Overall height	37.4in 950mm
Unladen weight	295lb 134kg

Performance
Top speed	71mph 115km/h
0–60mph	N/A

Price RM 2900

No. built 152

1920–1930: THE MOVE INTO MOTORCYCLES

1926–28 R42

The R42 replaced the R32, with an updated side-valve engine producing 12bhp. This engine, called the M43a, retained the 68mm bore/stroke but gained new alloy cylinder heads and an uprated carburettor, although it retained the same three-speed gearbox. It also gained uprated brakes with an expanding shoe front and a rear that operated directly on to the driveshaft, and had a new frame that cradled the engine lower and further back. The price,

The replacement for the R32, the R42 featured new alloy cylinder heads.

1926–28 R42

Engine	
Type	BMW air-cooled boxer twin
Internal code	M43
Block material	Cast iron
Head material	Aluminium
Bore and stroke	68 × 68mm
Capacity	494cc
Valves	Side-valve, 2 valves per cylinder
Compression ratio	4.9:1
Carburettor	1 × BMW Spezial 2 valve 22mm
Max. power (DIN)	12bhp @ 3,400rpm
Max. torque	N/A
Fuel capacity	3.07gall (14ltr)

Transmission	
Gearbox	3-speed, manual
Clutch	Single dry plate
Final drive	Shaft

Chassis	
Frame	Tubular steel twin loop
Front suspension	Plate spring
Rear suspension	Rigid

Tyres	26-3in cross-ply
Wheels	Wire spoke, steel rim
Rim width	2.5in

Brakes	
Type	Front 150mm drum, rear external shoe on shaft drive

Dimensions	
Wheelbase	55.5in 1410mm
Overall length	82.7in 2100mm
Overall width	31.5in 800mm
Overall height	37.4in 950mm
Unladen weight	277lb 126kg

Performance	
Top speed	59mph 95km/h
0–60mph	N/A

Price	RM 1510
No. built	6,502

■ 1920–1930: THE MOVE INTO MOTORCYCLES

too, was significantly less than the R32, although lights, speedo, pillion seat and horn were extra. Thanks to a price reduction of 30 per cent, the unit volumes of the BMW R42 more than doubled compared with the BMW R32 to more than 6,500 units sold.

1927–28 R47

The R47 succeeded the R37 as the sporting model in BMW's line-up, with 2bhp more and a little less weight. It had the same chassis as the R42 but produced 18bhp and was capa-

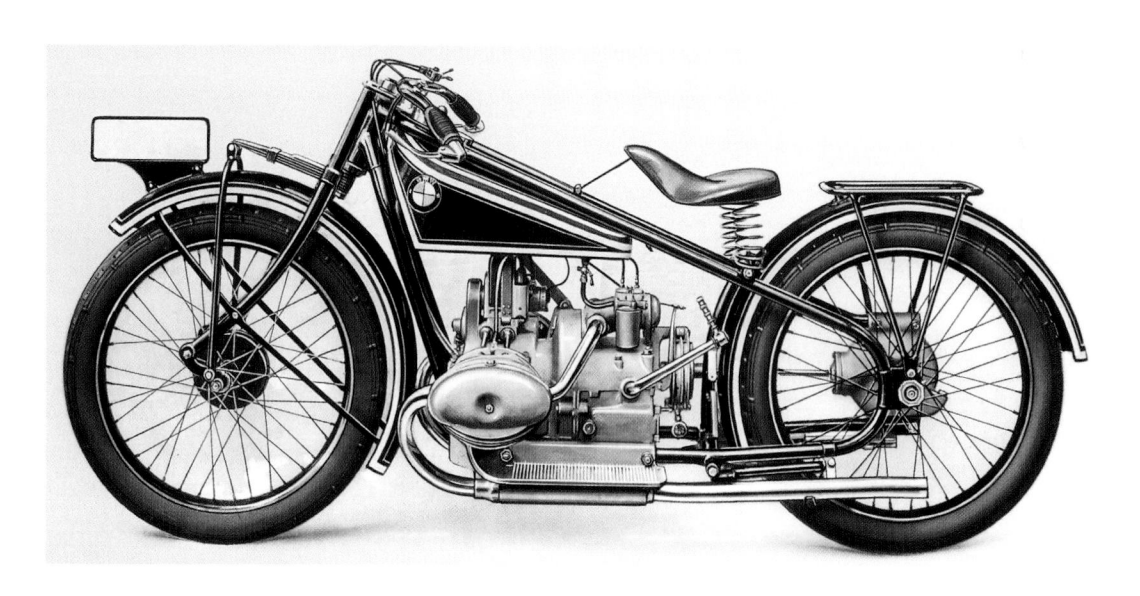

The overhead valve R47 succeeded the R37 and was the most powerful BMW yet.

1927–28 R47

Engine	
Type	BMW air-cooled boxer twin
Internal code	M51
Block material	Cast iron
Head material	Aluminium
Bore and stroke	68 × 68mm
Capacity	494cc
Valves	ohv, 2 valves per cylinder
Compression ratio	5.8:1
Carburettor	1 × BMW Spezial two valve 22mm
Max. power (DIN)	18bhp @ 4,000rpm
Max. torque	N/A
Fuel capacity	3.07gall (14ltr)
Transmission	
Gearbox	3-speed, manual
Clutch	Single dry plate
Final drive	Shaft
Chassis	
Frame	Tubular steel twin loop
Front suspension	Plate spring
Rear suspension	Rigid

Tyres	27-3.5in cross-ply
Wheels	Wire spoke, steel rim
Rim width	N/A
Brakes	
Type	Front 150mm drum, rear external shoe on shaft drive
Dimensions	
Wheelbase	55.5in 1410mm
Overall length	82.7in 2100mm
Overall width	31.5in 800mm
Overall height	37.4in 950mm
Unladen weight	286lb 130kg
Performance	
Top speed	68mph 110km/h
0–60mph	N/A
Price	RM 1850
No. built	6,502

ble of 68mph. While the R37 had been a niche model, the R47 was more mass-market, with more than 1,700 units sold. A number of them competed successfully on national and international race tracks.

1928–29 R52

The successor to the R42 had essentially the same tubular steel frame and chassis, albeit with a larger front drum brake.

The R52 succeeded the R42 and featured an uprated engine and front brake.

1928–29 R52

Engine		*Tyres*	26-3.5in cross-ply
Type	BMW air-cooled boxer twin	Wheels	Wire spoke, steel rim
Internal code	M57	Rim width	3in
Block material	Cast iron		
Head material	Aluminium	*Brakes*	
Bore and stroke	63 × 78mm	Type	Front 200mm drum, rear external
Capacity	486cc		shoe on shaft drive
Valves	Side-valve, 2 valves per cylinder		
Compression ratio	5.0:1	*Dimensions*	
Carburettor	1 × BMW Spezial two valve 22mm	Wheelbase	55.1in 1400mm
Max. power (DIN)	12bhp @ 3,400rpm	Overall length	82.7in 2100mm
Max. torque	N/A	Overall width	31.5in 800mm
Fuel capacity	2.74gall (12.5ltr)	Overall height	37.4in 950mm
		Unladen weight	334lb 152kg
Transmission			
Gearbox	3-speed, manual	*Performance*	
Clutch	Single dry plate	Top speed	62mph 100km/h
Final drive	Shaft	0–60mph	N/A
Chassis		*Price*	RM 1510
Frame	Tubular steel twin loop		
Front suspension	Plate spring	No. built	4,377
Rear suspension	Rigid		

1920–1930: THE MOVE INTO MOTORCYCLES

Although the engine was subject to a significant redesign, with a new bore and stroke of 63 × 78mm, to produce a capacity of 486cc, the performance was little changed.

1928–30 R57

The R57 was the successor to the R47 and shared much of its architecture and engineering. The new designation suggested a new model, but there were no major innovations and the R57 used the same 494cc engine and 18bhp performance. The only remarkable feature was a larger carburettor on the engine side, while an enlarged brake drum was now mounted in the front wheel. However, there was an improved transmission, with a twin-plate clutch replacing the single, an improved ignition and higher voltage electrical system. In addition, the wheelbase was shortened by 10mm, the fuel tank capacity reduced and brakes enlarged. The weight also increased.

The R57 succeeded the R47, with uprated front brake and transmission.

1928–30 R57

Engine	
Type	BMW air-cooled boxer twin
Internal code	M51
Block material	Cast iron
Head material	Aluminium
Bore and stroke	68 × 68mm
Capacity	494cc
Valves	ohv, 2 valves per cylinder
Compression ratio	5.8:1
Carburettor	1 × BMW Spezial two valve 22mm
Max. power (DIN)	18bhp @ 4,000rpm
Max. torque	N/A
Fuel capacity	2.74gall (12.5ltr)
Transmission	
Gearbox	3-speed, manual
Clutch	Single dry plate
Final drive	Shaft
Chassis	
Frame	Tubular steel twin loop
Front suspension	Plate spring
Rear suspension	Rigid
Tyres	26-3.5in cross-ply
Wheels	Wire spoke, steel rim
Rim width	3in
Brakes	
Type	Front 200mm drum, rear external shoe on shaft drive
Dimensions	
Wheelbase	55.1in 1400mm
Overall length	82.7in 2100mm
Overall width	31.5in 800mm
Overall height	37.4in 950mm
Unladen weight	330lb 150kg
Performance	
Top speed	71mph 115km/h
0–60mph	N/A
Price	RM 1850
No. built	1,005

1920–1930: THE MOVE INTO MOTORCYCLES

1928–29 R62

The first 750 boxer had a 745cc engine capable of 18bhp and 70mph, making BMW's new range-topper one of the quickest bikes of its day. It used the same cases, frame, suspension, and so on, as the cheaper 500cc R52, but a new crank, barrels, heads and pistons gave the larger capacity.

The R62 was the first 750cc BMW boxer and one of the fastest bikes of the day.

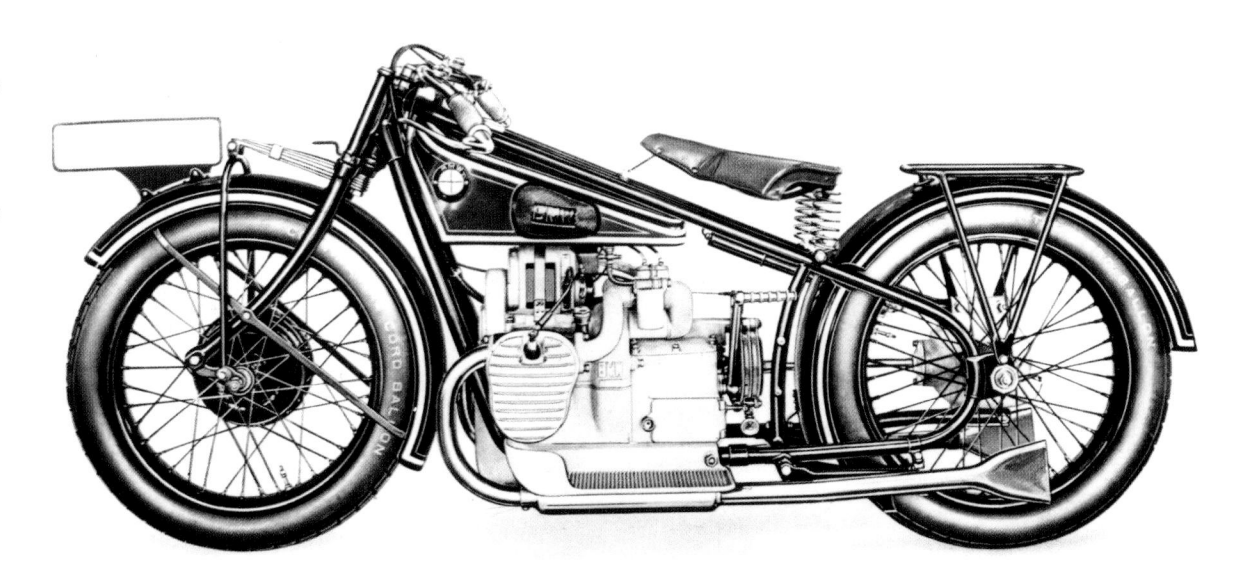

1928–29 R62

Engine	
Type	BMW air-cooled boxer twin
Internal code	M56
Block material	Cast iron
Head material	Aluminium
Bore and stroke	78 × 78mm
Capacity	745cc
Valves	Side-valve, 2 valves per cylinder
Compression ratio	5.5:1
Carburettor	1 × BMW Spezial two valve 22mm
Max. power (DIN)	18bhp @ 3,400rpm
Max. torque	N/A
Fuel capacity	2.74gall (12.5ltr)
Transmission	
Gearbox	3-speed, manual
Clutch	Single dry plate (2-plate later)
Final drive	Shaft
Chassis	
Frame	Tubular steel twin loop
Front suspension	Plate spring
Rear suspension	Rigid
Tyres	26-3.5in cross-ply
Wheels	Wire spoke, steel rim
Rim width	3in
Brakes	
Type	Front 200mm drum, rear external shoe on shaft drive
Dimensions	
Wheelbase	55.1in 1400mm
Overall length	82.7in 2100mm
Overall width	31.5in 800mm
Overall height	37.4in 950mm
Unladen weight	341lb 155kg
Performance	
Top speed	71mph 115km/h
0–60mph	N/A
Price	RM 1650
No. built	4,355

■ 1920–1930: THE MOVE INTO MOTORCYCLES

1928–29 R63

The first ohv 750 from Bavaria was effectively a development of the 500cc R57, with the cylinder bore increased to 83mm. The valve gear was completely enclosed and the front brake was enlarged but much of the rest was unchanged. The R63 was the sportiest of the BMW models until the end of the 1920s, although its relatively high price of 2100 reichsmarks meant that it remained an impossible dream for many motorcycle enthusiasts.

The 1928 R63 was the first ohv 750, but otherwise it was based on the R57.

1928–1929 R63

Engine
Type	BMW air-cooled boxer twin
Internal code	M60
Block material	Cast iron
Head material	Aluminium
Bore and stroke	83 × 68mm
Capacity	735cc
Valves	ohv, 2 valves per cylinder
Compression ratio	6.2:1
Carburettor	1 × BMW Spezial two valve 24mm
Max. power (DIN)	24bhp @ 4,000rpm
Max. torque	N/A
Fuel capacity	2.74gall (12.5ltr)

Transmission
Gearbox	3-speed, manual
Clutch	Single dry plate (2-plate later)
Final drive	Shaft

Chassis
Frame	Tubular steel twin loop
Front suspension	Plate spring
Rear suspension	Rigid

Tyres
	26-3.5in cross-ply
Wheels	Wire spoke, steel rim
Rim width	3in

Brakes
Type	Front 200mm drum, rear external shoe on shaft drive

Dimensions
Wheelbase	55.1in 1400mm
Overall length	82.7in 2100mm
Overall width	31.5in 800mm
Overall height	37.4in 950mm
Unladen weight	334lb 152kg

Performance
Top speed	74mph 120km/h
0–60mph	N/A

Price
	RM 2100

No. built
	800

1920–1930: THE MOVE INTO MOTORCYCLES

1929–34 R11

1929 saw the end of the boxers' welded tubular steel frames to be replaced with a distinctive pressed-steel arrangement both for the frame and front suspension. Developed specially for use with a sidecar, the new frame offered improved stability and made a positive impression. The robust look it provided began to be referred to as the 'German school' of motorcycle design. The engine was unchanged from the R62.

The 1929 R11 (along with the R16) saw the introduction of new pressed-steel frames.

1929–1934 R11

Engine
Type	BMW air-cooled boxer twin
Internal code	M56
Block material	Cast iron
Head material	Aluminium
Bore and stroke	78 × 78mm
Capacity	745cc
Valves	Side-valve, 2 valves per cylinder
Compression ratio	5.5:1
Carburettor	1 × BMW Spezial two valve 24mm
Max. power (DIN)	18bhp @ 3,400rpm
Max. torque	N/A
Fuel capacity	3.07gall (14ltr)

Transmission
Gearbox	3-speed, manual
Clutch	Single dry plate
Final drive	Shaft

Chassis
Frame	Pressed steel
Front suspension	Plate spring
Rear suspension	Rigid

Tyres
Wheels	26-3.5in cross-ply
	Wire spoke, steel rim
Rim width	3.5in

Brakes
Type	Front 200mm drum, rear external shoe on shaft drive

Dimensions
Wheelbase	54.3in 1380mm
Overall length	82.7in 2100mm
Overall width	35.03in 890mm
Overall height	37.1in 940mm
Unladen weight	356lb 162kg

Performance
Top speed	62mph 100km/h
0–60mph	N/A

Price	RM 1750
No. built	7,500

■ 1920–1930: THE MOVE INTO MOTORCYCLES

1929–34 R16

The ohv sports version of the R11 featured the same new pressed-steel chassis but with an uprated version of the overhead-valve engine which, from 1932, was also equipped with two carburettors, increasing output further to 33bhp.

The R16 was essentially the same as the R11, but with the ohv version of the engine.

1929–1930 R16

Engine
Type	BMW air-cooled boxer twin
Internal code	M60
Block material	Cast iron
Head material	Aluminium
Bore and stroke	83 × 68mm
Capacity	735cc
Valves	ohv, 2 valves per cylinder
Compression ratio	6.5:1
Carburettor	1 × BMW Spezial two valve 26mm
Max. power (DIN)	25bhp @ 4,000rpm
Max. torque	N/A
Fuel capacity	3.07gall (14ltr)

Transmission
Gearbox	3-speed, manual
Clutch	Single dry plate
Final drive	Shaft

Chassis
Frame	Pressed steel
Front suspension	Plate spring
Rear suspension	Rigid

Tyres	26-3.5in cross-ply
Wheels	Wire spoke, steel rim
Rim width	3.5in

Brakes
Type	Front 200mm drum, rear external shoe on shaft drive

Dimensions
Wheelbase	54.3in 1380mm
Overall length	82.7in 2100mm
Overall width	35.03in 890mm
Overall height	37.1in 940mm
Unladen weight	363lb 165kg

Performance
Top speed	74mph 120km/h
0–60mph	N/A

Price	RM 2200
No. built	1,006

CHAPTER THREE

1930–1940: BMW TAKES ON THE WORLD

After BMW emerged as a motorcycle manufacturer in 1923 there followed a period of consolidation through the remainder of the decade. Over the years, the Bavarian marque become renowned for its signature, touring-orientated air-cooled boxer twins, along with increasing innovation and performance, as well as race and sporting success.

But it was all nothing compared with what was to come next.

DIVERSIFYING TO SURVIVE

Up to 1930, BMW's greatest sporting success had been a handful of German 500cc championships and a first, but short-lived, world land speed record. Its greatest technological innovations, meanwhile, were the successive evolutions of its side- and overhead-valve boxer twins. Until 1928's R11 and 16 (which moved to radical pressed-steel frames from

The R16 and R11, with their pressed-steel frames, carried BMW motorcycles into the 1930s.

1930–1940: BMW TAKES ON THE WORLD

the previous tubular cradles), these had remained conservatively very akin to the original R32 of 1923. That was about to change.

After weathering the German economic crisis of the early 1930s, which not only helped sweep Hitler's National Socialist party to power but also forced BMW to diversify once more to ensure its survival, the rest of the decade was to be one of increasingly dramatic style, ever-more innovative technological advancement and world-beating sporting achievement. These developments are best exemplified, respectively, by BMW's stunning Art Deco-style R7 of 1934, the brilliant R5 of 1936, which introduced telescopic forks and 'modern' gearchanges, and the astonishing, supercharged Type 255 Kompressor, which reached its zenith in 1939 when it became the first foreign machine to win the Senior TT. Every one of them, naturally, was an air-cooled boxer twin.

The end of the decade, and the onset of the Second World War, brought all of that accomplishment and advancement to a crushing, catastrophic halt, but it did not diminish the achievements and significance of those, and other, boxer twins of the period. Neither did it negate the rise to world dominance of BMW motorcycles themselves.

Just ten years previously, however, such was German austerity that no one could have predicted the positive future that was to come. In 1930, although BMW's R11 and R16 boxer twins, with their novel and striking-looking pressed-steel frames and forks, were well regarded, their high price in a worsening economy meant that they were out of reach for many. BMW responded by taking the decision to change direction – at least in the short term. Alongside its premium, large-capacity boxer twins, they began to produce something very different – the small-capacity R2 model, which was powered by a 198cc single-cylinder engine. At that time in Germany, no licence was required to drive a smaller-capacity motorcycle with an engine up to 200cc, so the R2 proved very popular. Within two years, BMW had sold almost 15,000 of them. Two years later, the R2 was joined by a larger-capacity single-cylinder variant, the 398cc R4, a machine for which the growing German army placed a large order in 1933. It was bikes like these that kept BMW afloat during Germany's great depression.

In 1939, BMW claimed its first Senior TT win with its supercharged Kompressor.

1935–39 Type 255 Kompressor

Engine
Type	BMW supercharged air-cooled boxer twin
Internal code	Type 255
Block material	Magnesium
Head material	Aluminium
Bore and stroke	66 × 72mm
Capacity	492cc
Valves	DOHC, 2 valves per cylinder
Compression ratio	N/A
Carburettor	N/A
Max. power (DIN)	60bhp
Max. torque	N/A
Fuel capacity	N/A

Transmission
Gearbox	4-speed, manual
Clutch	Single dry plate
Final drive	Shaft

Chassis
Frame	Tubular steel double loop
Front suspension	Telescopic fork
Rear suspension	Plunger type

Tyres
Wheels	Wire spoke, steel rim
Rim width	N/A

Brakes
Type	Front 200mm drum, rear 200mm drum

Dimensions
Wheelbase	N/A
Overall length	N/A
Overall width	N/A
Overall height	N/A
Unladen weight	304lb 138kg

Performance
Top speed	140mph 220km/h
0–60mph	N/A

Price	N/A
No. built	N/A

With the company stabilized and prosperity returning, it was time for BMW once again to turn its attention to its boxer twins – and boy, did they do it in style!

THE R7: THE MOST TECHNICALLY ADVANCED MOTORCYLE EVER?

First, in 1934, came the almost mythical R7, a one-off prototype or concept machine built to explore new technologies and push the conventions of motorcycle design. One of its claims to fame was that it was the first BMW – indeed, the first motorcycle – fitted with telescopic forks. No motorcycle better displays the technical advances, bold styling ambition and sheer ability of BMW motorcycles during the 1930s. Yet, astonishingly, it is a motorcycle that few, apart from BMW cognoscenti, have even heard of, let alone seen.

The creation of visionary BMW engineer Alfred Böning, and powered by an all-new boxer engine designed by Leonhard Ischinger, the R7 was a motorcycle that was years ahead of its time – arguably the most futuristic, technically advanced and distinctive motorcycle ever. Conceived to challenge the 'powered bicycle' tradition of motorcycle design and styled at the height of the Art Deco period, its engineering was as radical as its styling was dramatic. It was also considered too extreme and expensive to manufacture, and never went into production. The only example ever built never even went on show and was 'lost' during the Second World War. (It was rediscovered in 2005, painstakingly restored by BMW and is now one of the stars at the BMW Museum in Munich, being run, ridden and displayed regularly at BMW events.)

ABOVE: **The one-off concept boxer, the R7, sadly never made it into production.**

LEFT: **The 1934 R7 was designed as a one-off concept machine by Alfred Böning.**

The R7's Art Deco-style streamlined look was typical of the 1930s.

50

1930–1940: BMW TAKES ON THE WORLD

ABOVE LEFT: **The R7's 'H-pattern' hand gearchange remains familiar today on many cars.**

ABOVE RIGHT: **Alfred Böning was the genius behind the R7's design.**

Streamlined 'faired-in' exhausts were a novel styling feature on the R7.

51

■ 1930–1940: BMW TAKES ON THE WORLD

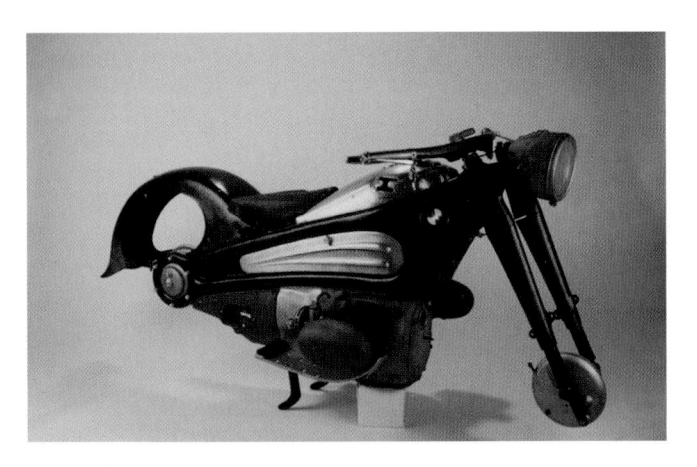

After rediscovering the sole example of the R7, BMW set about restoring it.

Some parts on the R7, including the distinctive mudguards, had to be remade from scratch.

Even the name of the R7 is a subject of debate, as it is referred to in some publications of the era as the R205 and elsewhere as a 'prototype R17 and R5'. In truth, the R7 was always conceived as a distinct, stand-alone model. The early 1930s was a time of huge ambition in the German automotive industry, partly influenced by the dramatic style of the Art Deco period and fuelled by the rise of National Socialism. The R7 was first conceived at around the same time as Ferdinand Porsche's Volkswagen Beetle. The brainchild of BMW engineer Alfred Böning, its purpose was to challenge the traditional concept of the motorcycle, which was, essentially, seen as a bicycle with an engine. It was built to showcase the design and engineering capabilities of BMW, with the aim of turning it into a production model.

If that suggested a radical departure from conventional motorcycles, the resultant R7 certainly delivered. Its enclosed bodywork, pressed-steel 'bridge' frame of the type used on many modern machines (and including some monocoque sections, which were incredibly rare at that time) and telescopic front forks were all firsts in motorcycling. Gone was the old, traditional, 'saddle' fuel tank; the tank was now re-located under the expansive, swoopy, Art Deco-inspired bodywork, as were all the electric components, which helped make the R7 far more durable than other bikes of the era. The rider sat on a sprung saddle and gripped the alloy side covers (which opened to reveal the electrics) with the knees, while the feet were housed in and protected on the alloy footboards.

Even the instruments and controls were different and radically new. The rotating disc digital speedo housed in the headlight section followed the style of prestige cars of the era. The chrome top cover housed the oil pressure gauge and, on the right-hand side, a car-style 'H-pattern' hand gearchange. (Changing gear by hand was the norm on motorcycles at the time, but never before had it been so neat and car-like.) Most bikes of the time had only three speeds, but the R7 had a four-speed gearbox, meshed with a dry, single-plate, cable-operated clutch.

Finally, the heart of the R7 was all new and, naturally, an opposed boxer twin. This masterpiece, designated M205/1, was the work of Leonhard Ischinger. The boxer twin layout was familiar, but it was intended to take BMW in a new direction via far more modern technology, with a number of features derived from car design. Accordingly, for the first time on a BMW motorcycle, the R7's engine was a one-piece 'tunnel' design with a forged, one-piece crankshaft. The con-rod big ends were split (like those used in car engines) and ran on plain bearings. In another radical development, the cylinders and heads were one-piece. One advantage of this was that there was no longer a need for a head gasket, which was a weak link in many engines of the period. Instead, the camshafts were located below the crank, in turn placing the push-rod tubes below each cylinder, which then improved the location for the valves and spark plugs.

These innovations, combined with a hemispherical combustion chamber, two valves per cylinder and a displacement of 790cc (a 500cc version was also proposed, as in BMW's tradition of the time, but never built) gave far better performance than other BMW motorcycle engines of the period, with an impressive 35bhp at 5,000rpm.

Finally, the attention to detail and finish was exquisite. The motor and the lower covers, along with the smooth rocker covers, formed a visually clean surface tapering down towards the non-rotating rear axle. This ran parallel to the upper bodywork and flowed into the rear mudguard and was highlighted by the uniquely shaped 'fish-tail' twin exhausts. There was extensive use of chrome and even the taillight was carefully sculpted, with the word 'Stop' illuminated in the lens.

Despite its bold ambition, technological advances and extraordinary styling, the R7 was deemed too heavy and expensive to go into production. Even before the prototype had been shown in public, BMW decided to change direction towards producing more sporting models. They backed Rudolf Schleicher's R5 design instead, although many of the novel features of the R7, most obviously the telescopic forks, lived on in its successor.

As for the R7 itself, in the late 1930s, the sole example was stripped of a few usable parts, then put into a box and placed into storage. In June 2005, the box was rediscovered and opened by BMW. The motorcycle was found to be 70 per cent complete, although its overall condition was very poor, with many parts having been severely damaged by rust and by corrosion caused by a damaged battery. BMW's Mobile Tradition department (now called BMW Classic and responsible for the marque's museum and historic vehicles) decided to commission a restoration. Although the project was managed by BMW, much of the specialist restoration work was undertaken by outside experts. Hans Keckeisen took care of the bodywork while Armin Frey, a doyen of classic boxer engines, worked on its powertrain. Their task was made slightly easier when the original R7 designs and blueprints were discovered in BMW's archive.

The engine was badly corroded, so parts were sought from various sources, some from contemporary models, others being remade entirely. The four-speed gearbox and shaft drive were stripped and the electrical system completely rebuilt.

The metalwork was in a bad way, too. The distinctive, flowing mudguards were almost beyond repair and had to be remade. The wheels and exhaust were missing and the unique frame needed a lot of work in order to be in a condition to support the engine.

With all the parts found or remade, and coats of lustrous black paint (complete with BMW's signature period pinstripes) applied, the project was finally completed in January 2008 and the R7 was returned to BMW. Today, it takes pride of place in the BMW Museum in Munich and is also regularly displayed on the road at classic events and rallies throughout Europe.

As for Alfred Böning, his R7 may not have gone into production but he himself became key to a whole raft of BMWs, right up to 1972. He had a hand in the R12 and R75 in the 1930s, later worked on BMW cars including the 328 and 501, and headed the /5 series motorcycle project launched in 1969, which set the template for the final generation of BMW airhead motorcycles and which featured many of the technical advances pioneered on the R7. He died in 1984.

GROUND-BREAKING TECHNOLOGY: R12, R17 AND R5

Although it never went into production, the R7 was hugely significant in helping to inspire the ground-breaking technology of the production models that followed. The first of these were the R12 and R17 of 1935, the successors to 1928's R11 and R16. Having broken fresh ground with those bikes' pressed-steel frames, BMW followed up with the introduction of a hydraulically damped telescopic front fork.

Motorcycle suspension in the 1920s and 30s was at best rudimentary and at worst non-existent – and this was at a time when roads were often shockingly poor. Of course, BMW's own early motorcycle suspension systems up to that time had been fairly basic, too. The R32 of 1923 had an unsprung rear end, just a few centimetres of front suspension travel and no damping whatsoever.

It was that poor suspension quality, combined with the general state of the roads and the increasing demands of racing, that spurred BMW's engineers to come up with some new solutions. Their eventual response was the hydraulically damped telescopic fork and BMW ultimately became the first manufacturer in the world to integrate such a system in a regular production motorcycle. The new system was first trialled in racing and then fitted to Böning's short-lived R7. From 1935, it went into production on the R12 and R17, replacing the previously customary cantilever spring.

Telescopic forks were not the only technological advance on those bikes. Unveiled at the Berlin Motor Show in February 1935, the 745cc side-valve R12 and ohv R17 also sported the world's first four-speed motorcycle gearbox and

1930–1940: BMW TAKES ON THE WORLD

After the introduction of the pioneering pressed-steel frames, the next technological breakthrough would be telescopic forks.

a strengthened crank. They also heralded the arrival of half-hub brakes integrated into their rear wheels.

The more mainstream and affordable side-valve R12 was probably the most significant in terms of popularity and significance, but in sporting twin-carbed R17 trim it produced 33bhp at 5,000rpm. This figure made it BMW's most powerful roadster until the arrival of the R68 of 1952. On the downside, priced at 2400 reichsmarks, the R17 was also the most expensive German motorcycle of its day, which partly explains why only 450 were made and it went out of production after just two years. Today, this rare and exclusive model is one of the most sought after of all pre-war BMW motorcycles.

1935–42 R12

The R12 was one of the most significant of all BMW boxers – the road model (along with its sister R17) that saw the introduction of oil-damped telescopic fork front suspension. Production numbers ultimately exceeded 36,000, making it the most widely adopted pre-war BMW motorcycle.

Developed from the preceding R11, the R12 was unveiled at the motor show in Berlin on 14 February 1935, along with the sportier, more expensive R17. Like the R11, it used a distinctive, Art Deco-style pressed-steel frame, but this time it had a pioneering hydraulically damped telescopic front fork. This brought a significant improvement in terms of comfort and rideability in comparison with the previous flat spring rocker.

The R12's side-valve 745cc boxer twin (the R17 used the ohv valve version) was also essentially that of the R11, but came in two forms: a single, SUM-carbed 18bhp version and one with twin Amal carburettors producing 22bhp. Another new addition was a four-speed transmission operated by a lever on the tank (with shaft drive down the right), plus a new rear drum brake in place of the brake on the shaft as before. This new brake design also meant that the front and rear wheels were interchangeable.

Although the R12 was primarily a civilian machine up to 1937, a military, single-carb version became adopted by the German army and was produced up to 1942 when it was superseded by the R75, one of the most significant motorcycles of the Second World War.

1930–1940: BMW TAKES ON THE WORLD

FRONT FORKS AND REAR SUSPENSION

The introduction of telescopic front forks in 1935 led to a crucial improvement in the riding characteristics of BMW motorcycles. Next would come rear suspension. Factory enduro rider Alexander von Falkenhauen was key to the adoption of this feature. As well as being contracted for racing in off-road events, von Falkenhausen worked as a designer on motorcycle frames. In 1936, he added rear-wheel suspension for the first time to his experimental R5 and promptly won gold medals in the toughest challenge of all, the International Six Days Trial (ISDT). This convinced his racing colleagues at BMW to stake everything on rear suspension for 1937, when they won again. A year later, his concept went into series production.

From 1938, a new model series with the types R51, R61, R66 and R71 was presented. The R51 replaced the R5 but retained the latter's engine, more or less unchanged. Instead, its defining feature was the new suspension. Although the larger R66 developed six horsepower more and was also 5km/h faster, the R51's agility and low weight ensured it handled better. It was also the basis for two competition versions: the R51 SS (Super Sport) with four horsepower extra and capable of a top speed of almost 160km/h; the R51 RS had a fully revised engine rated at 36bhp, which was enough for a top speed of 180km/h. By 1941, with the Second World War preventing the supply of motorcycles to civilians, BMW were producing the R12 and R75 models only for the military authorities. When BMW restarted motorcycle production after the war, the R51 became the new R51/2.

In parallel to this sporty 500, BMW also produced the side-valve 745cc R71, which, although not as powerful, had more torque and was better suited to use with a sidecar. A side-valve, 18bhp 600cc version, called the R61, also debuted this year as a successor to the short-lived R6.

The R71 was introduced along with the R51 and also featured new plunger rear suspension.

■ 1930–1940: BMW TAKES ON THE WORLD

1938–1941 R51

Engine
Type	BMW air-cooled boxer twin
Internal code	254/1
Block material	Cast iron
Head material	Aluminium
Bore and stroke	68 × 68mm
Capacity	494cc
Valves	ohv, 2 valves per cylinder
Compression ratio	6.7:1
Carburettor	2 × Amal 5/423
Max. power (DIN)	24bhp @ 5,500rpm
Max. torque	N/A
Fuel capacity	3.07gall (14ltr)

Transmission
Gearbox	4-speed, manual
Clutch	Single dry plate
Final drive	Shaft

Chassis
Frame	Tubular steel double loop
Front suspension	Telescopic fork
Rear suspension	Plunger type
Tyres	19-3.5in cross-ply
Wheels	Wire spoke, steel rim
Rim width	3in

Brakes
Type	Front 200mm drum, rear 200mm drum

Dimensions
Wheelbase	55.11in 1400mm
Overall length	83.8in 2130mm
Overall width	32.08in 815mm
Overall height	37.8in 960mm
Unladen weight	400lb 182kg

Performance
Top speed	87mph 140km/h
0–60mph	N/A

Price	RM 1595
No. built	3,775

1936–37 R5

The R12 and R17 were almost immediately followed, in 1936, by the even more innovative R5. No motorcycle could realistically be expected to match the sheer 'wow factor' of Alfred Böning's sensational but ultimately abortive R7 of 1934, but the R5 certainly came close. Like the prototype R7, the R5 was a completely new boxer twin, but slightly more conventional and with more of an emphasis on sporting ability. In terms of its design it looks to today's eyes more like a machine from the 1950s than the 30s. In terms of technological advancement, performance and significance, it is considered today as the very best of pre-war BMW boxer motorcycles. Indeed, its main designer, the innovative engineer Rudolf Schleicher, later referred to it as his most important design.

With a sophisticated look defined by a double-cradle frame and a state-of-the-art telescopic fork, the R5 boasted some of the qualities of later generations of motorcycle and had a lasting stylistic influence. What is more, thanks to a favourable performance from its new engine and light weight, the R5 was also one of the sportiest motorcycles of its day.

At its heart was a new version of the familiar BMW boxer twin. This was based on the foundation laid by the side-valve R series predecessors but with overhead valves actuated by twin chain-driven camshafts. The aim was to keep the length of the push-rods as short as reasonably possible, so as to raise the engine's rpm capabilities. It kept the old side-valve engine's dimensions with a square 68mm bore and 68mm stroke, giving 494cc capacity. Compression ratio was 6.7:1 and each cylinder breathed through its own Amal 5/423 carburettor, giving the engine a power output of 24hp at 5,500rpm.

This new engine was carried in an equally new, electrically welded, double-cradle frame made from tubular steel, which had been adapted directly from the works racing machine and offered excellent torsional stiffness. Combined with the hydraulically damped telescopic front fork, this gave the R5 outstanding directional stability and roadholding.

1930–1940: BMW TAKES ON THE WORLD

1938 R51 SS: BMW'S FIRST PRODUCTION RACER

BMW's 1938 R51, thanks to its powerful 494cc ohv boxer engine, lightweight chassis and the new addition of rear suspension, was already a capable sporting machine. However, that year BMW went a stage further by producing, in limited quantities, two competitive versions. These machines were effectively BMW's first 'production racers'.

The R51 SS (SuperSport) used cycle parts closely modelled on those of the works Kompressor racers but was normally aspirated rather than 'blown'. As such, it made around 4bhp more than the road R51 and was capable of a top speed of almost 160km/h. It was an ideal entry-level motorcycle for racing and also quite competitive at smaller, local events.

By contrast, the engine of the R51 RS was completely reworked, and made 36bhp, enough for a top speed of 180km/h. Although this was still far from the factory racing machines of Georg Meier, it still won victories in numerous grand prix and national championships. Just 17 were made and, instead of being put up for sale, were allocated to up-and-coming young talented riders.

The 1938 R51SS racer was based on the Kompressor, but normally aspirated.

ABOVE: **Although the chassis was similar, the engine of the R51SS racer was almost completely reworked.**

LEFT: **Along with the R51RS, the R51SS was considered to be BMW's first production racer.**

57

■ 1930–1940: BMW TAKES ON THE WORLD

The R12 used a 750cc version of BMW's side-valve air-cooled boxer twin.

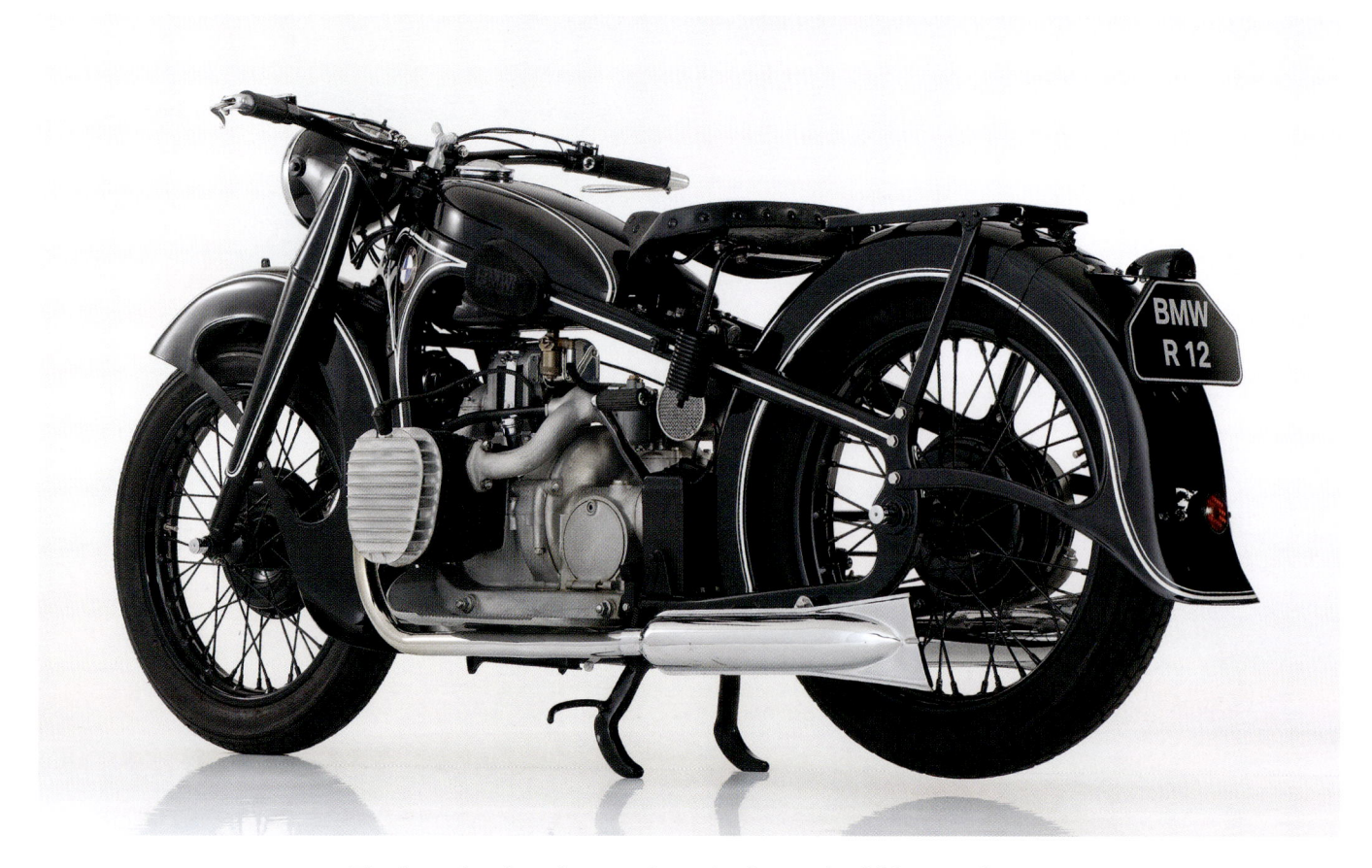

The introduction of a rear drum brake on the R12 was a first.

ABOVE: **Instrumentation, as on most bikes of the time, was simple but effective.**

LEFT: **Oil-damped telescopic forks were another advanced technological feature.**

The R12 was one of the most significant of BMW's early air-cooled boxer twins.

■ 1930–1940: BMW TAKES ON THE WORLD

Like its R11 predecessor, the R12 used a distinctive pressed-steel frame.

The 1936 R5 is today considered one of the most important of all pre-war BMWs.

1930–1940: BMW TAKES ON THE WORLD

The R5 was on sale for less than two years. Only 2,652 had been built when production came to an end in 1937 to make way for the new and improved the R51, which came complete with new rear suspension. The R5 had carried a hefty price tag of 1550 reichsmarks – which was enough to buy a small car at the time – but it still attracted a devoted following, particularly in later years. One of its fans was the grandfather of Lord March, of the Goodwood motor circuit. Decades later, his grandson stumbled across the bike purely by chance and was able to buy it back.

The 500cc engine of the R5 was a familiar boxer twin, but was an all-new design.

BELOW: **Its frame was a new, electrically welded, tubular steel double cradle.**

■ 1930–1940: BMW TAKES ON THE WORLD

Its headlamp nacelle contained the warning lights, key and speedometer.

Clever design and minimal weight helped give the R5 exceptional handling.

1930–1940: BMW TAKES ON THE WORLD

Final drive was by a familiar 'Cardan' shaft-drive unit.

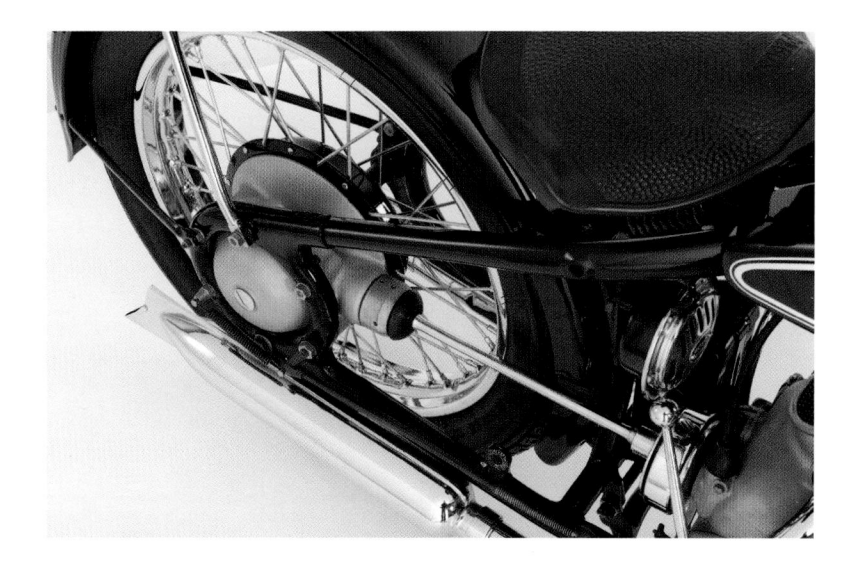

BELOW: **Rudolf Schleicher's R5 in 1936 was the most advanced BMW boxer yet.**

SPORTING SUCCESS

The availability of bikes such as these, and the support of the Nazi government in Germany, led to a series of sporting successes. Neither the world land speed records nor the historic TT win in 1939 would have been possible without BMW's development of possibly the most extreme 'boxer' of all – the Type 255 Kompressor.

BMW was one of the first motorcycle manufacturers to experiment with forced induction, waiting a mere two years after the marque's debut (in 1923) to bolt a supercharger to an overhead-valve racing machine. In part because of the deep connections with aero engine practice, BMW racing motorcycles were subject to continuous development with 'blowers', but initially achieved only limited success in road racing. Created purely as a factory racing machine and never

63

1930–1940: BMW TAKES ON THE WORLD

1936–1937 R5

Engine
Type	BMW air-cooled boxer twin
Internal code	254
Block material	Cast iron
Head material	Aluminium
Bore and stroke	68 × 68mm
Capacity	494cc
Valves	ohv, 2 valves per cylinder
Compression ratio	6.7:1
Carburettor	2 × Amal 5/423
Max. power (DIN)	24bhp @ 5,500rpm
Max. torque	N/A
Fuel capacity	3.29gall (15ltr)

Transmission
Gearbox	4-speed, manual
Clutch	Single dry plate
Final drive	Shaft

Chassis
Frame	Tubular steel twin loop
Front suspension	Telescopic fork
Rear suspension	Rigid
Tyres	19-3.5in cross-ply
Wheels	Wire spoke, steel rim
Rim width	3in

Brakes
Type	Front 200mm drum, rear 200mm drum

Dimensions
Wheelbase	55.1in 1400mm
Overall length	83.8in 2130mm
Overall width	31.5in 800mm
Overall height	37.4in 950mm
Unladen weight	363lb 165kg

Performance
Top speed	87mph 140km/h
0–60mph	N/A

Price RM 1550

No. built 2,652

The racing supercharged 255 Kompressor was the most advanced BMW boxer yet.

1930–1940: BMW TAKES ON THE WORLD

sold to the public, the ultra-exotic, magnesium-built, supercharged BMW Type 255 Kompressor (also known as the 500 Kompressor, RS255, and Type 255 RS500) debuted in 1935. It went on to virtually dominate road racing in the late 1930s. The successor to the earlier WR750 racer displaced 492cc, had aluminium cylinders and magnesium crankcases and, with the help of a Zoller supercharger, was capable of producing around 65bhp. It was a phenomenal output for the era.

The Kompressor's first landmark achievement was in setting a new world land speed record for motorcycles. On 12 October 1936, in the hands of stalwart factory rider and racer Ernst Henne, it achieved a speed of 272.11km/h. Henne was the rider who had first claimed the record for BMW eight years previously. A little over a year later, on 28 November 1937, Henne took a specially adapted and fully faired example to 279.5km/h on a closed section of the new Frankfurt-Darmstadt autobahn. That record would stand for 14 years.

Henne was an ideal ambassador for BMW and its world-beating boxer twins, but he was certainly not the only one. In 1938, fellow BMW rider Georg 'Schorsch' Meier was also making a name for himself aboard the 255, riding to victory in both the German and European 500cc road racing championships in his debut year with the Bavarian marque. That success gave both 'Schorsch' and BMW the confidence to go for the Senior TT, the biggest road-racing prize of all. In the following year, aboard a further refined 255 and ably assisted by British teammate Jock West, he made history by becoming the first rider from outside the British Isles to win the Isle of Man Senior TT for 500cc machines. West, meanwhile, rounded out BMW's dominance by coming second.

The 1930s was a golden age of grand prix racing, with the European motorcycle factories regularly vying for dominance on newly built, high-speed racing tracks. On one side were the British stalwarts of single-cylinder, overhead camshaft development – Norton and Velocette especially – who had honed their light and reliable racers since the mid-1920s with great success. They combined light weight, good handling, high speed and durability. On the other side, as the decade unfolded, a new breed of supercharged, multiple-cylinder machines was emerging.

ABOVE: **Eight years on from his first world speed record, BMW's Ernst Henne was at it again.**

In 1937, Henne rode a streamlined Kompressor to a new record of 173.7mph.

■ 1930–1940: BMW TAKES ON THE WORLD

The supercharger on the 255 Kompressor was integrated into the front of the engine.

Today, one of the few remaining examples holds pride of place at the BMW Museum.

1930–1940: BMW TAKES ON THE WORLD

GEORG MEIER AND THE 1939 SENIOR TT

Georg 'Schorsch' Meier is probably the most famous of all the early BMW boxer racers.

In what was arguably the greatest sporting achievement of BMW's airheads, Georg Meier became the first foreign winner of the prestigious Senior TT, the blue riband event of the Isle of Man TT races. He was riding the racing version of BMW's boxer twin, the supercharged Type 255 Kompressor. The feat was all the more impressive because 'Schorsch' (a common Bavarian nickname for Georg) had only begun road racing two years previously. He was also the first motorcycle racer to lap a grand prix course at an average speed of over 100mph, which he achieved at the Belgian Grand Prix that same year, again on a BMW 255.

Georg Meier was born in 1910 in Bavaria. After leaving school at 14, he became an apprentice at a local motorcycle shop and at 19 he joined the new Bavarian state police motorcycle unit. It was there that he began competing in motorcycle trials and enduro events. In 1937, he was selected for the German team for the International Six Days Trial, where, despite having no road racing experience, he won the speed trial element. He was quickly approached by the BMW team for the 1938 season. Throughout that year, Meier rode the BMW 255 Kompressor in both the European and German championships, winning both. However, in the Senior TT, a stripped spark plug thread ended his race just after the start. Teammate Jock West finished fifth.

The 1939 Senior TT has gone down in BMW history.

continued overleaf

■ 1930–1940: BMW TAKES ON THE WORLD

GEORG MEIER AND THE 1939 SENIOR TT *continued*

'Schorsch' Meier led from the start in the 1939 Senior TT, building a 52-second lead on the first lap.

Meier's British teammate Jock West went on to finish second in the Senior TT.

1930–1940: BMW TAKES ON THE WORLD

The following year, the BMW team, encouraged by the Nazi government to prove the superiority of German engineering, arrived on the island early to take advantage of 14 full days of race practice.

Tragedy struck on 2 June, when the third member of the BMW team, Karl Gall, crashed at Ballaugh Bridge on his first practice lap. He died from his injuries, exacerbated by the onset of pneumonia, 11 days later. Meier and West had decided to continue. In Friday's Senior race, Meier stormed off, posting a record 90.33mph average from a standing start and registering a 52-second lead by the end of the first lap, from teammate West and Velocette-mounted Stanley Woods.

On lap two, West took a five-second lead over Woods and Meier went even faster, with an average of 90.75mph. West increased his advantage over Woods in lap three to 15 seconds, then Woods lost time in a fuel stop when his engine took more than half a minute to fire. Meier, meanwhile, after matching his opening lap of 90.33mph, had opened up a lead of a minute and a half.

On lap five Meier proved fastest again, his lead extending to two minutes ahead of West and more than three in front of Woods. On lap six, the gap between the three leading riders closed again, with West being reeled in by the chasing Woods by seven seconds, although he was still behind by 58 seconds. It was too late.

After a fuel stop by West at the start of the seventh and final lap, Meier took the win by two minutes and 20 seconds.

There is a postscript to this story, however. Although Meier and West took a historic 1-2, the tragic death of Karl Gall meant that, with no official third team member, BMW did not qualify for the team prize. The Bavarian team had co-opted the only other BMW runner that year – privateer Tim Reid – into the squad for the Senior race, riding his own R51 SS over-the-counter racer, one of only three to be exported to the United Kingdom. Sadly, Reid did not finish what would turn out to be his one and only TT race.

Later that year Meier also won the Dutch TT at Assen and the Belgian GP, however the European championship (there was no world championship in those days) went to the new four-cylinder Gilera.

With the onset of the Second World War, racing was suspended. Meier was deemed unfit for military service, due to a back injury, so he spent the war as a motorcycle instructor for the German Military Police. After the war, Germany was excluded from the new world championships. Meier won the German championships six times on a modified 255, and was also elected German sportsman of the year in 1949.

Meier retired from racing in 1953 to run a BMW motorcycle dealership. He did return to the Isle of Man, in 1989, to ride a lap of honour aboard the 255, marking the fiftieth anniversary of his remarkable achievement. Although the 1939 race was derided by some as 'the Nazi TT', it remains one of the TT's – and BMW's – most striking wins. Georg Meier died in 1999.

By the flag, Meier had built up a lead of over two minutes.

1930–1940: BMW TAKES ON THE WORLD

'Schorsch' Meier's 1939 Senior TT victory was another world first.

In 1935, things took a radical turn. BMW's new Type 255 integrated the supercharger at the front of the engine, rather than atop the gearbox, as had been the case previously. The 'blower' now sent pressurized air past valves operated by twin overhead camshafts, encased in a remarkably tidy and compact magnesium cylinder head cover. The 255 also saw the introduction of the new, modern telescopic front fork, which would also soon debut on the R5 roadster.

In 1937 it was improved further still with springing at the rear using a coil-sprung plunger system (which would subsequently debut on the R51 road machine). An additional friction damper kept the undamped bounce under control on the racers.

Meanwhile, as BMW's 'Rennsport' (hence the 'RS') racing department found increasing power, a strict focus on weight control began to pay dividends in terms of handling and acceleration. One of the key methods for achieving this was to make the wheel hubs and engine casings out of ultra-light magnesium rather than conventional aluminium alloy. The weight of the frame, meanwhile, was kept to a minimum by using lightweight, tapered tubing with as few lugs as possible. The result of these changes was an impressive 60bhp at 7,000rpm which was enough to power the BMW to speeds of over 220km/h (137mph).

In 1938 it all came to fruition when, in the hands of works rider Georg 'Schorsch' Meier, the RS255 won both the German and European championships. However, the team managed only 5th spot at that year's TT, with British rider Jock West on board; the ultimate prize, the Senior TT, still eluded it. Success in the premier event finally came in the following year, when the two Kompressors of Meier and West grabbed a historic 1-2. However, just as quickly as it had gained the greatest prize, the 255's reign was over. The Second World War brought an end to all racing while post-war regulations banned the use of superchargers.

Today, the few remaining Kompressors are the rarest and most desirable of all motorcycles. One example was auctioned in 2013 for $480,000, the second-highest price ever paid at auction for a motorcycle.

It was a historic moment. BMW had now etched its name on to every major national and international trophy, confirming its position as a world leader in motorcycle sport. It was not bad for a firm that had produced its first bike just 16 years previously.

1930–1940: BMW TAKES ON THE WORLD

WHAT ABOUT AERO ENGINES?

Although during the 1930s motorcycles and cars became more and more important to BMW, it continued making aero engines, particularly with German re-armament during the 1930s.

Among its most successful designs during this period was the BMW 132, a nine-cylinder radial engine built from 1933. It was developed from a licence for a similar unit built by Pratt & Whitney and was primarily used in the Junkers Ju 52 transport plane.

Another of BMW's engines during this period was the 801 14-cylinder radial, which went on to be the most produced German radial engine of the Second World War. It was most famously used in the Focke-Wulf Fw 190 fighter.

ABOVE: **The wartime Ju 52 transport planes used BMW radial aero engines.**

RIGHT: **The nine-cylinder Type 132 was developed from a Pratt & Whitney design.**

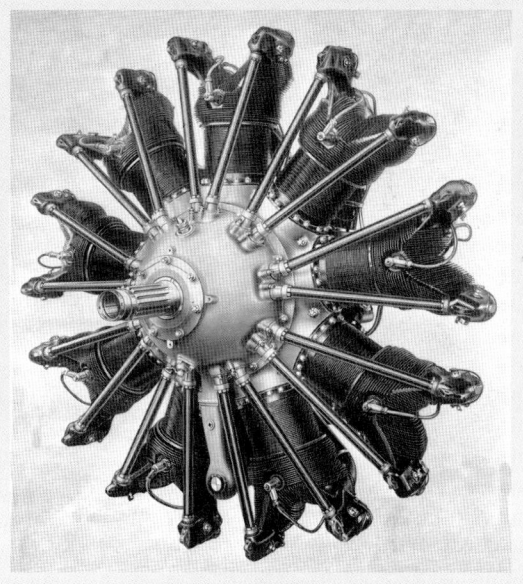

DEVELOPMENTS IN THE ROAD MODELS

The company's success in racing inevitably had an influence on BMW's series-produced road models. First, following the impact made by the 500cc R5, in 1937 BMW introduced a 600cc version, which combined a new 600cc engine with the gearbox and chassis of the R5.

Much more was to come the following year, which would prove to be not just a massive year for Meier but for all of BMW's boxer range. In 1938, the marque introduced a raft of new models, comprising not just the updated R23 single but also, more significantly, the R51 500cc sportster, which replaced the pioneering R5. The 600cc R61 was an update of the short-lived, 600cc R6, while the R71 750cc tourer replaced the R12 and the R66 replaced the range-topping 750cc sportster, the R17.

The key development on all of these models was, following the previous introduction of telescopic fork suspension at the front, the adoption of plunger suspension at the rear, as successfully developed by works rider and frame engineer Alexander von Falkenhausen in the International Six Days Trial. The combination of the two systems offered exceptional levels of comfort, which served to cement BMW's reputation as the kings of touring machines. All also adopted foot gearchanges and footrests to suit in place of footboards.

The R12 and R51 in particular proved hugely successful and formed the foundation for the boxer twins that

■ 1930–1940: BMW TAKES ON THE WORLD

In 1938, a range revamp saw the R66 replace the R17.

BELOW: **The new twin-carbed R39 proved a particular success.**

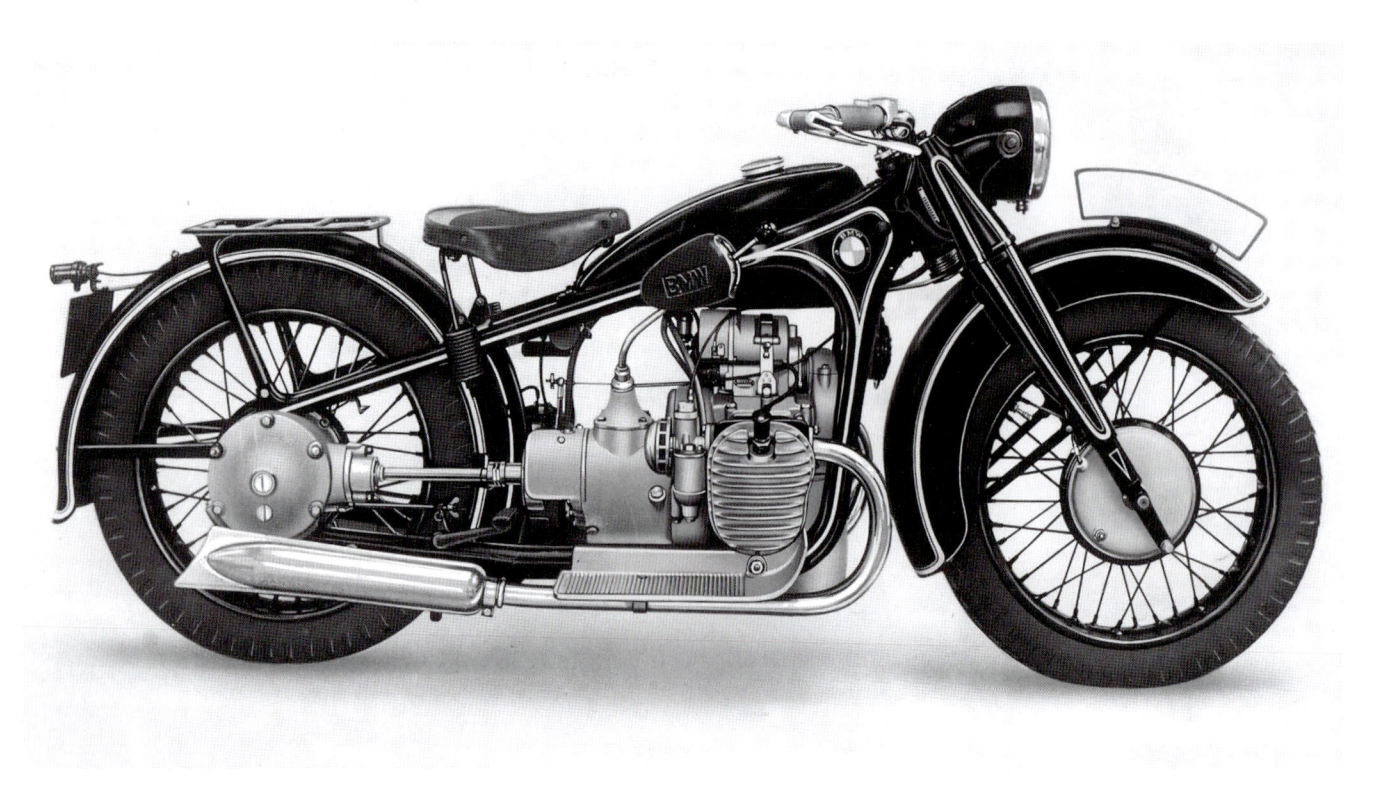

1935–37 R12

Engine
Type	BMW air-cooled boxer twin
Internal code	M 56 S or 212
Block material	Cast iron
Head material	Aluminium
Bore and stroke	78 × 78mm
Capacity	745cc
Valves	Side-valve, 2 valves per cylinder
Compression ratio	5.2:1
Carburettor	1 × SUM 25mm
Max. power (DIN)	18bhp @ 3,400rpm
Max. torque	N/A
Fuel capacity	3.07gall (14ltr)

Transmission
Gearbox	4-speed, manual
Clutch	Twin dry plate
Final drive	Shaft

Chassis
Frame	Pressed steel
Front suspension	Telescopic fork
Rear suspension	Rigid
Tyres	19-3.5in cross-ply
Wheels	Wire spoke, steel rim
Rim width	3in

Brakes
Type	Front 200mm drum, rear 200mm drum

Dimensions
Wheelbase	54.33in 1380mm
Overall length	82.6in 2100mm
Overall width	35.4in 900mm
Overall height	37.0in 940mm
Unladen weight	407lb 185kg

Performance
Top speed	68mph 110km/h
0–60mph	N/A

Price	RM 1630
No. built	36,000

The 1935 R12 saw the introduction of the hydraulically damped telescopic fork.

would follow later. However, all the models helped BMW's production numbers reach new heights during the period, easing past the 100,000 mark before the outbreak of the Second World War. In 1939 alone, more than 20,000 BMW motorcycles were sold. While motorcycles remained a secondary business to BMW's aero engines, they were now firmly established. However, with the clouds of war looming once again, all that was about to change…

1930–1940: BMW TAKES ON THE WORLD

KEY MODELS

1935–37 R17

The sports variant of the R12 (and successor to the R16) came with the powerful ohv version of the now 745cc boxer twin, which enabled it to achieve an incredible top speed of 140km/h. As such, it is not only the fastest pre-war production German motorcycle, it was the most expensive German motorcycle of its day and BMW's most powerful ever, only eventually surpassed by the R68 of 1952.

The ohv R17 was BMW's fastest pre-war production machine.

1935–37 R17

Engine
Type	BMW air-cooled boxer twin
Internal code	M 60
Block material	Cast iron
Head material	Aluminium
Bore and stroke	83 × 68mm
Capacity	736cc
Valves	ohv, 2 valves per cylinder
Compression ratio	6.5:1
Carburettor	2 × Amal 76/424
Max. power (DIN)	33bhp @ 5,000rpm
Max. torque	N/A
Fuel capacity	3.07gall (14ltr)

Transmission
Gearbox	4-speed, manual
Clutch	Twin dry plate
Final drive	Shaft

Chassis
Frame	Pressed steel
Front suspension	Telescopic fork
Rear suspension	Rigid
Tyres	19-3.5in cross-ply
Wheels	Wire spoke, steel rim
Rim width	3in

Brakes
Type	Front 200mm drum, rear 200mm drum

Dimensions
Wheelbase	54.33in 1380mm
Overall length	82.7in 2100mm
Overall width	32.08in 900mm
Overall height	37.0in 940mm
Unladen weight	363lb 165kg

Performance
Top speed	87mph 140km/h
0–60mph	N/A

Price	RM 2400
No. built	434

1930–1940: BMW TAKES ON THE WORLD

1938–41 R66

The successor to the top-of-the-range 750cc R17 sportster gained an ohv version of the 600cc engine from the short-lived R6 which produced 30bhp, enough to propel it to an impressive 145km/h. It also received the same update by way of new rear suspension.

The R66 was the successor to the short-lived R6; shared much with the R5 but used the ohv 600cc engine.

1938–1941 R66

Engine	
Type	BMW air-cooled boxer twin
Internal code	266/1
Block material	Cast iron
Head material	Aluminium
Bore and stroke	69.8 × 78mm
Capacity	597cc
Valves	ohv, 2 valves per cylinder
Compression ratio	6.8:1
Carburettor	2 × Amal 6/420 S
Max. power (DIN)	30bhp @ 5,300rpm
Max. torque	N/A
Fuel capacity	3.07gall (14ltr)

Transmission	
Gearbox	4-speed, manual, footshift
Clutch	Single dry plate
Final drive	Shaft

Chassis	
Frame	Tubular steel double loop
Front suspension	Telescopic fork
Rear suspension	Plunger type
Tyres	19-3.5in cross-ply
Wheels	Wire spoke, steel rim
Rim width	3in

Brakes	
Type	Front 200mm drum, rear 200mm drum

Dimensions	
Wheelbase	55.11in 1400mm
Overall length	83.8in 2130mm
Overall width	32.08in 815mm
Overall height	37.8in 960mm
Unladen weight	407lb 187kg

Performance	
Top speed	87mph 140km/h
0–60mph	N/A

Price	RM 1695
No. built	1,669

CHAPTER FOUR

1940–1949: WAR TAKES ITS TOLL

The Second World War fundamentally redirected BMW, in terms of both aero-engine manufacturing and motorcycle production. The ultimate outcome would be a complete reorganization and restructuring of the company and its products.

MILITARY-SPECIFIC MOTORCYCLES

In the very early years of the decade, production of some of the boxer twins, including the R51, continued. Over time, however, the emphasis changed. Since 1935, the increasingly re-armed German military had begun using the radical R12 boxer twin, along with the smaller, single-cylinder R4, as army vehicles. However, as militarization increased and war clouds loomed, in the mid-to-later 1930s, there was a rise in demand from the army. All German motorcycle manufacturers, including BMW, began to recognize the need to produce military-specific motorcycles.

Military Demands

In 1937, rivals Zündapp and BMW received a request from the German army to produce a purpose-built motorcycle and sidecar. The specification was precise: it had to be able to carry a payload of 500kg (the equivalent of three fully equipped soldiers); it had to be capable when fully loaded of cruising on autobahns at 80km/h, with a top speed of 95km/h; it had to be able to run at a minimum of 4km/h alongside marching troops; it had to use 4.5 x 16inch cross-country tyres; it had to have a minimum ground clearance of 150mm with enough mudguard clearance to use snow chains; the minimum range attainable by its fuel capacity had to be 350km; and, finally, and crucially, it had to have substantial off-road ability, including being able to ford shallow waters and climb steep inclines.

Until then, all motorcycles used by the military had been derived from civilian models. However, the need for a fast-moving army in the upcoming *Blitzkrieg* meant that no expense was to be spared in the creation of a motorcycle and sidecar combination that was extremely versatile, well-performing and dependable.

BMW, already involved with the military with its R12, took part in the tender. The first prototype, using the side-valve engine from the R71, suffered overheating problems, so BMW decided to develop a stand-alone overhead-valve engine with an extensively ribbed aluminium cylinder head for effective cooling even at marching speed in great heat. Work began in 1938.

Over the next two years, Zündapp and BMW developed their own machines – Zündapp the KS-750 and BMW the all-new boxer twin R75. After extensive testing, it was decreed that the KS-750 was far superior, and BMW was asked to build it. BMW refused, but agreed to adopt some of Zündapp's features, such as the rear wheel drive, hydraulic brakes and wheels. After both manufacturers agreed to standardize as many components as possible, such as the sidecars, in order to streamline production and the delivery of spare parts, both machines were commissioned. With the specifications confirmed, in 1941 production of both the KS-750 and the R75 began.

From this point on, BMW's motorcycle production was restricted solely to military machines, particularly the R75, while much of the rest of its production capability was turned over to the manufacture of aero engines. Eventually,

THE CONTROVERSY OF WARTIME

As early as 1940, BMW was using foreign workers in its production processes. After 1942, criminals, prisoners of war from Eastern Europe, forced workers mainly from Western Europe and detainees in concentration camps had to work in BMW's factories. The proportion of foreigners in the BMW workforce increased from around 3 per cent in 1940 to some 51 per cent in 1944. In common with most of German industry at the time, a technocratic concept of efficiency guided the approach taken by BMW managers and the use of forced labour was tacitly accepted and approved.

BMW AG first raised the issue in the public domain in 1983, in *The BMW Story – A Company in its Time*, by Horst Mönnich. In 1999, BMW joined forces with other companies in the German economy to establish the 'Remembrance, Responsibility, Future' foundation. Former forced labourers were paid compensation through the foundation, and the companies also engaged with the inequities of the past in numerous publications.

More recently, during a ceremony in Munich to mark its 100th birthday, BMW expressed 'profound regret' for the 'enormous suffering' caused by using Nazi slave labour during the Second World War, admitting that 'under the National Socialist regime of the 1930s and 40s, BMW AG operated exclusively as a supplier to the German arms industry'.

During the war, in common with much of German industry, BMW resorted to the shameful practice of using forced labour.

BMW was instructed by the government to abandon production of civil aero engines and automobiles.

Delivery of the first R75 took place in July 1941 with production shifting from Munich to Eisenach the following year. Just over three years later, in October 1944, after nearly 16,000 had been built, production ceased. This was due first to repeated air raids and then to the American occupation in April 1945.

■ 1940–1949: WAR TAKES ITS TOLL

The military R75 motorcycle and sidecar, ridden by Alexander von Falkenhausen.

BELOW: **The R75 military motorcycle and sidecar was BMW's only wartime motorcycle.**

R75: 1941–1946

The R75 was a military motorcycle and sidecar powered by an ohv flat twin boxer engine with driven sidecar and reverse gear and was BMW's only production motorcycle between 1941 and 1944. Famously used in the desert of North Africa by Rommel's Africa Corps and against the Soviet Union (1941–1945) it became widely admired and, later, commonly copied.

When the first prototype exhibited overheating problems during trials, it was decided that the old side-valve engines

1940–1949: WAR TAKES ITS TOLL

The R75's design was in response to a very detailed specification from the German military.

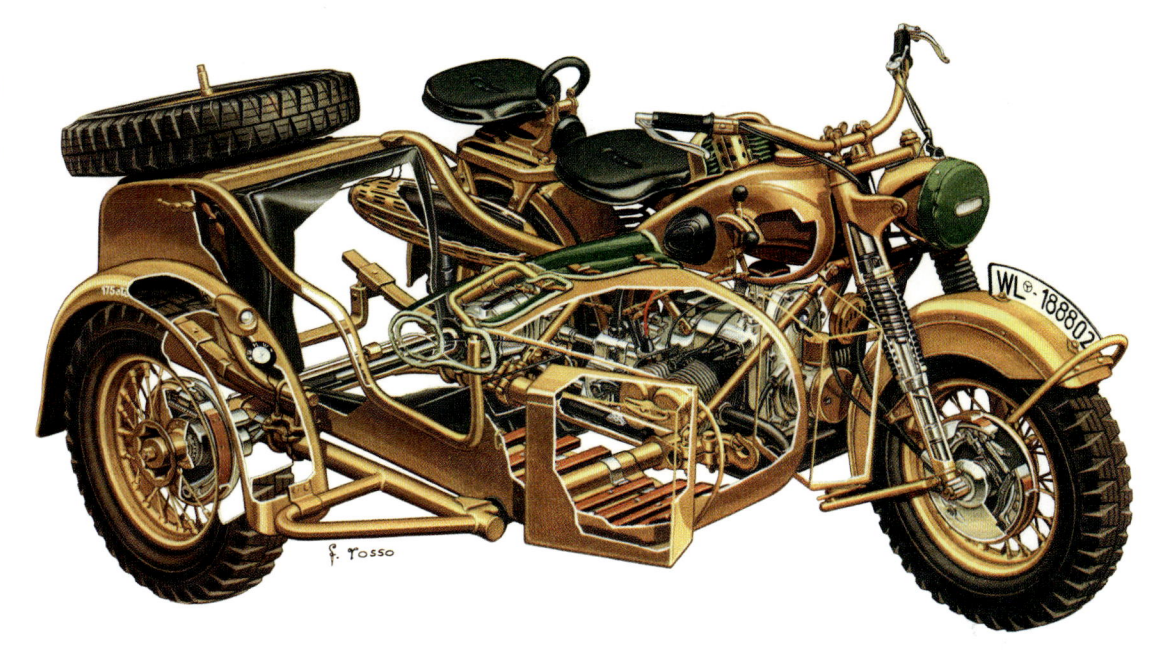

1941–1946 R75

Engine		Rear suspension	N/A
Type	BMW air-cooled boxer twin	Tyres	N/A
Internal code	N/A	Wheels	N/A
Block material	Cast iron	Rim width	N/A
Head material	Aluminium		
Bore and stroke	78 × 78mm	*Brakes*	
Capacity	745cc	Type	N/A
Valves	ohv, 2 valves per cylinder		
Compression ratio	N/A	*Dimensions*	
Carburettor	N/A	Wheelbase	N/A
Max. power (DIN)	26bhp	Overall length	N/A
Max. torque	N/A	Overall width	N/A
Fuel capacity	N/A	Overall height	N/A
		Unladen weight	930lb 420kg
Transmission			
Gearbox	4-speed, manual	*Performance*	
Clutch	Single dry plate	Top speed	N/A
Final drive	Shaft	0–60mph	N/A
Chassis		Price	N/A
Frame	N/A		
Front suspension	N/A	No. built	16,500

79

1940–1949: WAR TAKES ITS TOLL

used on the previous model R71 would not do. Instead, an all-new 750cc engine was created using overhead valves. Following the war, this engine went on to become the basis of all BMW boxer twins.

The R75 had not only attachments for a sidecar but also the means to drive the sidecar wheel as well as the motorcycle's rear wheel. This rear-wheel set-up featured a locking differential, selectable on-road/off-road gear ratios and also a reverse gear.

Although it was less well regarded than Zündapp's version of a military motorcycle, the R75 was very successful in the long run, proving to be highly manoeuvrable and reliable in the dust, sand and mud of battlefield conditions. It was also cheaper to make and more reliable than its rival. In fact, it so impressed the British, Americans and Russians that all were persuaded to try to imitate it at the end of the war. In Britain, the imitator was the Douglas Mark V, complete with shaft drive. In the US, after an approach by the US Army, Harley-Davidson produced the XA, which was more a copy of the BMW R71 side-valve, while Indian came up with the Indian 841. In both cases, the prototype bikes had 740cc side-valve engines and shaft drives; neither was put into full-scale production. The Soviets, on the other hand, quietly imported five BMW R75s via intermediaries in neutral Sweden, reverse-engineered them, and made their own, which they named the Dnepr M-72. This motorcycle was the father of the Russian Ural and the Chinese ChiangJang CJ750, and also a direct predecessor to the modern Ural.

Although production of the R75 officially ceased in 1944, in 1946, under Russian control, around 100 more machines were built at the Eisenach plant and shipped to Russia as war reparations.

BMW ENTERS THE JET AGE

Most of BMW's production capacity during the Second World War was dedicated to the manufacturer of aero engines, notably radial piston engines such as the 132 and 801 models. However, from 1940 BMW was also a pioneer in jet aero engines, although with limited success.

Its 003 axial-flow turbojet was first tested in, then rejected for, the Messerschmitt Me 262, which went on to become the most effective jet fighter of the war. It was used in the Heinkel He 162 in 1944, but its use was always limited and cut short by the end of the war.

Although the company was a pioneer in jet aviation, BMW's early versions were not hugely successful; here it is seen fitted to the He 162 fighter.

THE POST-WAR PERIOD

After the war, the truth about BMW's production of the R75 became debatable. The Russians took over the Eisenach factory in July 1945, as it was located in the newly designated Russian zone, and Marshal Zhukov ordered production to restart in October. The first delivery of eight 'new' R75s to Russia took place in January the following year. In total, however, only 106 R75s were built that year under Russian control, with all of them being shipped to Russia as war reparations.

The post-war situation with the rest of BMW was similarly shambolic. While the Eisenach factory was now in Russian hands, BMW's Munich factory, in the western zone, had been completely destroyed. In addition, most of BMW's engineers were taken to the US or the Soviet Union to continue the work they had done on jet engines with BMW during the war. On top of all that, the terms of Germany's surrender forbade BMW from manufacturing motorcycles.

During the period immediately following the war, what was left of BMW in Munich was used either to service American military vehicles, or to make pots and pans from borrowed machine tools and salvaged equipment and materials. This was later expanded to other kitchen supplies and bicycles. How far the mighty had fallen…

In 1947, the US authorities in Bavaria granted BMW permission to restart production of sub-250cc motorcycles. The trouble was that they had nothing to build – all the tooling had been lost and all the plans, blueprints and schematic drawings were now out of reach, in Eisenach. They were forced to restart from scratch. What they came up with was the 250cc single-cylinder R24 of 1948, which, while no boxer twin, was undoubtedly the machine that, by keeping BMW alive, enabled all the boxer twins that followed.

The R24 was created basically by copying one of the pre-war bikes. An old R23 was located, measured, reverse-engineered and given a few improvements – and a new name. The simple, 'old school' design meant that the R24 was the only post-war BMW without rear suspension, but in war-ravaged Germany that hardly mattered. The country needed basic, affordable, utility transport and the R24 proved a great success. In 1949, 9,200 were built, a figure that almost doubled the following year, to 17,000.

The R24 was not the only 'BMW' motorcycle of the late 1940s. In Soviet-controlled eastern Germany, the Eisenach plant was not only producing the war reparation R75 boxers in limited numbers, it was also manufacturing R35 singles. In other words, around 1948, there were effectively two 'BMW' motorcycle companies – one the genuine article, in Munich in Western Germany, the other in Soviet-controlled Eisenach.

Eventually, in 1952, this bizarre situation was resolved after the Soviets ceded control of the Eisenach plant to the East German government. Following a trademark lawsuit, it was renamed EMW (for Eisenacher Motoren Werke) and the BMW blue-and-white roundel was changed to a virtu-

The Munich factory was a prime target for Allied bombers and was almost completely destroyed.

1940–1949: WAR TAKES ITS TOLL

After the war, the first motorcycle **BMW** produced was the single-cylinder R24.

In 1949 alone, 9,200 R24s were built; they proved vital for German re-mobilization.

1940–1949: WAR TAKES ITS TOLL

By 1950, the production figure for the R24 had almost doubled to 17,000.

The success of the R24 was not bad for a machine that had been 'reverse-engineered' from the old pre-war R23.

■ 1940–1949: WAR TAKES ITS TOLL

ally identical 'EMW' one, but in red and white. It is worth remembering that no motorcycles made in East Germany after the Second World War were manufactured under the authority of BMW in Munich, simply because there was no need for an occupying power to gain such authority. As such, all BMW R35 motorcycles were produced in Eisenach until 1952, when they became EMW. That, however, and the rest of the 1950s, is another story…

KEY MODEL: 1948–1950 R24

Although it is no boxer twin, it is impossible to discuss BMW motorcycles of the post-war era without mentioning the R24, BMW's first of that category.

Permission to restart German manufacture of motorcycles came only in 1948, and was restricted to sub-250cc single-cylinder machines. BMW's devastated Munich factory, with no tooling or designs available, 'reverse-engineered' a pre-war

Although a single rather than a boxer twin, the R24 is fundamental to the story of post-war BMW.

The R24's simple, push-rod, shaft-driven 250cc single was a development of pre-war designs.

84

1940–1949: WAR TAKES ITS TOLL

R23 single, updating its engine with centrifugally governed ignition advance and rocker supports mounted on separate heads. Also new was the four-speed transmission with ratchet foot control and a Bing carburettor. The result was the R24.

Although its design was primitive (it was to be BMW's only post-war motorcycle without rear suspension, for example), the R24 was simple, affordable and exactly the sort of mobile solution that war-torn Germany needed. It was a huge success, with over 7,000 built in its first year and almost double that the year after. It was enough to get the whole BMW business back on its feet.

As was the fashion, instruments and warning lights were held in the headlamp nacelle.

BELOW: **The simple, affordable, rugged design of the R24 was crucial for getting war-ravaged Germany mobile again.**

■ 1940–1949: WAR TAKES ITS TOLL

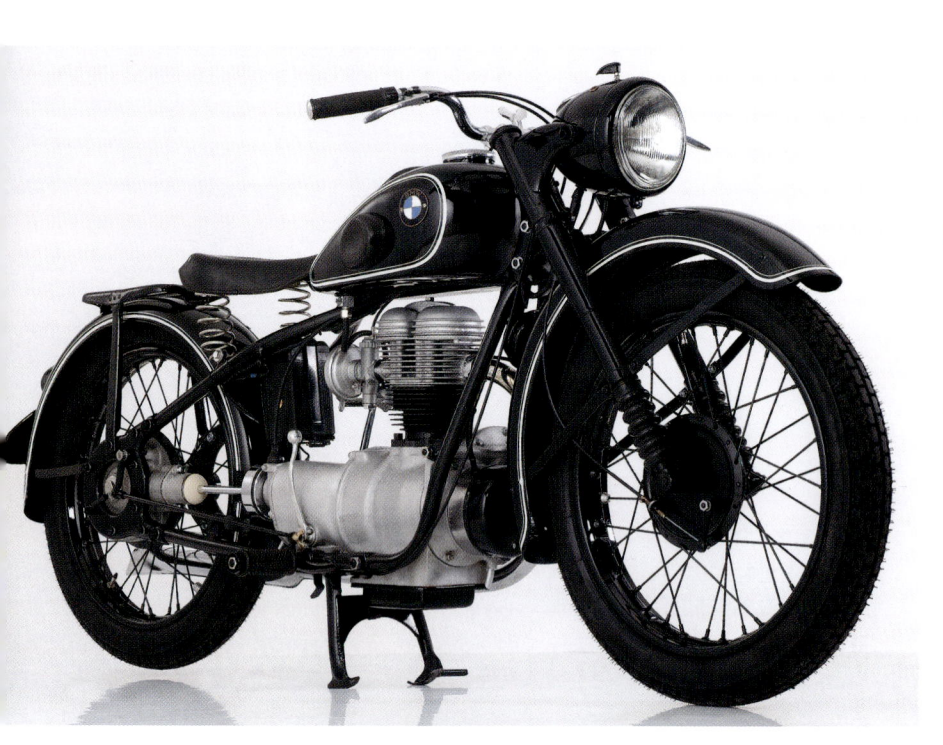

ABOVE: **The R24's shaft final drive was rugged and required little by way of maintenance.**

LEFT: **Suspension-wise, the R24 made do with rudimentary forks and a sprung saddle.**

1948–1950 R24

Engine	
Type	BMW air-cooled single
Internal code	224/1
Block material	Cast iron
Head material	Aluminium
Bore and stroke	68 × 68mm
Capacity	247cc
Valves	ohv, 2 valves per cylinder
Compression ratio	6.75:1
Carburettor	1 × Bing AJ 1/22/140 b
Max. power (DIN)	12bhp @ 5,600rpm
Max. torque	N/A
Fuel capacity	2.63gall (12ltr)
Transmission	
Gearbox	4-speed, manual
Clutch	Single dry plate
Final drive	Chain
Chassis	
Frame	Tubular steel double loop
Front suspension	Telescopic fork
Rear suspension	Rigid
Tyres	19-3in cross-ply
Wheels	Wire spoke, steel rim
Rim width	2.5in
Brakes	
Type	Front 160mm drum, rear 160mm drum
Dimensions	
Wheelbase	N/A
Overall length	79.5in 2020mm
Overall width	29.5in 750mm
Overall height	27.9in 710mm (saddle)
Unladen weight	286lb 130kg
Performance	
Top speed	59mph 95km/h
0–60mph	N/A
Price	DM 1750
No. built	12,020

CHAPTER FIVE

1950s: FROM BOOM TO BUST

After the devastation of the Second World War, BMW, along with much of German industry, had to rebuild from virtually nothing. In 1946, all the remnants of the Munich factory could manage was the making of a few pots and pans out of scavenged tools and materials and acting as a repair depot for the military vehicles of the occupying US forces. BMW's former automobile plant at Eisenach was less damaged and more serviceable, but it was now in the hands of the Russians and out of BMW control.

It was a situation that makes BMW's transformation and re-emergence over the next decade, in the 'post-war German economic miracle', all the more astonishing. From producing not one single motorcycle in 1946, by 1954, at the height of the German motorcycle boom, the Munich-based concern was able to sell some 30,000 – but it was not to last.

R51/2 AND R51/3, R67, R67/2 AND R68

A template had been established in the 1920s and continued through the 1930s and 40s: the more utilitarian and affordable 250cc and 400cc singles sold extremely well, and proved crucial for re-mobilizing Germany, but it was the

In the immediate post-war period, it was **BMW's** singles that got the company back on its feet.

1950s: FROM BOOM TO BUST

signature boxer twins that were at the heart of BMW's revival. Although BMW's post-war motorcycle production had recommenced in 1948 with the R24 250cc single, which was 'reverse-engineered' from the pre-war R23, US regulations prohibited the manufacture of anything larger or with more cylinders. It was not until 1950 that the first post-war boxer twin – the R51/2 – became available.

As its name suggests, the R51/2 was based on the pre-war R51. The engine of the R5 offered a robust foundation for the resumption of development work in the post-war period and the R51/2 incorporated various new features, such as a single oil circuit for both cylinders, slanted carburettors and finned valve covers. Other improvements included a two-way damped telescopic front fork, gearbox mainshaft damper and strengthened frame.

In truth, the R51/2 was only a stop-gap model intended to get production under way while BMW worked on something more modern. As such, it was only made for one year, with just over 5,000 examples being built. As the sales figures climbed, BMW engineers began to enjoy greater licence to innovate and the R51/2's replacement, the 500cc R51/3, despite the similarity in designation, was a far more modern machine. It was unveiled at the Amsterdam show in February 1951 alongside the 594cc R67. The duo featured the first of an entirely new and much neater-looking generation of engines, which would go on to form the basis of all BMW's boxer engines right up to 1969.

In contrast to the R51/2 boxer twin, with its two chain-driven camshafts, there was now a single, central camshaft driven by gearwheels from the crank. The engine was also more handsome in design, with smooth surfaces and one-piece valve covers. Placing the magneto and the generator behind the front cover made the unit more compact. Finally, the new Noris magneto ignition complete with automatic advance and retard enabled the engine to run particularly smoothly. However, although it was all new and improved, with a compression ratio of only 6.3:1, power output was actually unchanged from the 24bhp of the R51/2.

In terms of the chassis, the frame retained the familiar suspension designs that dated from 1938, namely, a telescopic fork at the front and plunger units at the rear. The half-width 200mm-diameter brake hubs also came from the earlier models but were uprated.

While the R51/3 was primarily aimed at the sporting solo rider, the torquier R67 was conceived more with sidecar enthusiasts in mind. A 594cc capacity was the result of a bore

The first post-war boxer twin was the R51/2 of 1950, here with sidecar.

1950s: FROM BOOM TO BUST

ABOVE: **The R51/2's successor came in 1951 and was far more modern.**

The R51/3 was primarily aimed at the sporting rider.

and stroke of 72 x 73mm, but with an even lower compression ratio of 5.6:1 it produced only 26bhp and also featured a higher final drive ratio.

In their first test reports, the motorcycling press were generally very complimentary about the R51/3 and the R67, praising the results achieved by BMW's engineers – particularly the smoothness of the engines and the excellent handling of the bikes. In fact, when it was entered for the International Six Days Trial in 1951, the R51/3 came through with flying colours.

The R67 was built for only one year. In 1952, BMW gave the R51/3 a 200mm twin leading shoe front disc brake and

89

■ 1950s: FROM BOOM TO BUST

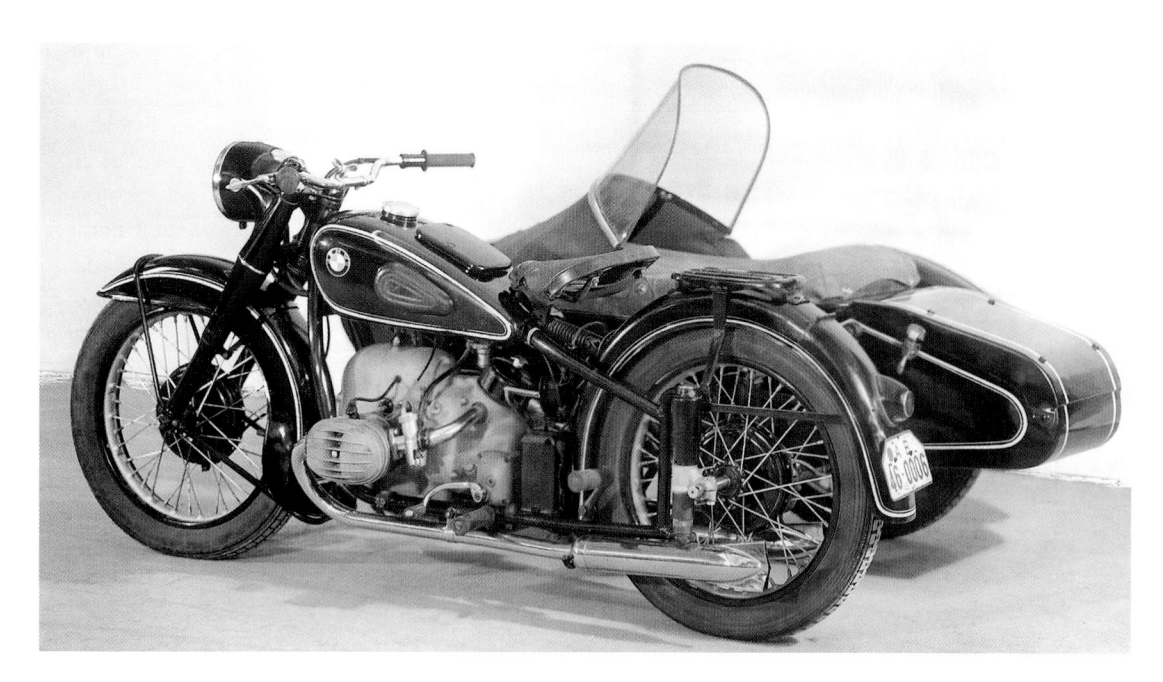

Where the R51/3 was designed as a solo, its sister machine, the R67, was designed for sidecar use.

rubber gaiters on the front forks in place of the pre-war style steel covers. The same updates were passed on to the R67, which was then renamed as the R67/2. This version was built until 1954 and in far bigger numbers. In total 4,234 were built.

The year 1952 also saw the debut of the R68, which, with a 600cc twin-cylinder engine developing 35bhp, was Germany's first production motorcycle capable of 160km/h (100mph). With its presentation at the International Bicycle and Motorcycle Show of that year, BMW demonstrated its return to the top class of international motorcycle construction. The R68 would ultimately be regarded as BMW's most prestigious model of the 1950s.

The most important innovations of 1954 were the introduction of full-width hub brakes and new light-alloy wheel rims, instead of the previous steel ones with their two-

The R67 was only built for one year before being replaced by the R67/2.

90

1950s: FROM BOOM TO BUST

tone paint finish. The previous 'fishtail' silencers were also replaced by a less complex, cigar-shaped design.

In short, BMW, and its boxer twins in particular, seemed to be going from strength to strength, enough for annual production to top 30,000 motorcycles for the first time, in 1954.

ON THE RACE TRACK

BMW's success on the road was mirrored elsewhere – in motorsport. Although Germany was banned immediately after the war from the sort of international racing competition in which BMW had achieved so much just before the war, the boxer twins were still raced successfully in domestic series, by the likes of 'Schorsch' Meier. Going into the 1951 season, international motorcycle racing's governing body, the FIM, lifted its ban on German riders competing in its events. Forced-induction engines remained firmly on the blacklist, however, so BMW was obliged to replace its successful supercharged Type 255 Kompressor for international competitions with new, naturally aspirated units.

For 1954, BMW delivered a new 45bhp, DOHC, 500cc boxer twin, complete with gear-driven shaft final drive and, in a move away from telescopic forks, an Earles-type leading-link front suspension system. This would become a BMW signature for the years to come.

The all-new RS54 racing machine sported some of the most advanced technology of the era, and this level of engineering was reflected in its performance on the race track. Although just 24 RS54s were produced that year, it became an instant hit, primarily with privateer racers. Its engine later also took a star turn in sidecar racing. On the international stage, Walter Zeller was runner-up in the 1956 world championship with a BMW factory machine and Dickie Dale finished 1958 in third position. Even more spectacular, however, was the run of victories in sidecar racing, started by Wilhelm Noll and Fritz Cron who won BMW's first sidecar world championship that year.

That was just the start. Between 1954 and 1974, BMW collected no fewer than 19 riders' sidecar world championship titles and 20 manufacturers' crowns. The BMW pairing of Klaus Enders and Ralf Engelhardt alone accounted for six of those triumphs in the late 1960s and early 1970s. Never before had one manufacturer dominated a category of motorsport in such a fashion. This extraordinary period of success also saw BMW set 21 world records, including Wilhelm Noll's 1955 absolute world speed record of 280.2km/h (174.1mph) on a BMW sidecar machine.

The RS54 racer demonstrated some of the most advanced engineering of the era.

■ 1950s: FROM BOOM TO BUST

WILHELM NOLL – SIDECAR KING

On 12 September 1954 at the Italian Grand Prix at Monza, car mechanic Wilhelm Noll, with telephone engineer Fritz Cron in the sidecar, secured the world sidecar championship. It was not just BMW's first road racing world championship but also the first for the BMW boxer twin.

For the two riders from Kirchhain near Marburg, it was their third win of the season, after success in Germany and Switzerland. Those wins were complemented by two second places – at the Ulster GP at Belfast and Belgian GP at Spa-Francorchamps – and a third at the Isle of Man TT. The BMW team had been on the podium at all six world championship races that year, breaking the long-standing dominance of Norton.

At the beginning of the season, none of this had looked likely. Four-times world champion and defending title-holder Eric Oliver had won the first three races on his faired works Norton, with passenger Les Nutt. Following an injury to his arm in the subsequent, non-championship Feldbergrennen race, however, Oliver was ruled out of the next round in Germany. Noll and Cron on their fuel-injected RS seized the opportunity and claimed BMW's first-ever world championship race win. They then repeated the feat in Switzerland. With Oliver managing just two points there, the rivals were level on 26 points heading into the final round. As Oliver's arm injury required it to be put back into plaster, he could not race, so all Noll had to do was score.

Even so, the German duo did not take it easy. Lining up at Monza with their own now fully faired version of the BMW sidecar, they hit the front from the start before carving out a lead of more than four seconds. By doing so, they had proved that they were worthy world champions.

The first title marked the start of a unique run of success for the BMW boxer in motorcycle sidecar racing. Although they had to settle for the runners-up slot the following year, in 1956 Noll and Cron won the title again, and then the duo retired from racing. The RS54 boxer went on to claim 19 drivers' and 20 constructors' world championship titles up to 1974, a feat that remains a record up to this day.

Passenger Fritz Cron, along with rider Willhelm Noll, became sidecar world champions in 1954.

1950s: FROM BOOM TO BUST

Pictured early in the 1954, Cron and Noll's machine used the BMW RS54 engine.

Later in 1954, Cron and Noll's machine had gained aerodynamic bodywork.

continued overleaf

■ 1950s: FROM BOOM TO BUST

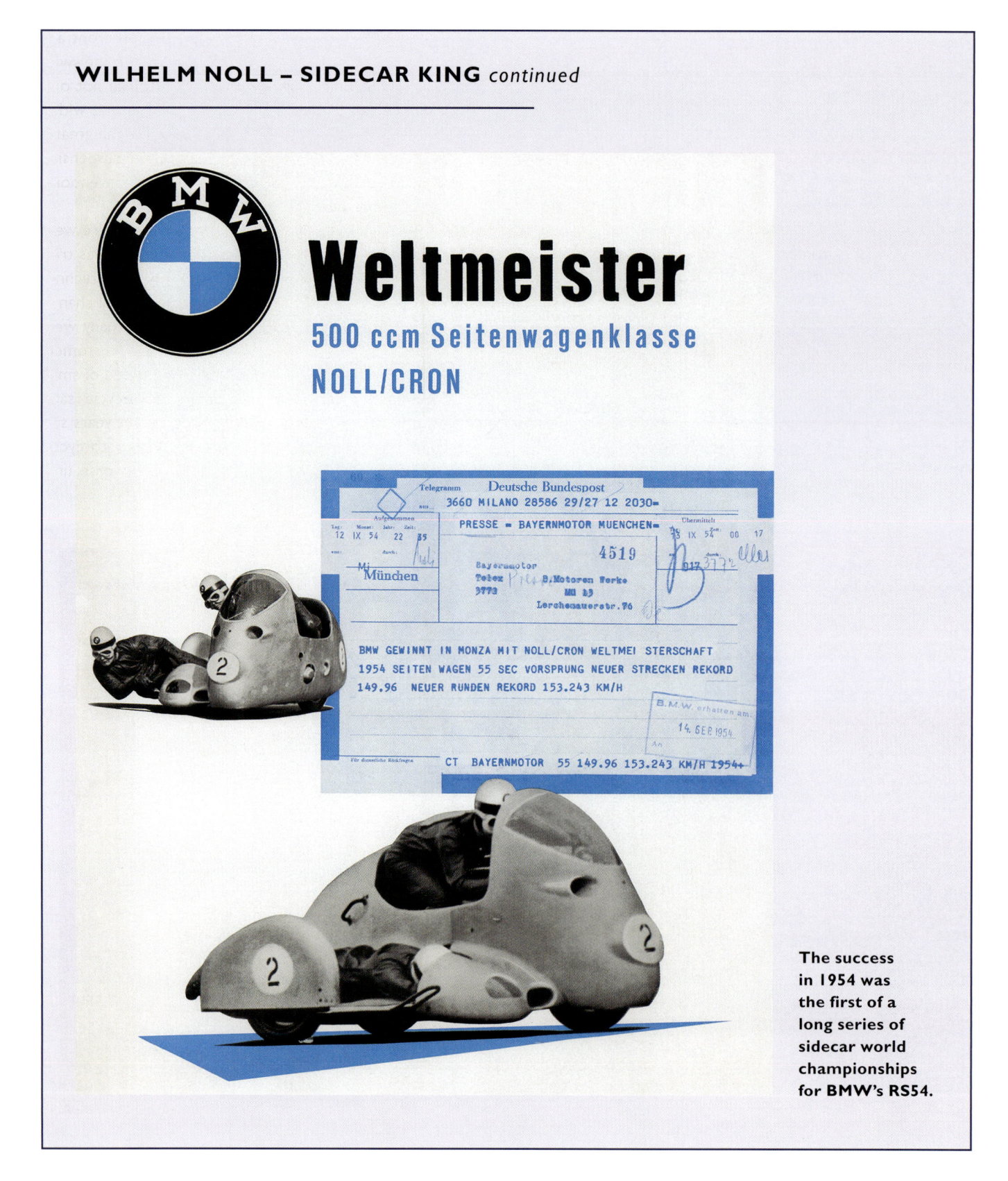

WILHELM NOLL – SIDECAR KING *continued*

The success in 1954 was the first of a long series of sidecar world championships for BMW's RS54.

THE MID- TO LATE 1950s: BAD TIMES

The racing motorcycles' combination of Earles-type suspension for the front wheel and swing arm at the rear, combined with two hydraulic shock absorbers front and rear, was the next big technological step and was adopted by BMW's production road boxer twins from 1955. The 500cc R50, 600cc R60 and R69 (and, from 1956, the single-cylinder BMW R26) replaced the R51/3, R61/3 and R68 respectively and all utilized full swinging-arm suspension front and rear. A new benchmark had been set in terms of comfort and directional stability.

Meanwhile, BMW continued production of the old R67/3, the only model still with telescopic forks, as a budget motorcycle primarily intended for police force use. Despite a 4.00 x 18inch rear tyre intended to make it even more suitable for sidecar use, it proved one of the least popular of all BMW's post-war boxers, and only 700 were produced in 1955 and 1956.

On the new 1955 models, along with the new front and rear suspension, the driveshaft was integrated into the swing arm for the first time. This new driveline featured not only a new three-shaft transmission but also a driveshaft with a front universal joint. The new design catered for the greater angular displacements caused by increased rear suspension travel, which could no longer be handled by a conventional flexible elastomer disc.

These developments may have suggested that there were exciting times ahead at BMW. In fact, the opposite was true. Although the mid-1950s proved a period of great technological advancement, it was also one of huge cultural change, especially for motor transport. Motorcycling for many went from boom to bust, as increasing numbers of customers eschewed two (or three) wheels for the new breed of small, affordable motor cars. Although BMW motorcycle sales peaked at around 30,000 in 1954, the subsequent years saw a huge decline. In 1955, the number of BMW motorcycles produced fell to 23,531, and it went from bad to worse, until it had fallen as low as 5,429, in 1959.

The all-new R50 family from 1955 introduced swinging arm rear suspension.

■ 1950s: FROM BOOM TO BUST

BMW was not the only manufacturer affected, of course. During 1957, many German motorcycle manufacturers, including Adler, DKW and Horex, went to the wall. BMW was supported in part by its car business and managed to struggle on, but the economic crisis also meant that, following the introduction of the innovative R50 series in 1955, BMW carried out virtually no motorcycle development for almost five years.

By 1959, with motorcycle sales plummeting and its sales of luxury cars proving incapable of covering production and development costs, BMW faced bankruptcy. Even the manufacture of the novel Isetta 'bubble car', from 1955, was unable to resolve the firm's deep-seated financial crisis.

It all came to a head at a landmark BMW shareholders' meeting later that year. There was a proposal on the table from the management to sell the company to Daimler-Benz. Instead, a small group of shareholders led by industrialist Dr Herbert Quandt changed their minds at the last minute, due to opposition from the workforce and trades unions. Against the advice of his bankers and risking much of his own personal wealth, Quandt decided to increase his share of BMW from 10 to 50 per cent. After taking control in this way, he quickly put into practice an alternative plan for rationalizing the group. His new plan for a car range focusing on sporty small and mid-range cars instead of luxury ones quickly led to an upswing in sales, reversed the company's fortunes and revitalized BMW as the world headed into the 1960s.

BMW's direction changed again at a vital shareholders' meeting in 1959.

HERBERT QUANDT – BMW SAVIOUR

One man is regarded as having saved BMW from the brink of bankruptcy and sale in 1959 – German industrialist Herbert Werner Quandt. Herbert's father, Günther, was a successful businessman, who made his first fortune supplying uniforms to the German army in the First World War. He subsequently diversified into a range of businesses, from battery manufacture and metal fabrication to potash mining, and when he died, in 1954, the Quandt group comprised about 200 businesses. Quandt also owned about 10 per cent of Daimler-Benz and 30 per cent of BMW. On his death, the assets passed to Herbert and his half-brother Harald.

When the ailing BMW company came close to being sold to Daimler-Benz in 1959, the Quandts decided not to sell out. Instead, they increased their share to 50 per cent, to take control of the company, and became instrumental in reversing its fortunes. When Harald died, in 1967, Herbert became BMW's majority shareholder. Herbert Quandt died in 1982 but his descendants retain a controlling interest in BMW today. They remain one of Germany's richest familiies.

Herbert Quandt (right), pictured later with BMW chairman Kurt Golda, is credited with rescuing BMW in 1959.

KEY MODELS

1951–1954 BMW R51/3: 'The First Modern Boxer Engine'

The 494cc R51/3 was introduced in 1951 and with a production run of nearly four years and almost 20,000 built, it proved to be one of most important boxers of the 1950s. It was unveiled at the Amsterdam show in February 1951, along with the 600cc R67, both featuring significantly updated engines.

By contrast to BMW's first post-war flat twin, with its two chain-driven camshafts, there was now a single, central camshaft driven by gearwheels from the crankshaft. The new engines were also far more handsome, smoother designs with one-piece valve covers. Placing the magneto and generator behind the front cover made the engine more compact, while the new Noris magneto ignition automatic advance and retard enabled the engine to run particularly smoothly.

The frame retained the familiar suspension designs dating from 1938 with a telescopic fork at the front and plungers at the rear, while the brakes were uprated slightly. In 1952, the leading and trailing shoe brake were replaced by a two leading shoe pattern and from 1953 rubber gaiters were fitted to the telescopic forks in place of the metal covers. The most important innovation in 1954 was the switch to full-width hub brakes and new light alloy wheel rims in place of the previous steel ones. The fishtail silencers were also replaced by a less complex cigar-shaped design.

While the R67 had been conceived mostly to be used in combination with a sidecar, the R51/3 was aimed very much at the sporting rider.

■ 1950s: FROM BOOM TO BUST

The R51/3 was one of the most important BMW motorcycles of the 1950s.

BELOW LEFT: **The all-new air-cooled boxer twin was a far smoother, more integrated design.**

BELOW RIGHT: **Rear suspension on the R51/3 was still a plunger design but brakes and wheels were updated.**

1952–1954 BMW R68: 'The First 100mph Boxer'

The demand for more performance in the early 1950s led to the creation of one of the finest BMW boxers of the 1950s. By 1951, the Bavarian marque realized that its boxers were being outperformed by the latest British parallel twins from Triumph and BSA. The response was the launch of a 'hotted-up' R67. Introduced by BMW as the '100mph motorcycle' at the International Bicycle and Motorcycle Show (IFMA) in Cologne in 1952, the R68 was the company's top sporting model of the day and paved the way for the R69 of 1955.

Designed for the sporting rider, almost 20,000 examples of the R51/3 were built.

LEFT: **The R51/3's instrumentation still followed the simple template of a single dial plus warning lights in the headlamp nacelle.**

BELOW: **Lean, clean and effective, the R51/3 proved very popular.**

1950s: FROM BOOM TO BUST

1951–1954 R51/3

Engine
Type	BMW air-cooled boxer
Internal code	252/1
Block material	Cast iron
Head material	Aluminium
Bore and stroke	68 × 68mm
Capacity	494cc
Valves	ohv, 2 valves per cylinder
Compression ratio	6.3:1
Carburettor	2 × Bing 1/22/41
Max. power (DIN)	24bhp @ 5,800rpm
Max. torque	N/A
Fuel capacity	3.73gall (17ltr)

Transmission
Gearbox	4-speed, manual
Clutch	Single dry plate
Final drive	Shaft

Chassis
Frame	Tubular steel double loop
Front suspension	Telescopic fork
Rear suspension	Plunger type
Tyres	19-3.5in cross-ply
Wheels	Wire spoke, steel rim
Rim width	3in

Brakes
Type	Front 200mm drum, rear 200mm drum

Dimensions
Wheelbase	55.11in 1400mm
Overall length	83.8in 2130mm
Overall width	31.1in 790mm
Overall height	38.7in 985mm
Unladen weight	418lb 190kg

Performance
Top speed	83mph 135km/h
0–60mph	N/A

Price DM 2750

No. built 18,420

With a top speed of 100mph, the R68 was BMW's best-performing sporting model of the day.

1950s: FROM BOOM TO BUST

The R68 was derived from the R67, but with a 'hotted'-up engine producing 35bhp.

1952–1954 R68

Engine
Type	BMW air-cooled boxer
Internal code	268/1
Block material	Cast iron
Head material	Aluminium
Bore and stroke	72 × 73mm
Capacity	594cc
Valves	ohv, 2 valves per cylinder
Compression ratio	8.0:1
Carburettor	2 × Bing 1/26/9
Max. power (DIN)	35bhp @ 7,000rpm
Max. torque	N/A
Fuel capacity	3.73gall (17ltr)

Transmission
Gearbox	4-speed, footshift
Clutch	Single dry plate
Final drive	Shaft

Chassis
Frame	Tubular steel double loop
Front suspension	Telescopic fork
Rear suspension	Plunger type
Tyres	19-3.5in cross-ply
Wheels	Wire spoke, steel rim
Rim width	3in

Brakes
Type	Front 200mm drum, rear 200mm drum

Dimensions
Wheelbase	55.11in 1400mm
Overall length	83.8in 2130mm
Overall width	32.08in 815mm
Overall height	38.7in 985mm
Unladen weight	422lb 190kg

Performance
Top speed	99mph 160km/h
0–60mph	N/A

Price	DM 3950
No. built	1452

1950s: FROM BOOM TO BUST

Developed from the touring R67, the R68 had different valve covers and narrower mudguards. Internal changes in the engine included larger valves, bigger 28mm Bing carburettors, a different camshaft, a higher compression ratio of 7.7:1 and needle-bearing rocker arms. Performance was significantly boosted to 35bhp, making it the most powerful production boxer yet built.

The R68 came in two guises, one for the road and one for off-road competition. It was particularly popular in the important International Six Days Trial; this version had an upswept, 'siamesed' exhaust, wider bars, separate pillion and raised rear number plate.

1954 BMW RS54: 'The Bevel-Drive Production Racer'

BMW had captured global attention before the Second World War by repeatedly breaking the motorcycle world land speed record, via Ernst Henne and its supercharged streamliners. It had also won the European championship in 1938 and the Isle of Man Senior TT in 1939 with Georg 'Schorsch' Meier. The post-war situation was very different. In the immediate aftermath of hostilities, all German factories (BMW, NSU, DKW, and so on) were barred from international competition. However, they all carried on developing their old supercharged designs and racing for domestic championship honours. BMW was particularly successful, with Meier winning the German 500cc championship on a modified pre-war supercharged RS255 in six years out of seven, between 1947 and 1953.

Germany was re-admitted to worldwide FIM-sanctioned events in 1950, albeit with superchargers now banned. BMW was buoyed up by the accelerating sales of its production motorcycles under the German post-war 'economic miracle', and set about upgrading its pre-war supercharged RS255 into a modern, normally aspirated GP racer.

In 1950, Alfred Böning, Eberhard Wolff, Leonard Ischinger and Rudolph Schleicher set to work on the neutered RS500 engine, in order to gain more performance from the now normally aspirated boxer. Their first result was the RS53, which featured a proper swinging arm rear suspension system with twin hydraulic shock absorbers, and with the shaft drive running down the right-hand tunnel. Towards the end of 1953, a revised version, dubbed the RS54, was shown, with a significantly revised engine and front suspension.

Although the new design retained much of the old Kompressor, with twin gear-driven camshafts hidden in the cylinder heads, in reality the engine was virtually all new. Initially, it had a bore and stroke of 66 × 72mm, giving 492cc; with later development, it became 'square' at 68 × 68mm, while the works machines eventually used 70 × 64mm. Camshafts were driven by a shaft-and-bevel system, running on needle roller bearings while, to keep the cylinder head short, the exhaust cam (driven from the engine) was geared direct to the inlet cam and drove the valves by short, flat rockers. Valves were set at a wide 82-degree angle in the semi-spherical heads, using duplex coil springs held by stepped aluminium keepers.

The RS54 was a purpose-built boxer racer built as a successor to the 255 Kompressor.

Although the RS54 was based on the old 255, the 492cc engine was ultimately an all-new design.

ABOVE: **Lean, lithe and nimble, the RS54 was designed by Alfred Böning, Eberhard Wolff, Leonard Ischinger and Rudolph Schleicher.**

The chassis of the RS54 was even more advanced, with a swinging arm rear and Earles-type forks at the front.

Amal-Fischer 30mm TT carburettors (made under licence since the 1930s) were mounted at 15 degrees downdraught. The crankshaft ran in three main bearings inside a one-piece cast crankcase, at the front of which gears drove the oil pump and magneto, which sat atop the engine. The connecting rods had a flat section, as tests had showed cracking with a more typical 'I'-section rod. Forged Mahle pistons with only an 8:1 compression ratio ran inside cast aluminium cylinders, with either a shrunk-in iron liner, or chrome-plated plain barrel with six-stud crankcase fixing. The typical BMW engine-speed flywheel clutch drove a four-speed gearbox, and the final driveshaft was housed inside the right-hand swing arm tube, although, unlike the later production models, the swing arm did not hold oil.

BMW made an even bigger step forward with the RS54's chassis. This comprised a full loop, all-welded lightweight frame with proper rear swing arm suspension and hydraulic damped shocks instead of plunger units at the rear, plus, in place of telescopic forks, a new, ultra-rigid fork design, which comprised its own swing arm and two shocks, as licensed from Englishman Ernie Earles. This quickly became known as the 'Earles fork' and, from 1955, would become standard across BMW's boxers right through the 1960s.

103

1950s: FROM BOOM TO BUST

Braking-wise, an aluminium 200mm twin leading shoe full-width drum was used at the front, with a single leading shoe drum at the rear. A hydraulic version, as fitted to the later works racers and sidecars, was also sometimes used.

Another surprise had been BMW's announcement, in 1953, that limited examples of their new racing machine would also be offered for sale. These were to be closely modelled on the works machines, but, ultimately, only 24 were actually built, along with 50 extra engines, which were made available to sidecar racers.

The RS54 was a 130kg (286lb), DOHC, dedicated racing machine producing 45bhp, which on paper compared well with its main competition, the 50bhp, single-cylinder Norton Manx. It proved to be a superb racing motorcycle in national races throughout the next decade, although it never quite claimed the 500cc Grand Prix world championship. However, it more than made up for it on three wheels, becoming the most successful sidecar competition machine in the history of the sport. In its first year, 1954, Wilhelm Noll and Fritz Cron won the world sidecar championship, repeating the feat in 1956. In fact, between 1954 and 1974, RS54-powered sidecars secured 19 world sidecar championships.

What is more, the technological advances demonstrated by the RS54, and particularly its Earles-type leading-link front forks, passed over to BMW's road boxers, setting the template for BMW's machines for the next decade.

Today, the RS54 is among the most sought-after and collectable of all BMW boxer twins. In 2013, one example – chassis no. 254007 – sold for well over US$167,000 at Bonhams Las Vegas Motorcycle Auction.

1954 RS54	
Price	N/A
Engine	dohc boxer twin
Capacity	492cc
Output	45bhp
Wet weight	130kg
Top speed	N/A
No. built	24

1955–1960 BMW R50: 'The First Modern Chassis'

The R50 was introduced at the Brussels show in January 1955 alongside the R60 and R69 and was significant mostly for using an all-new chassis that, being derived from that of the RS54 racer, moved completely away from pre-war designs for the first time. As such, it was not only the first production BMW boxer twin to feature a proper swinging arm rear suspension system along with twin shock absorbers, which replaced the previous 'plunger'-type rear suspension, it also discarded the now ageing front telescopic forks for the new leading-link Earles type. Although most commonly used on sidecars up to that time, the Earles forks reduced dive under braking and delivered an improved ride. Together, this set the template for every BMW boxer chassis up to 1969.

The engine of the R50 was essentially that of the R51/3 but with four- rather than five-ring pistons to provide a slightly higher compression ratio, and two larger Bing carburettors, which together helped slightly increase peak power to 26bhp.

The 1955 R50 was the first production BMW with swinging arm rear suspension.

Also new was a three-shaft gearbox (in place of the preceding two) and a diaphragm-spring clutch. The external hand lever had disappeared and the four-speed gearbox gained revised ratios.

The driveshaft was now enclosed in the right-hand arm of the swing arm, with the universal joint moved to the gearbox end of the driveshaft to cope with the increased movement of the rear suspension.

Despite the addition of the new swing arm, the frame still resembled quite closely that of the previous 'plunger' machines but with a slightly stronger steel spine and steering head. A side stand was added in 1955, after which the boxer frame remained virtually unchanged up to 1969. A new fuel tank, meanwhile, was more rounded than before and held 17 litres.

The R50 was replaced by the updated R50/2 in 1960.

1955–1960 R50

Engine

Type	BMW air-cooled boxer
Internal code	252/2
Block material	Cast iron
Head material	Aluminium
Bore and stroke	68 × 68mm
Capacity	494cc
Valves	ohv, 2 valves per cylinder
Compression ratio	6.8:1
Carburettor	2 × Bing 1/24/45
Max. power (DIN)	26bhp @ 5,800rpm
Max. torque	N/A
Fuel capacity	3.73gall (17ltr)

Transmission

Gearbox	4-speed, manual, footshift
Clutch	Single dry plate
Final drive	Shaft

Chassis

Frame	Tubular steel double loop
Front suspension	Earles fork
Rear suspension	Swing arm, twin shock
Tyres	18-3.5in cross-ply
Wheels	Wire spoke, steel rim
Rim width	3in

Brakes

Type	Front 200mm drum, rear 200mm drum

Dimensions

Wheelbase	55.7in 1415mm
Overall length	83.6in 2125mm
Overall width	25.9in 660mm
Overall height	38.1in 980mm
Unladen weight	429lb 195kg

Performance

Top speed	87mph 140km/h
0–60mph	N/A

Price	DM 3050
No. built	13,510

The R50 was replaced by the updated R50/2 in 1960.

CHAPTER SIX

1960s: FROM BOOM TO BERLIN

CHANGING FORTUNES

Following BMW's financial crisis of 1959, its nearly being sold to Daimler-Benz and the subsequent restructuring under new majority shareholder Herbert Quandt, the fortunes of the company – and its products – changed dramatically. The catalyst for much of this was not initially a new boxer motorcycle, but a new boxer-powered car. BMW's 700, a new, small, affordable car powered by an enlarged, 697cc boxer twin motorcycle engine, developed from that of the R67, was launched in August 1959. It proved an immediate success and remained in production until November 1965. With almost 200,000 sold, the 700 fuelled a massive turnaround in BMW's fortunes.

In the context of BMW's ageing boxer twin motorcycles, the immediate effect was to encourage the development of a new line of machines. The first fruits of this came in late 1960 and early 1961 with the new R50/2 and R 60/2 and their more sporting variants, the R50S and R69S. Outwardly, these newcomers looked generally little different from their predecessors and retained the characteristic swinging arm and Earles-type rear and front suspension systems of those bikes, respectively. However, internal engine changes were significant, delivering greater reliability. The results were machines that formed the backbone of BMW's motorcycling output through most of the 1960s.

The 1960s was a decade of great social and consumer change. As the austerity of the post-war years began to subside and the appeal of motorcycles as utility transport waned in favour of a new breed of small, affordable cars, the rise in disposable income and the increase in leisure time led to motorcycling becoming more of a hobby than a means of transport. Against this background, BMW's aspirational premium and reliable tourers and sports machines were in increasing demand.

The US market was a key factor in all of this. Buyers there traditionally had an interest in large-capacity, twin-cylinder tourers, which had the ability to cover large distances in comfort. BMW's big boxer twins fulfilled this brief perfectly and became increasingly popular.

There was one BMW casualty in all of this: the German company's more affordable and utilitarian single-cylinder machines. The final 250cc version, the R27, was also introduced in 1960 as the successor to the R26 but ceased production in 1966. From then up to the introduction of the controversial K series threes and fours, in 1983, BMW only produced variations of its air-cooled boxer twins. It would not resume making singles until the launch of the Rotax-powered, Aprilia-built F650 Funduro in 1993.

At the end of the 1960s, as BMW's motorcycle production was moved from Munich to Berlin, the Bavarian company did it again, introducing the all-new /5 series of boxer twins that would become the basis of all of its machines through the following decade.

UPDATES FOR A NEW DECADE

Back at the beginning of the 1960s, however, things had been very different. The mood at the Cologne IFMA (International Bicycle and Motorcycle Exhibition) in the autumn of 1960 was particularly bleak, with many German motorcycle manufacturers having gone bankrupt in the previous few years and others left fighting to survive. The offer on BMW's stand was therefore all the more surprising. The entire model range had been updated and extended. There was the new R50/2 and R60/2, a new sports 500, the R50S, and the highlight of them all, the new R69S.

ABOVE: **In August 1960, against a backdrop of crisis in the motorcycling industry, BMW introduced the R60/2.**

RIGHT: **Although it was outwardly similar, the revised engine of the R60/2 boosted peak power to 30bhp.**

BELOW: **A new, deeply padded bench seat in place of the old sprung saddle led to much-improved comfort for the rider of the R60/2.**

■ 1960s: FROM BOOM TO BERLIN

The sporty new R69S was even bigger.

BELOW: **Higher compression and other internal changes helped boost the R69S's power to 42bhp.**

Although these new machines looked very similar to their predecessors, there were significant changes internally, with new cam followers, a beefier crankshaft and camshaft, stronger bearing housings, a new clutch plus new three-ring pistons. Those in the R60/2 provided a higher 7.5:1 compression ratio, which helped boost peak power to 30bhp at 5,800rpm.

Although the biggest seller of these new models would prove to be the R50/2, the most exciting of the newcomers were undoubtedly the two new sporting versions, the R50S and, particularly, the R69S, the replacement for the R69.

Based on the R69, the R69S had new, higher-compression (9.5:1) pistons, larger inlet ports and a larger-volume air filter, along with improved crankcase ventilation and a less restrictive exhaust. These changes combined to boost peak power for the 69S from 35 to 42bhp at 7,000rpm, the highest output yet from a production boxer. It was enough to generate a top speed of 175km/h, a speed that only a few motorcycles were capable of achieving even in the international market and that made it the fastest German production motorcycle ever. The R50S, meanwhile, produced the same power as the earlier R69 – 35bhp at 7,650rpm.

Another new feature on the sports versions was a hydraulic steering damper, which could be shut down if not required. This, together with the proven swinging-arm suspension at both wheels, ensured a high level of directional stability even at high speeds.

Comfort levels, meanwhile, were also given a notable boost by the jettisoning of the old-fashioned sprung saddle in favour of a now obligatory and deeply padded dual bench seat.

108

1960s: FROM BOOM TO BERLIN

The R69S was the first modern sports road boxer.

The comfort and performance of the R69S helped to establish BMW among motorcycling's sporting elite.

All in all, the new models, and particularly the sporting R50S and R69, proved exactly the right bikes at the right time and helped establish BMW among the motorcycling sporting elite, not just in Europe but in the US as well.

Leading US magazine *Cycle World* was particularly impressed by the R69S:

Whatever the BMW's merits in a contest of speed, it is still the smoothest, best finished, quietest and cleanest motorcycle it has ever been our pleasure to ride. To be honest, we think that anyone who would worry much over its performance-potential is a bit of a 'booby'. The R69S is fast enough to handle any encounter, and it has attributes that are, in touring, infinitely more valuable than mere speed. All things considered, if we were planning a two-wheel style vacation/tour, the BMW would have to be our choice of mount.

However, not all the reviews were as positive. While the R69S went on to re-emphasize its qualities with a string of

1960s: FROM BOOM TO BERLIN

successes in endurance racing, the less dazzling R50S was quietly discontinued during 1962 after the production of just 1634 examples.

SEARCHING FOR PERFECTION

As the decade unfolded, the changes kept coming. The BMW engineers' search for perfection was evident in various detail improvements over the coming years. Early reliability problems with the R69S led to a few tweaks for 1962, with new pistons and cylinders. To further differentiate it from the old R69, it was also given new 'R69S' badges, most notably on the rear mudguard. In September 1963 BMW also added a rubber-mounted vibration damper to the front of the crankshaft in order to ensure the engine's reliability on long runs at high speed.

The touring /2 versions, however, required very few updates, gaining only slightly longer push-rods in mid-1965, rotating valves from October 1966, a lightly modified crank in 1967 and revised spark plug mounts in 1968.

Despite their initial success, these last Earles-fork BMWs were, by the mid-1960s, looking increasingly antiquated. Conspicuously heavy, due to their robust frames and forks that had largely been developed for a sidecar use that was now out of fashion, especially in the US, their performance was at best merely adequate and their solo handling was idiosyncratic.

To address this, from 1967 BMW produced updated versions, with 36mm BMW-designed telescopic forks and all the sidecar lugs removed from the frame. These were designated the R50US, R60US and R69US. Unfortunately, however, although they had been modified specifically with the US market in mind, the changes did not particularly improve the bikes' fortunes Stateside.

Bigger changes were planned for the end of the decade. By 1966, along with the decision to can its single-cylinder machines and relocate production to Berlin, BMW was in the early stages of developing the successors to the Earles-forked machines. They unveiled the fruits of their labours in autumn 1969. These were the three models of the all-new, Berlin-built models in the company's /5 series: entry-level R50/5, mid-range R60/5 and the flagship R75/5.

It cannot be overstated how much of a leap forward these machines were. In terms of technology, no stone was left unturned: not only did the engine belong to a new era, so did the chassis and design.

1969's all-new /5 series, topped by the R75/5, lifted BMW to another level again.

1960s: FROM BOOM TO BERLIN

In terms of the chassis, there was a new, dual-cradle tubular frame made of steel, a swinging arm with two oil pressure struts at the rear and, most conspicuously, an extensively revised, BMW-designed telescopic fork replacing the heavy and outdated Earles fork. This new fork's longer spring travel, much-increased ground clearance and excellent agility gained unanimous praise in the motorcycle press as well as among customers.

High-end light alloy wheel rims contributed to a reduced unsprung mass, while amply sized, full hub brakes guaranteed reliable and stable deceleration.

The rest of the new /5 series was just as innovative. Development of the all-new engine, designated the Type 247, was overseen by Alex von Falkenhausen and Ferdinand Jardin, and the result was considered to be the first true modular BMW unit. The twin-cylinder boxer provided an output of 32bhp in the R50/5, 40bhp in the R60/5 and 50bhp in the top model, the R75/5. All three models used the new engine. The main difference was that the cylinder bore size was changed according to capacity, with a stroke of 70.6mm being retained throughout. In addition, the engine took on a more curvaceous look overall, which made it appear more modern. It was a successful styling exercise built on the need to utilize the latest technological advances and create a new, up-to-date template upon which all future BMW motorcycles would be based.

Reliability was at the forefront of the new engine design rather than outright power. Oil pumping, oil scavenging feed and return design were key points and these were reflected in the Eaton-type oil pump, which could deliver 1,400 litres of oil at 6,000rpm. Fuel delivery was taken care of by Bing carburettors carefully selected for each capacity. For example, the R50/5 used two slide carburettors while the R75/5 ran with two of the latest constant vacuum (CV) types. This gave the R75/5 an outstandingly direct throttle response and excellent acceleration, yet respectably low fuel consumption.

The /5 engine's taller crankcase now rose up to the fuel tank, and also had the electric starter motor located within it. The traditional push-rods, meanwhile, were now placed under the cylinders. This left the topside of the cylinders free from clutter and also allowed greater airflow across the cooling fins. This was achieved by placing the camshaft under the crankshaft and having it driven by a duplex chain, so the pipes for the valve activation tappets were now underneath the light alloy cylinders. The crankshaft itself was a one-piece item for rigidity emphasized with increased bearing journal diameters.

New telescopic forks and lighter weight helped to improve handling and stability.

■ 1960s: FROM BOOM TO BERLIN

The /5 series was the first true modular BMW series, comprising the R50/5, R60/5 and R75/5.

Meanwhile, the new steel double-cradle frame, complete with a rear swing arm with twin oil-damped shock absorbers, made a significant contribution to the new bikes' ride comfort and safety.

BMW even showed itself to be a pioneer of modern instrumentation with the R75/5. The lamp bowl of the headlamp now housed a circular instrument that combined speedometer and engine speed display in a single unit. And the top-of-the-range R75/5 even had an electric starter for the first time.

The /5 series was well received straight away and BMW's boldness was quickly rewarded, with production figures at the new BMW plant in Berlin growing rapidly: in 1970, 12,287 motorcycles left the Spandau factory. The flagship R75/5, was particularly popular – by 1973, BMW had sold over 38,000 units of its first post-war 750cc motorcycle. For the first time, the most powerful variant of a BMW motorcycle model series was also the best-selling.

With the /5 series, BMW was well equipped to serve the rapidly growing motorcycle market of the 1970s, while the all-new chassis and engine offered great potential for further development. The prospects for the future included even more powerful and dynamic models to come.

Producing the new /5 series in the still-divided city of Berlin, BMW was able to send out its very own message of individualism and freedom. When the /5 series was discontinued, in July 1973, BMW had built a total of 68,956 motorcycles in Berlin, and in that same year the company celebrated '50 years of BMW Motorrad' with the manufacture of the 500,000th BMW motorcycle. It was a success story that looked set to continue thoughout the 1970s…

SPANDAU FACTORY

BMW's automobile production in Munich began to increase rapidly in the mid-1960s, and in 1969 the company decided to shift its motorcycle operations to Berlin. This was partly because space was running out in its factories in Bavaria, but also in order to take advantage of financial incentives offered by the government to companies looking to manufacture in Berlin.

BMW had a long history at the Berlin site anyway. Originally built as an aero engine factory by Siemens in 1928, it was acquired by BMW in 1939, when the company was still producing aero engines alongside its motorcycles and cars. Among the assemblies produced at the plant were the engines for the JU 52 transport plane.

At the end of the Second World War, the plant's equipment was largely destroyed, but it returned to full operations in 1949, constructing motorcycle components for the BMWs assembled in Bavaria and, from 1958, components for its car production, too.

The late 1960s saw the move of motorcycle production to the Spandau factory in Berlin.

Although lavish government subsidies were undoubtedly a factor, by the mid-1960s BMW was already considering reorganizing its production facilities due to a significant increase in its car production. The existing facility in Berlin had its attractions, not least a skilled workforce and adjacent land that was available to build a new assembly hall. With government assistance in place, a plan was set in motion.

On 13 May 1969, a motorcycle rolled off the Munich production line for the last time, and all future BMW motorcycle production was moved to the expanded Berlin plant. This began in September, with the all-new /5 series, which was built according to a new modular approach, with many components being shared between models. In those early days, the workforce of around 400 employees would turn out 30 motorcycles per day – all made by hand. Only the development and testing departments were left behind in Munich, where they remain today.

The popularity of these new machines meant that production figures in Berlin increased rapidly. In 1970, no fewer than 12,287 units came off the production line and by July 1973, when the /5 model series reached the end of production, 68,956 motorcycles had left Berlin – a five-fold increase in just three years. That year also saw the Berlin plant complete production of the 500,000th BMW motorcycle in the company's history.

Following the introduction of the even more successful /6 series, including the flagship R90S, the 100,000th BMW built in Berlin-Spandau rolled off the production line in January 1975. In 1976, these models were superseded once again by the new /7 series, itself rounded off with the landmark R100RS, the world's first production motorcycle with a full fairing. The continued success of these bikes led to the DM 200 million construction of a further assembly hall at Spandau, raising the Berlin plant's motorcycle production capacity to 60,000 machines a year.

Although the last air-cooled boxer rolled out of Spandau in 1996, the Berlin plant remains at the heart of BMW's motorcycle business. Today, the Spandau site covers roughly 178,000 square metres (almost two million square feet) and employs a workforce of 1,900. Up to 700 motorcycles per day roll out through the doors of the plant, which is consistently expanded and modernized. It also produces more than six million brake discs every year for BMW's cars. In 2001, the Berlin plant built the one-millionth BMW motorcycle and just 10 years later that figure had already passed the two million mark.

■ 1960s: FROM BOOM TO BERLIN

KEY MODELS

1960–1969 R69S: 'The First BMW Superbike'

In 1960, when the German motorcycle industry was virtually dead, BMW launched the R69S. In producing a machine that was capable of 175km/h, the company was elevating its reputation to the top ranks of world motorcycle manufacturers, particularly in the important US market. Today, the R69S is considered the definitive BMW of the pre-1970 era and one of the most collectable and desirable classic BMWs of all.

Based on the more sedate R69, which was produced between 1955 and 1960, the R69S was intended from the outset to be BMW's flagship sports bike. As such, it would benefit from the firm's extensive racing experience and even some of its race technology. To boost its performance from the R69's 35bhp to 42bhp, the highest yet from a production boxer, BMW fitted new, higher-compression (9.5:1) pistons, larger inlet ports, a larger air filter and a less restrictive exhaust. A year later, after some reliability problems from the high-performance engine, the pistons and cylinders were redesigned, a vibration damper was fitted to the end of the crankshaft and the main bearings were remodelled to withstand whip and flex in the crank.

Chassis-wise, its twin loop tubular steel frame featured BMW's full swinging arm, which was signature at the time, with twin shock absorbers at the rear plus BMW's licensed Earles forks at the front. One new addition was a hydraulic steering damper. Another was the plush and deeply padded bench seat. BMW's stylists strove to give the machine a distinctive visual impact, in order to set it apart from the touring models. There was a striking white paint option (until then only available to the likes of the police), which was enhanced in subsequent years with extra chromework and badging.

The result was not only the fastest German production machine of the era but also one renowned for its smooth handling, reliability, build quality and finish – not to mention its classic, clean looks. All in all, the R69S was truly deserving of its 'flagship' status. As the last of the Earles-type, pre-/5 series machines, it is also considered today to be the ultimate boxer twin of the era and one of the most desirable of all post-war BMWs.

The 1960 R69S was arguably BMW's first true superbike.

1960s: FROM BOOM TO BERLIN

The performance, quality and comfort of the R69S made it a big hit in the USA.

The R69S's significantly reworked engine produced 42bhp, making it the most powerful airhead yet.

BMW also broke with tradition with the R69S by offering it not in the usual black, but in white!

115

1960s: FROM BOOM TO BERLIN

The 'R69S' chrome badge on the rear mudguard was a later touch of quality.

A stylish speedometer dial and chrome steering damper were other quality touches.

1960–1969 R69S

Engine
Type	BMW air-cooled boxer
Internal code	268/3
Block material	Cast iron
Head material	Aluminium
Bore and stroke	72 × 73mm
Capacity	594cc
Valves	ohv, 2 valves per cylinder
Compression ratio	9.5:1
Carburettor	2 × Bing 1/26/75
Max. power (DIN)	42bhp @ 7,000rpm
Max. torque	N/A
Fuel capacity	3.73gall (17ltr)

Transmission
Gearbox	4-speed, manual, footshift
Clutch	Single dry plate
Final drive	Shaft

Chassis
Frame	Tubular steel double loop
Front suspension	Earles fork
Rear suspension	Swing arm, twin shock
Tyres	18-3.5in cross-ply
Wheels	Wire spoke, steel rim
Rim width	3in

Brakes
Type	Front 200mm drum, rear 200mm drum

Dimensions
Wheelbase	55.7in 1415mm
Overall length	83.6in 2125mm
Overall width	28.4in 722mm
Overall height	38.1in 980mm
Unladen weight	444lb 202kg

Performance
Top speed	108mph 175km/h
0–60mph	N/A

Price	DM 4030
No. built	11,317

1960s: FROM BOOM TO BERLIN

1969–1973 R60/5: 'An All-New Series for an All-New Era'

From the mid-1960s, light slowly began to appear at the end of the tunnel of the motorcycle crisis. As is often the case, a new trend initially developed in the US market, where the motorcycle was now increasingly regarded as an aspirational leisure vehicle rather than a mere means of transport. This moved the motorcycle away from its greasy image and the luxury motorcycle became increasingly fashionable. BMW's response was to create the all-new /5 series, to reflect the spirit of these times.

The R60/5 was typical of 1969's all-new /5 series family and its middle member.

The /5 series was designed by Hans-Gunther von der Marwitz to be a fashionable, luxury motorcycle.

117

■ 1960s: FROM BOOM TO BERLIN

ABOVE LEFT: **Telescopic forks, complete with protective rubber gaiters, replaced the old Earles front-end items.**

ABOVE RIGHT: **The R60/5's engine was all new and based around new one-piece aluminium crankcases (note the model badging).**

LEFT: **A long bench seat also ensured that the R60/5 was a superb touring machine.**

Former Porsche designer Hans-Gunther von der Marwitz was tasked with creating the /5 series. An enthusiastic motorcyclist, he wanted to follow in the tradition of racers Rudolf Schleicher and Alexander von Falkenhausen, by using racing technologies to design a machine that was fast and reliable. Another key feature was handling; von der Marwitz had been personally disappointed with the handling of the Earles fork /2 series.

What he came up with was clearly a classic BMW air-cooled boxer twin with shaft drive, but it also featured a host of technological innovations. It was fundamentally lighter than before and it performed better, yet it maintained the BMW values of quality, durability and comfort.

The first key difference was the capacity of each member of the three-strong family. By the mid- to late 1960s, 750s were becoming common as range-topping machines, not only

1960s: FROM BOOM TO BERLIN

Instrumentation followed the traditional layout but now also included a tachometer.

in twin-cylinder form, but also in a new breed of multi-cylinder machines from Japan. Thus, BMW's flagship performance /5 model would be 750cc. At the other end of the scale, more utilitarian, affordable and basic 500s were still popular, particularly with government agencies such as the police. A 600cc version, meanwhile, would occupy the middle ground.

With a requirement for increased performance, the engine to be used by all three would be all-new, although still very much a traditional BMW flat twin. New one-piece aluminium crankcases housed a one-piece forged crankshaft running in plain bearings. The camshaft was situated underneath the engine, driven by a duplex chain from the front of the crankshaft, while the valve actuation push-rods were now underneath the cylinders, giving the engine a cleaner, more modern look. Aluminium, incidentally, was used extensively to reduce weight and now formed the barrels but with cast-iron sleeves. The gearbox was a new four-speed, three-shaft unit bolted on to the rear of the engine.

The chassis, too, was all-new and designed for the first time specifically for solo riding rather than for use with a sidecar. It comprised an all-new tubular steel double-loop frame, but its strength was questionable as it was constructed of variable section tapered and oval tubing with a bolt-on rear subframe – von der Marwitz was convinced that too much frame stiffness was detrimental for a street motorcycle. This, combined with the /5 series short swing arm, meant that it was less stable than previous BMW flat twins, earning it the unflattering nickname 'rubber cow'.

Suspension, meanwhile, came from the BMW-designed but Fichtel & Sachs-built, leading-axle 35mm telescopic forks,

which had debuted on 1967's R69US, with twin Boge shock absorbers at the rear. Further modernizing touches included a fully updated electrical system with a pioneering electric starter (an option on the R50), and a whole new range of colours, including some metallics, instead of the traditional BMW plain black or white.

It was all enough for the new series to be a big hit from the outset. R60/5 production commenced at Spandau in September, with the R75/5 in October and the R50/5 in November. All were successful, although the R50/5, aimed mostly at government agencies, was overshadowed by its larger brothers, to the extent that, when the family was upgraded in the mid-1970s into the /6 series, the R50 version was dropped.

Overall, however, the comparatively sporty, dynamic, modern and yet comfortable, reliable and practical new /5 series was a huge success. After their launch at the end of 1969 it was soon obvious that demand for the bigger R60/5 and R75/5 models was exceeding all expectations and, while the R75/5 was the undisputed flagship, the R60/5 delivered a happy compromise of both price and performance. Instead of the intended R50, the R60/5 quickly became the motorcycle of choice for the German police, who soon dubbed it the 'Weiße Maus' ('white mouse'), because of its basic colour combined with that of its Gläser full fairing.

During 1970, 12,346 examples of the /5 series were sold – the best overall production figures since 1955.

1969–1973 R75/5: 'BMW's First Sports 750'

While 1969's new /5 series trio were all a success, the highlight for many was the flagship R75/5. With the 750cc class becoming the benchmark sporting displacement at the end of the 1960s, BMW, keen to re-establish its sporting credentials, built its first 750cc flat twin since the wartime R75. The resulting bike was so well received it became the best-seller of the trio – a first for a new BMW series.

Although the 75 was obviously based on the same engine block and chassis architecture as all three /5 series machines, its engine was significantly different. As well as the larger cylinder dimensions, it also boasted larger inlet and exhaust valves (42 and 38mm respectively compared to the R60/5's 38 and 34mm and R50/5's 34 and 32mm). It had more radical camshafts, too, as well as innovative Bing constant vacuum (CV) carburettors, in place of the Bing concentric carburettors of the smaller versions.

■ 1960s: FROM BOOM TO BERLIN

1969–1973 R60/5

Engine
Type	BMW air-cooled boxer twin
Internal code	N/A
Block material	Cast iron
Head material	Aluminium
Bore and stroke	73.5 × 70.6mm
Capacity	599cc
Valves	ohv, 2 valves per cylinder
Compression ratio	9.2:1
Carburettor	2 × Bing 1/26/11
Max. power (DIN)	40bhp @ 6,400rpm
Max. torque	N/A
Fuel capacity	5.27gall (24ltr)

Transmission
Gearbox	4-speed, manual
Clutch	Single dry plate
Final drive	Shaft

Chassis
Frame	Tubular steel double loop
Front suspension	Telescopic fork
Rear suspension	Swing arm, twin shock

Tyres	19-3.25in cross-ply front, 18-4.00 cross-ply rear
Wheels	Wire spoke, steel rim
Rim width	N/A

Brakes
Type	Front 200mm drum, rear 200mm drum

Dimensions
Wheelbase	54.52in 1385mm
Overall length	82.67in 2100mm
Overall width	33.46in 815mm
Overall height	40.94in 1040mm
Unladen weight	462lb 210kg

Performance
Top speed	103mph 167km/h
0–60mph	N/A
Price	DM 3996
No. built	22,721

The top-of-the-range R75/5 produced a healthy 50bhp – BMW's highest output yet.

The result was a peak power figure of 50bhp, another best-ever for a production BMW. Although this still lagged a little behind the 75's very latest rivals (Honda's new four-cylinder CB750, for example, produced 68bhp), and its top speed of 175km/h was no better than that of the outgoing R69S, it was enough, combined with lighter, more nimble, problem-free handling, to ensure its huge popularity. BMW's continuing reputation for reliability and maintenance friendliness was a great help, too. No longer was a big BMW boxer twin a staid, stodgy motorcycle only for the initiated diehard. Instead, for any rider interested in long-distance, comfortable, high-speed travel, it was the obvious choice. Here was a motorcycle that could reliably cruise all day at 100 miles per hour, with all the conveniences expected of a modern machine.

When renowned German motorcycle journalist Ernst 'Klacks' Leverkus tested the new R75/5 against Honda's new 750 four around the famous and feared Nürburgring, the BMW was actually faster, despite its power deficiency. BMW found itself firmly in the top league of the new superbike category, and it would build and capitalize on that position as the 1970s progressed. By the end of its production run, in 1973, a total of 68,956 /5 series machines had been built in Berlin. The following year, the new /6 series would take things further still.

The uprated performance and chassis of the R75/5 resulted in a true high-speed cruiser.

1969–1973 R75/5

Engine
Type	BMW air-cooled boxer twin
Internal code	N/A
Block material	Cast iron
Head material	Aluminium
Bore and stroke	82 × 70.6mm
Capacity	745cc
Valves	ohv, 2 valves per cylinder
Compression ratio	9.0:1
Carburettor	2 × Bing CV 64/32/4-3
Max. power (DIN)	50bhp @ 6,200rpm
Max. torque	N/A
Fuel capacity	5.27gall (24ltr)

Transmission
Gearbox	4-speed, manual
Clutch	Single dry plate
Final drive	Shaft

Chassis
Frame	Tubular steel double loop
Front suspension	Telescopic fork
Rear suspension	Swing arm, twin shock

Tyres	19-3.25in cross-ply front, 18-4.00 cross-ply rear
Wheels	Wire spoke, steel rim
Rim width	N/A

Brakes
Type	Front 200mm drum, rear 200mm drum

Dimensions
Wheelbase	54.52in 1385mm
Overall length	82.67in 2100mm
Overall width	33.46in 815mm
Overall height	40.94in 1040mm
Unladen weight	462lb 210kg

Performance
Top speed	108mph 175km/h
0–60mph	N/A

Price	DM 4996
No. built	38,370

CHAPTER SEVEN

1970s: FROM SPANDAU TO SUPERBIKES

The 1970s marked the beginning of a whole new era for BMW's airhead boxer twins, characterized by innovative ideas, technological developments and a new, single-minded focus on sports performance. Cockpits and full fairings made their debut, increasing rider comfort, and even sportier bikes were introduced, in particular the R90S, enabling a return to race success.

The decade had begun with the new /5 series, launched in 1969. This represented a major departure for BMW with a number of innovative features that had not been seen before on a traditional boxer twin. The aim was to increase its appeal to the growing sports-bike market, while at the same time hopefully not alienating its traditional touring market, where riders had come to love the marque for its long-distance comfort and reliability. In this, BMW was an undoubted success – at least at first. In 1971, a total of 18,000 BMW motorcycles rolled off the assembly line in Berlin.

INCREASED CAPACITY AND UPDATED STYLING

By 1973, and despite the /5 series proving BMW's most successful model family in over a decade, updates were due. Fuelled by its success, BMW took the opportunity of the 50th anniversary of the original R32 to make wholesale changes, including yet more ambitious technological innovations. The fact that the year also saw the production of the brand's 500,000th two-wheeler simply gave even more impetus to the changes.

The new /6 series of 1973 was this time extended from three to four models, with the largest being a flagship, sport-

The 1970s ushered in a new era of motorcycles as leisure machines rather than transport.

ing 'S' variant. At the same time, the capacities of all were increased in response to the growing popularity of larger machines such as Kawasaki's recent 900cc Z1. This was effectively achieved by dropping the old R50 variant and adding a new, 900cc R90 at the top of the range.

ABOVE: **In the early 1970s the BMW group as a whole went from strength to strength. This picture shows a busy shift change at the Milbertshofen plant in Munich**

In 1970, bolstered by the success of the new /5 series, **BMW** began building its new HQ in Munich. It opened in 1973 and clerical workers are pictured here inside its distinctive curved walls. It became known as the 'four-cylinder building' and remains a distinctive Munich landmark to this day. **BMW**'s museum is now next door.

1970s: FROM SPANDAU TO SUPERBIKES

1970 saw the production of the 10,000th motorcycle manufactured at Spandau.

One of the key changes across the new /6 series was updated styling, including a new 18-litre tank that made the machines look more streamlined and elegant. Buyers also had the option of a larger, 24-litre touring tank, and this was taken up by many. Alongside engine upgrades, there were new instruments with separate dials to show speed and revs, new handlebar controls, a five-speed gearbox (on some models) and hydraulic brakes with perforated discs at the front wheel. The top-of-the-range R90S even had two of these.

The new R60/6 replaced the old R50/5 as BMW's entry-level model. It retained conventional drum brakes in the front wheel, to keep the price down, and a slide carburettor. The R60/6 was not perceived as a particularly modern machine compared with its bigger variants, but over 13,000 were sold during its model life, both to private enthusiasts and government agencies.

The R75/6 succeeded the successful R75/5 at the same time. In contrast to the 60/6, it was consistently revised and featured a greater number of updates such as a front disc brake and a new five-speed gearbox.

Meanwhile, the updates that had been made to the /5 series during its last production year, including a 50mm extension of the swing arm, were also carried over to the /6 models. This helped improve stability of the R75/6 at high speed, particularly when a pillion or luggage were added. A lack of stability had been the main criticism levelled against the older bike. The torque reaction of the shaft drive, combined with the long travel of the front and rear suspension, were still present and still created a sense of understeer on the R75/6 when accelerating through fast, winding corners.

THE R90S

Along with the new R60 and R75, when the revised /6 series was launched in October of 1973, BMW also entered the 900cc capacity class for the first time, with not just one, but two new models.

The new R90/6 was intended to appeal to fans of long-distance travel as a comfortable and torquey tourer, while the added performance of the R90S was designed to keep pace with the latest competition as the flagship model of BMW's new series.

In engineering terms, the chassis and the design of the engine of the R90/6 matched that of the smaller R60/6 and R75/6, with BMW continuing to work using the proven modular principle. However, BMW also became the first motorcycle manufacturer to equip the two 900s with the new and

1970s: FROM SPANDAU TO SUPERBIKES

Following the success of the /5 series, the updated /6 series, headed by a new 90/6, was introduced for 1973.

BELOW: **Best of all, though, was the new range-topping R90S, launched to coincide with BMW Motorrad's 50th anniversary in 1973.**

Powerful and with a pioneering fairing, the R90S was a BMW for the modern age.

AERODYNAMIC PIONEERS

The fairing of the R100RS was aerodynamically developed in Pininfarina's wind tunnel.

BMW's engineers had been investigating drag and its effect on motorcycle performance ever since the 1930s, when Ernst Henne and other BMW works riders were chasing the motorcycle world land speed record. The record of 279.5km/h, set by Henne on 28 November 1937, riding a 500cc supercharged BMW motorcycle with streamlined fairings, was not broken until 14 years later.

Thirty years later, BMW launched a new, full-scale aerodynamics research programme involving extensive wind-tunnel testing. The results were initially used mainly in racing, but they also included the development of the world's first mass-production motorcycle with a handlebar-mounted fairing – the R90S. It was a milestone in the history of aerodynamic development.

The wind-tunnel research was then applied even more systematically in the development of the R100RS, which debuted in 1976. This was the world's first production motorcycle with a full fairing developed in a wind tunnel. Its frame-mounted fairing provided unprecedented protection against the elements, and allowed riders to travel long distances at high speed in an upright position.

innovative halogen H4 bulb, combined with a large 200mm headlamp. The R90/6 was also offered with an optional second front disc brake, which proved especially popular. It was offered as standard on the flagship R90S.

Overall, the R90/6 appealed to BMW's loyal base of customers and was successful. To the general public, however, it was completely overshadowed by the other new model of 1973: the striking, top-of-the-range sports version, the R90S. Although the R90/6 actually sold 3,600 units more than the R90S, and was technically refined with plenty of positive qualities, it is the landmark S that is by far the most collectable classic today. Its redesigned appearance and enhanced performance grabbed the public's attention, and it immediately became the 'poster bike' of BMW's new range. And the upcoming racing success of the R90S would cement its legacy in the history books.

Presented on the occasion of the 50th anniversary of BMW Motorrad, in the autumn of 1973, the R90S caused a sensation. Performance came via an uprated version of the R90/6's 898cc boxer twin, which, thanks to the assistance of new, twin Dell'Orto carburettors, produced 67bhp. It was the most powerful BMW so far and had a top speed of 200km/h (124mph). The chassis was also uprated to match,

HELMUT DÄHNE, TT WINNER

Helmut Dähne rode an extensively modified R90S to victory at the TT in 1976.

In May 1976, when he set off across the Irish Sea to take part once again in the TT, German rider Helmut Dähne was already a very experienced long-distance racer, with TT racing knowledge and expertise gained at Germany's own Nürburgring.

His mount in 1976 was the R90S, in the familiar Daytona Orange colour scheme. Much modified, extensively tuned and fitted with uprated suspension, it was 30kg lighter than the road bike and was dubbed the R90SS.

Dähne was backed by a strong team made up of mechanic Helmut Bucher and second rider Hans Otto Butenuth. A hugely experienced racer from Dortmund, Butenuth was familiar with both the BMW and the island circuit, so he was well qualified for the role of co-rider.

'We were the fastest in practice,' said Dähne later, 'so I thought I had a good chance of winning the race.' But then rain set in and the start was postponed several times. When the race finally got under way, conditions were ideal.

In those days, the production race comprised a massive 10 laps covering a total of nearly 400 miles of the Mountain Course. Dähne took the lead right away, outrunning his rivals on the specially prepared R 90S. After three laps it was time for the first fuel stop and rider change. Here the BMW team had another ace up its sleeve, having developed its own fast-filler system, which significantly accelerated the fuelling process. While Dähne arrived in the pits 30 seconds behind, Butenuth actually rejoined the race with a 10-second lead. The two subsequent stops also went smoothly and the pair ran out winners of the 1000cc Production class. 'The fact that Rolf Steinhausen and Josef Huber also won the sidecar class at the 1976 TT perfectly rounded off the success as far as BMW was concerned,' said Dähne.

■ 1970s: FROM SPANDAU TO SUPERBIKES

REG PRIDMORE, 1976 AMA SUPERBIKE CHAMPION

Reg Pridmore won the first of his AMA Superbike championships aboard a R90S, also in 1976.

The R90S went on to achieve a number of racing successes in 1976, the first of which was Steve McLaughlin's ride to victory in the Daytona 200, with teammate Reg Pridmore in second. Arguably, however, the greatest achievement of that year was Pridmore's crowning as US Superbike champion.

This was the very first year of the AMA Superbike championship and, while Pridmore won only three AMA Superbike races during his four seasons on the circuit, it was his uncanny consistency that earned him championship success. He went on to repeat the achievement (this time on Kawasakis) in 1977 and 1978, rarely finished outside of the top five and more often than not was on the podium.

It may come as a surprise, then, to note that he was not even American. Reginald Charles Pridmore III was born in London on 15 July 1939 and began racing in the early 1960s. He won his first race at Silverstone in 1961 on a Triumph 500 Tiger before, at 25, deciding to move to the United States, settling in Santa Barbara in California.

'I had a clean change of underwear, $250 and a dream to live in the sunshine,' Pridmore remembered later.

He soon gravitated towards production racing and began competing in a few AMA Nationals on Nortons in 1971. In 1972, he switched to BMW and, by the time superbikes became a recognized AMA National championship event, in 1976, Pridmore had the jump on his competitors with a wealth of experience racing production bikes.

'Superbike became a recognized national class by the AMA in 1976,' Pridmore remembered. 'By then, I already had five or six years of experience racing that type of motorcycle in club races of California.'

At the very first AMA Superbike race, at Daytona on 5 March 1976, McLaughlin pipped Pridmore (both on Butler & Smith BMW R90Ss) to the line by less than half a wheel. But it was Pridmore who would win the championship. On 1 August, at Laguna Seca, Pridmore won his first AMA Superbike race. Two months later, he won the final round at Riverside and claimed the crown.

'I look back on what we achieved by our success on that bike,' he reflected later. 'I beat a lot of the big boys and the Japanese and Italian factories. It made a lot of people sit up and say, "On a BMW?"'

Pridmore's consistent finishes earned him two more titles, and he won his final AMA Superbike Championship in 1978 at the age of 39, making him the oldest AMA Superbike champion to this day. He retired from professional racing after the 1979 season.

with twin-disc front brakes, all without compromising the all-round touring qualities that were so typical of a BMW.

The R90S's most conspicuous innovation was its distinctive fairing – it was the world's first production machine with a cockpit fairing attached to the handlebars. BMW had taken the novel approach of commissioning an industrial designer, Hans A. Muth, to create the bike's styling. The result set the R90S apart from all other motorcycles – not just a handlebar fairing but also a tank penned with flowing contours and a characteristic bench seat with a unique tail fairing, all finished in a specially developed silver smoked metallic livery that highlighted the machine's contours and exclusivity.

The positive response received from customers encouraged BMW to provide a second livery, Daytona Orange, as part of an update in 1975. This colour scheme has remained a favourite among collectors to this day. This later version of the R90S also returned BMW to glory on the track. Hans-Otto Butenuth and Helmut Dähne rode a R90S to a class win in the 1976 Production TT, Steve McLaughlin celebrated victory in the Daytona 200 on the same machine, and teammate Reg Pridmore was crowned US superbike champion the same year.

THE /7 SERIES: A NEW MODEL GENERATION

On 1 January 1976, BMW grouped its motorcycle activities into a new company, BMW Motorrad GmbH, and took the opportunity to fully revise its motorcycle line-up once again. With the arrival of machines such as Honda's GL1000 and Kawasaki's Z1000, it had become clear that the market trend was for ever-larger displacements. So, after a production run of just three years, BMW's /6 series was replaced by an upgraded new model generation – the /7 series. Along with a new R60/7 and R75/7, BMW introduced not just the new R100/7, with a full litre engine capacity, but also the stunning new R100RS. The latter, the world's first production motorcycle with a full fairing, which helped it to achieve a top speed of 200km/h (124mph) from its 70bhp power unit, while at the same time offering a level of protection from wind and weather that had never been seen before.

The /7 series featured a number of detailed improvements and modifications. The most striking visual difference was a new 24-litre tank, as previously only fitted on the R90S. However, this time it featured a small but very effective modification. The filler cap cover was now in a recessed position and was additionally fitted with a roll-over valve, which prevented petrol from flowing out in the event of a crash. This modification also allowed more convenient fixing and use of a tank bag, a popular accessory at the time.

The more elegant and modern look of the /7 series was enhanced not only by the new tank but also by a new front mudguard, which now did without a supporting strut. The valve covers on the engines also had a new, squarer shape and a greater wall thickness to increase their impact resistance. There were no changes to the power of the R60/7 entry-level model but a number of modifications were made inside the engine. These changes primarily related to noise generated from the operation of the valves. The front wheel also received a more advanced, perforated disc brake.

Although the new 1000cc models deservedly attracted most of the attention, the entry-level R60/7 enjoyed good sales figures as it proved popular with government agencies. Indeed, over its two-year production run, it significantly outperformed its sister model, the R75/7.

Alongside the launch of the modified /7 series, in 1976, BMW once again marketed a traditional 750cc model. Like the smaller R60/7, the R75/7 was also fitted with the new 24-litre tank complete with recessed safety tank filler pipe (as on the R60/7) and front wheel mudguard with no strut. This meant that the only visual difference from the R60/7 was the Bing constant-pressure carburettors.

Apart from the optimized valve drive designed to reduce noise, the R75/7 was powered by the same engine from the previous R75/6. The engineering of the previous series had been regarded as exceptionally robust and mature, so no significant changes to the gearbox and chassis were deemed necessary, apart from the perforated front disc.

The R75/7 shared the fate of the R60/7 and was discontinued from the range after a production run of just two years. At this point, plans for a new, smaller air-cooled boxer series were already very advanced. This new smaller series was to be positioned below the larger boxers. Accordingly, the 600cc R60/7 was discontinued in 1978 while the 750cc R75/7 was enlarged to 800cc. This reinstated the gap downwards to the new 'small' (*kleine*) series as well as that upwards to its larger boxers.

THREE NEW BOXERS

The biggest news of all in 1976 was the introduction of not just one, but three new 1000cc boxers. Alongside a new R100S and R100RS, BMW presented a new unfaired R100/7.

1970s: FROM SPANDAU TO SUPERBIKES

Although it was a conventional tourer, its weight of just 215kg (with a full tank) placed it among the lightest 1000cc motorcycles then available. With its torquey, 60bhp twin-cylinder boxer engine, it delivered impressive performance, but BMW's highlights at the International Bicycle and Motorcycle Show (IFMA) in Cologne in 1976 were the two other R100s. The first was the new R100S, the successor to the legendary R90S. That model was, however, overshadowed by BMW's decision not to steal the RS's thunder by replacing the R90S's Dell'Orto carburettors with the lower-priced, more conventional Bing constant-pressure type (which reduced the engine's output by 2bhp), and also by not offering the exclusive Silver Smoke and Daytona Orange liveries that had so distinguished the R90S. it also suffered as a result of the media frenzy surrounding the R100RS.

These factors meant that, in spite of all its sporty characteristics, the R100S never attained the lustre and reputation of the R90S. An increase in power carried out in a model update for 1978 made little impact.

Instead, it was the new, range-topping R100RS that stole all the plaudits in 1976. The third BMW with a 1000cc boxer engine was also the world's first production bike equipped with a full fairing, which was optimized aerodynamically by Pininfarina and finished in a striking bluish sheen of Silver Metallic. Fixed to the frame, the fairing not only offered protection from the wind and rain but also allowed the rider to travel long distances at high speeds in an upright position. The bike underlined this unique ability by conducting world record runs on the Nardo circuit in Italy.

BMW also increased the power of the 1000cc boxer engine in the R100RS to 70bhp, to highlight its status as the flagship model. However, this was mainly reflected by improved acceleration and torque compared with the other two 1000cc boxers, the R100/7 and the R100S. The interpretation of the suffix 'RS', meanwhile, was quickly changed from 'Rennsport' for 'racing sport' to 'Reisesport' (for 'tourer sport').

Otherwise, BMW made use of the proven modular principle and installed the same chassis and brake technology in the RS that had been used on its sister models. This helped generate impressive sales and enabled BMW to sell more than 33,000 RS models. In the first ever readers' poll carried out by the leading German motorcycle magazine *Das Motorrad*, the RS was voted 'Motorcycle of the Year'.

In 1976, the range was updated again and gained a new flagship, the R100RS.

1970s: FROM SPANDAU TO SUPERBIKES

The RS had not only been boosted and restyled, it also had the world's first production full fairing.

The RS was most commonly offered in silver, but other colours were made available later.

131

■ 1970s: FROM SPANDAU TO SUPERBIKES

BMW claimed that the RS was 'the best superbike in the world'. For a while, they were right.

1970s: FROM SPANDAU TO SUPERBIKES

ABOVE: **Not only was the RS fast, it also handled decently.**

In 1977, the new R80/7 was the successor to the R75/6.

133

■ 1970s: FROM SPANDAU TO SUPERBIKES

1976–84 R100RS: 'THE FIRST FULLY FAIRED MOTORCYCLE'

BMW AG began 1976 with a restructuring of its motorcycle activities, the creation of BMW Motorrad GmbH gave BMW's motorcycle wing a standalone corporate identity and one of its first moves as a wholly-owned subsidiary was to continue its model line-up with a push into the one-litre class. The new R100/7 and R100S were powered by a boxer engine with 980cc capacity, but it was the R100RS that turned the most heads, as the world's first series-produced motorcycle with a full fairing.

Developed in a wind tunnel by Pininfarina, as well as following aerodynamic principles, the fairing's primary goal was to protect the rider from wind and bad weather. As such, when it unveiled at the show in Cologne, the new RS offered a unique rider experience, with exceptionally high average speeds in a relaxed sitting position. With its striking looks enhanced by a bluish sheen of silver metallic, BMW had once again created a sensation. In the years that followed, wherever there was an RS, it became the focus of attention. Even onlookers with no particular interest in motorcycles admired the big BMW.

The world in 1976 had never seen anything quite like the R100RS's fairing, which was striking, effective and different.

ABOVE: There was more to the RS than just that fairing; the engine, bodywork, wheels, and more, had all been uprated, too.

ABOVE RIGHT: By producing 70bhp, the new R100RS was the most powerful air-cooled boxer yet.

The console was uprated, too, with an oil temperature gauge and ammeter joining the twin dials.

134

1970s: FROM SPANDAU TO SUPERBIKES

The RS immediately overtook the R90S as the 'poster bike' of the BMW range.

The R100RS was not just a desirable, effective performer; for many, it became the dream bike of a generation.

135

■ 1970s: FROM SPANDAU TO SUPERBIKES

1976–1984 R100RS

Engine		Tyres	19-3.25in cross-ply front, 18-4.00 cross-ply rear
Type	BMW air-cooled boxer twin	Wheels	Cast alloy
Internal code	N/A	Rim width	N/A
Block material	Cast iron		
Head material	Aluminium	*Brakes*	
Bore and stroke	94 × 70.6mm	Type	Front. twin 260mm disc, rear 200mm drum (later single disc)
Capacity	980cc		
Valves	ohv, 2 valves per cylinder		
Compression ratio	9.5:1	*Dimensions*	
Carburettor	2 × Bing CV 94/40/105	Wheelbase	57.67in 1465mm
Max. power (DIN)	70bhp @ 7,250rpm	Overall length	83.85in 2130mm
Max. torque	N/A	Overall width	29.37in 746mm
Fuel capacity	5.27gall (24ltr)	Overall height	51.8in 1300mm
		Unladen weight	506lb 230kg
Transmission			
Gearbox	5-speed, manual	*Performance*	
Clutch	Single dry plate	Top speed	124mph 200km/h
Final drive	Shaft	0–60mph	4.6secs
Chassis			
Frame	Tubular steel double loop	Price	DM 11,210
Front suspension	Telescopic fork		
Rear suspension	Swing arm, twin shock	No. built	33,648

NEW ENTRY-LEVEL MODELS AND A NEW FLAGSHIP

More changes were to come. First, in 1977, BMW presented the R80/7 as the successor to the R75/7. The increase in capacity was achieved by a larger bore, with the stroke remaining unchanged. Combined with an increase in compression to 9.2:1, the new 800cc engine generated a healthy 55bhp at 7,000rpm.

Then, in 1978, BMW sprang another surprise at the International Bicycle and Motorcycle Show (IFMA) in Cologne, by introducing its entirely new small (*kleine*) air-cooled boxer series. These, the BMW R45 and R65, were intended to plug the gap in BMW's range as its entry-level machines.

(Incidentally, as a result of these two developments, plus the discontinuation, in 1979, of the old R60/7, the R80/7 assumed the role of the new mid-range bike in BMW's boxer line-up. Over the course of its production up to 1984 it received numerous upgrades and modifications, the most important being the addition of twin-disc brakes in 1978, plus modern cast-alloy rims and the sportier S-shaped bench seat in 1979.)

The new R45 and R65 were big news as both the engine and the double-loop frame had been completely redesigned. The new, smaller engine, designated the 248/1, was significantly narrower than that of the bigger-capacity boxers and the frame appeared much smaller and lighter.

The R45, with a displacement of 473cc, came in both 27 and 35bhp versions. The former was designed to benefit from a favourable German insurance class and this helped it quickly become BMW's best-selling model in its home range. In fact, in 1979, it was the biggest-selling motorcycle in Germany. The 35bhp version, meanwhile, was mostly built for export.

1970s: FROM SPANDAU TO SUPERBIKES

In line with BMW's modular approach, the engineering of the R65 was identical to that of the R45, save for cylinder capacity. In fact, the only visual characteristic distinguishing the two was the lettering on the side covers. However, the R65's 647cc helped it generate an output of 45bhp at 7,250rpm. Unfortunately, this meant that neither could it take full advantage of the new 50bhp insurance category introduced in Germany a short time previously, nor could it match the output of most of its Japanese rivals. Its lower weight and good handling did help to make it respectably popular both in Germany and abroad, however. When the model was revised in 1981, its output was raised to 50bhp. Ultimately, however, the complex construction made production of this smaller series more expensive than originally envisaged and the series was dropped from BMW's product range in 1985.

LEFT: **In 1978, two new smaller boxers arrived – the R65 and R45.**

BELOW: **Lighter and smaller than the big boxers, the newcomers were intended to appeal to more novice riders.**

■ 1970s: FROM SPANDAU TO SUPERBIKES

R100RT AND R100T

Also introduced in 1978 was a motorcycle that was to become another signature BMW boxer over the coming decades. Encouraged by the success of the R100RS, BMW presented another version of the torquey 1000cc boxer, this time with a full touring fairing. The R100RT (the 'RT' designation representing 'Reisetourer') was intended to enhance the top end of BMW's range and take on the role of new flagship model. The main difference between the RS and RT was mainly in the upper section of the fairing, which was designed to be higher and wider in the RT. This, along with a higher and wider windshield and higher handlebars, allowed the RT rider to adopt a more upright seating position than on the RS, while a special feature enabled the windscreen to be angled manually to suit the needs of the individual user.

Another RT innovation was the adoption of two separately configured vents, which allowed the rider to direct a stream of cooling fresh air as desired. The idea was that, particularly in summer, this would aid rider comfort, especially as more engine heat would now be trapped behind the new fairing.

The RT was also fitted as standard with a luggage rack behind the bench seat plus pannier brackets, both of which further enhanced its touring capability. Matching panniers and a tank bag were also available as optional extras. This was unusual at a time when most travel accessories were available only from independent suppliers, and were often not specifically designed for each particular motorcycle.

This RT's 'purpose-built' touring ability was quickly recognized as its strength. It was a machine that retained its stability even when fully equipped with luggage and a pillion, and it was very agile. As a result, it quickly gained a loyal following, which it retains to this day.

The RT was not BMW's only 'tourer' that year. In 1978, the previous basic 1000cc boxer, the R100/7, was replaced by a modified version to coincide with the presentation of the R100RT. The R100T (with T for 'Touring') was intended to appeal to customers who were looking for a comfortable touring motorcycle capable of covering long distances but without the RT's new full fairing. Harmonized BMW accessories, meanwhile, including a large windshield and integrated panniers, meant that the R100T could also be upgraded to a fully fledged touring motorcycle if the owner so required.

In 1978, the old R100/7 was replaced by the new R100T.

138

1970s: FROM SPANDAU TO SUPERBIKES

The R100T's engineering unsurprisingly came primarily from its 1000cc sister models, the R100RS and R100RT, with the difference that the R100T had to make do with an engine output of 65bhp in order to maintain the gap with the flagship models.

Later, in 1981, the 'T' designation was removed, to create the R100, which gained an additional 2bhp, to bring it closer to the flagship models. Further modifications were made to its chassis at that point, including the introduction of lightweight cast-alloy wheels and a more advanced front disc brake.

The late 1970s also saw another significant development with BMW's boxer twins, one probably less apparent at the time but which over the decade to come would have huge ramifications for the German firm. Fuelled by the enthusiasm of a group of BMW's own engineers, the company was once again making headway into off-road motorcycle sport – and particularly enduro in the 500cc+ class – with a spate of home-brewed boxer twin specials. In 1979, a BMW won the German championship. It was an achievement that would lead directly to one of the greatest boxer twins of all, the GS. But that is a story for another chapter.

The 1970s, for BMW's boxer twins, had had it all: a 50th anniversary, innovative technology including aerodynamic fairings; a return to winning ways in racing; and some of the most significant and successful boxer models of all. The only question was: could the success be continued into the 1980s?

KEY MODELS

1973–76 R90S: 'A Design Classic'

The R90S was a BMW boxer of firsts: along with the R90/6, the first BMW boxer with a cylinder capacity over 750cc; the first BMW to achieve a top speed of over 200km/h; and the first production motorcycle with both a cockpit fairing and twin-disc front brake set-up. It is rightly regarded as a design classic of the 1970s.

Launched at the end of 1973 to coincide with BMW Motorrad's 50th anniversary, the R90S was conceived as the flagship model of the revised /6 series. It attracted significant attention not just in the German press, but also internationally, where enthusiastic testers even referred to it as the 'Super BMW'.

The S's impressive top speed of 200km/h was achieved by enlarging its twin-cylinder boxer engine to 900cc, which, with the assistance of new twin Dell'Orto carburettors, helped generate a robust 67bhp. And in order to keep that increased performance under control, BMW provided the

ABOVE LEFT: **1973's new R90S immediately stood out, thanks to its cockpit fairing and Daytona Orange colour scheme.**

ABOVE RIGHT: **Twin Dell'Orto carburettors helped the enlarged engine produce an impressive 67bhp.**

■ 1970s: FROM SPANDAU TO SUPERBIKES

ABOVE: **The instruments now comprised twin dials for the speedometer and tachometer, with a strip of warning lights in between.**

LEFT: **The two-tone smoked metallic paint scheme of the R90S proved a big hit.**

The radical styling of the R90S was by renowned designer Hans A. Muth, of Target Design.

R90S with a twin-disc front brake, another innovation of the time.

Another first was the commissioning of a designer to assist with the styling. The result – flowing contours and the characteristic bench seat with unique tail fairing, along with special paintwork – confirmed its flagship status and completely set the R90S apart. It remains today a firm favourite with collectors, particularly in the stunning Daytona Orange livery.

140

1970s: FROM SPANDAU TO SUPERBIKES

At the front, twin disc brakes were another first and helped haul the powerful R90S down.

1973–1976 R90S

Engine
Type	BMW air-cooled boxer twin
Internal code	N/A
Block material	Cast iron
Head material	Aluminium
Bore and stroke	90 × 70.6mm
Capacity	898cc
Valves	ohv, 2 valves per cylinder
Compression ratio	9.5:1
Carburettor	2 × Dell'Orto PHM 38
Max. power (DIN)	67bhp @ 7,000rpm
Max. torque	N/A
Fuel capacity	5.27gall (24ltr)

Transmission
Gearbox	5-speed, manual
Clutch	Single dry plate
Final drive	Shaft

Chassis
Frame	Tubular steel double loop
Front suspension	Telescopic fork
Rear suspension	Swing arm, twin shock
Tyres	19-3.25in cross-ply front, 18-4.00 cross-ply rear
Wheels	Wire spoke, steel rim
Rim width	N/A

Brakes
Type	Front. twin 260mm disc, rear 200mm drum

Dimensions
Wheelbase	57.67in 1485mm
Overall length	85.8in 2180mm
Overall width	29.13in 740mm
Overall height	47.63in 1210mm
Unladen weight	473lb 215kg

Performance
Top speed	124mph 200km/h
0–60mph	4.8secs

Price DM 9130

No. built 17,465

■ 1970s: FROM SPANDAU TO SUPERBIKES

1978-84 R100RT

The R100 RT launched in 1978 was developed from the R100RS and took the new faired concept to its logical next stage. Focusing fully on the requirements of touring in terms of aerodynamics, ergonomics and comfort, the RT's full fairing was adapted to deliver even greater comfort while a bespoke luggage system was also offered, making it the ideal motorcycle for discerning touring riders.

The RT's larger windscreen could be angled to suit the needs of individual riders and fresh air could be directed behind the fairing through air vents. The RT was also fitted with a luggage rack behind its bench seat and pannier racks on each side to enhance its touring credentials further. The acronym selected was 'RT' to represent the new concept of 'Reisetourer'. Today those two letters remain synonymous with the comfortable touring bikes in the BMW range.

Following the success of the sports tourer RS, BMW introduced the touring RT in 1978.

1978–1984 R100RT

Engine
Type	BMW air-cooled boxer twin
Internal code	N/A
Block material	Cast iron
Head material	Aluminium
Bore and stroke	94 × 70.6mm
Capacity	980cc
Valves	ohv, 2 valves per cylinder
Compression ratio	9.5:1
Carburettor	2 × Bing CV 94/40/105
Max. power (DIN)	70bhp @ 7,250rpm
Max. torque	56lb ft @ 5,500rpm
Fuel capacity	5.27gall (24ltr)

Transmission
Gearbox	5-speed, manual
Clutch	Single dry plate
Final drive	Shaft

Chassis
Frame	Tubular steel double loop
Front suspension	Telescopic fork
Rear suspension	Swing arm, twin shock

Tyres	19-3.25in cross-ply front, 18-4.00 cross-ply rear
Wheels	Wire spoke
Rim width	N/A

Brakes
Type	Front. twin 260mm disc, rear single 260mm disc

Dimensions
Wheelbase	57.67in 1465mm
Overall length	87in 2210mm
Overall width	29.37in 746mm
Overall height	57.67in 1465mm
Unladen weight	515lb 234kg

Performance
Top speed	118mph 190km/h
0–60mph	5.0secs

Price	DM 11,480
No. built	18,015

1978–84 R45

BMW's entirely new 'small' (*kleine*) boxer series was introduced at the International Bicycle and Motorcycle Show (IFMA) in 1978. Aimed at the 'entry-level' rider in the popular 500 and 600cc capacity class, the R45 and R65 had a completely new, narrower boxer engine held in a redesigned twin loop frame. The R45 had a displacement of 473cc and came in both 27 and 35bhp versions. It quickly become the best-selling model in the BMW motorcycle range and, in 1979, it was the biggest-selling motorcycle in Germany.

Despite this, the R45 proved complex to make and too expensive to produce, and the series was dropped from BMW's product range in 1985.

1978's smaller, lighter, slimmer R45 was designed to appeal to entry-level boxer fans.

1978–1984 R45

Engine	
Type	BMW air-cooled boxer twin
Internal code	N/A
Block material	Cast iron
Head material	Aluminium
Bore and stroke	70 × 61.5mm
Capacity	473.4cc
Valves	ohv, 2 valves per cylinder
Compression ratio	9.2:1
Carburettor	2 × Bing CV 64/28/303
Max. power (DIN)	35bhp @ 7,250rpm
Max. torque	26.6lb ft @ 5,500rpm
Fuel capacity	4.83gall (22ltr)
Transmission	
Gearbox	5-speed, manual
Clutch	Single dry plate
Final drive	Shaft
Chassis	
Frame	Tubular steel double loop
Front suspension	Telescopic fork
Rear suspension	Swing arm, twin shock
Tyres	18-3.25in cross-ply front, 18-4.00 cross-ply rear
Wheels	Cast alloy
Rim width	N/A
Brakes	
Type	Front. single 260mm disc, rear 200mm drum
Dimensions	
Wheelbase	54.72in 1390mm
Overall length	83.07in 2110mm
Overall width	27.08in 688mm
Overall height	42.51in 1080mm
Unladen weight	451lb 205kg
Performance	
Top speed	100mph 160km/h
0–60mph	7.4secs
Price	DM 5880
No. built	28,158

CHAPTER EIGHT

1980s: AN AGE OF ADVENTURE

The onset of a new decade saw another huge change in the fortunes of BMW Motorrad and, as a result, in the types of air-cooled boxer motorcycles it offered.

Despite the initial success and popularity of new, more sporting litre-class machines such as 1973's R90S and the subsequent R100RS, which debuted in 1976, as the 1970s ended, these were quickly overshadowed by a tidal wave of ever more sophisticated and powerful rivals, particularly from Japan. As a result, sales of the big 1000cc air-cooled boxer stagnated and those generated by BMW's new smaller boxers, such as the R45, were lower than expected. Most importantly of all, Japanese competitors were launching a stream of bigger and more powerful four-cylinder and even six-cylinder models on the market. BMW simply could not compete.

By 1979, BMW Motorrad was in such deep trouble that there was even talk of its complete closure in favour of the blossoming car business. Could the new management team installed in early 1979 find a way forward? Convinced that the traditional air-cooled boxers had no hope of competing in the future with the new wave of Japanese machines, they

From humble beginnings, 1980's R80G/S would change the face of BMW.

gave the green light to a new generation of machines powered by a radical, longitudinally mounted, all-new family of liquid-cooled, four-cylinder and three-cylinder engines.

The plan was to launch a four-cylinder motorcycle powered by a 1000cc engine as the first model in the new series, positioned above the boxer models. In order to highlight the distinctiveness of the new series, the bigger 1000cc boxers would then be phased out after a transitional period, with only the smaller boxers remaining in the range as BMW's entry-level machines.

The trouble was, as the new decade approached, these new multi-cylinder machines were still years away. Sales of the traditional bikes were poorer than expected and, in the short term, BMW needed a sales hit – and fast.

THE R80G/S: A NEW SEGMENT

The necessary boost came at the very start of the 1980s, from a completely unforeseen source, and resulted in a bike that was not just a radical departure for BMW but also proved such an immediate hit that it completely changed the direction of the company. The R80G/S was the very first of what became known as BMW's GS series, which not only caused a sensation in terms of sales, but also achieved significant racing success and went on to provide the catalyst for the whole 'adventure bike' class. They were best-sellers across the globe and became the very backbone of BMW's modern motorcycle range.

The origins of the first G/Ss were surprisingly humble. The revolutionary R80G/S came about not so much via the long-distance 'adventures' with which its modern incarnation is so closely associated, but more from amateur weekend off-road racing. It was a sport that was enjoyed by a number of employees in BMW Motorrad's testing department, including off-road enthusiast Laszlo Peres.

In the 1950s, 60s and 70s, amateur enduro competition, using largely road-derived machines, was hugely popular. The Europe-wide International Six Days Trial was its pinnacle event, attracting such celebrities as movie star and bike enthusiast Steve McQueen, aboard a specially adapted Triumph twin. On a domestic level in Germany in the 1960s, home-brewed BMW machines, based on the robust big-displacement boxer twins, were often raced by the likes of Herbert Schek and Laszlo Peres. In the mid-1970s, BMW's larger boxer twins became contenders when the German motorsport authorities introduced an over-750cc class in off-road competition for the first time, starting in 1978.

Peres and a BMW team came up with a prototype for the 1978 over-750cc off-road championships, and promptly rode it into second place. The bike was further developed into the GS800 and, encouraged by the successes of Peres and his colleagues, BMW commissioned a limited run of this new motorcycle for the following year. The factory team went one better in 1979, claiming the championship in the large-capacity class with rider Richard Schalber, and going on to win a brace of gold medals in the ISDT in Siegerland, West Germany, with riders Fritz Witzel Junior and Rolf Witthöft.

At around the same time, BMW Motorrad's sales had suffered a dramatic downturn after almost a decade of growth. The causes were identified as a weak dollar, which was hindering performance in the main export market of the USA, and an excessively conservative model strategy. Karl Heinz Gerlinger was head of sales and marketing at BMW Motorrad GmbH at the time:

…the competition from the Far East was overwhelming. The Japanese manufacturers were the dominant force in world markets, both where motorcycles provided purely a mode of transport and where they were already being used for leisure purposes. The Japanese brands offered something for every taste, at every price level, and occupied every conceivable market niche. New products were rolled out in rapid succession, and the resultant sale of old stocks led to an extreme drop-off in prices. The motorcycle market was booming, but BMW could only look on from the sidelines as sales tumbled. For BMW dealers, it was like being left off the guest list for the biggest party in town; they were demoralized. BMW Motorrad was in danger of becoming a 'nostalgia brand'.

With its boxer models of the time perceived as too conservative, BMW was under massive pressure. At this point, the three- and four-cylinder K series machines, with their state-of-the-art engine technology, were still three to four years away; the far-reaching project to develop a totally new model series had been launched just a few months earlier. The obvious course of action was to highlight the virtues of the proven boxer engine but to new customers, as Gerlinger explains:

Part of the solution came from within the walls of the development department, where a BMW enduro quietly took shape. A boxer with a single-sided swing arm – what a wonderful new creation! However, the sense of excitement was tempered by a host of questions. Can boxers really 'fly'? Was it possible to present such a large motorcycle to customers – credibly – as an enduro?

THE FATHER OF THE G/S

If any one person can be credited with the inspiration for, if not exactly the creation of, the revolutionary BMW R80G/S, it is surely former development engineer and enthusiastic off-roader Laszlo Peres.

In 1977, it was announced that there would be a new 750cc+ category in the German enduro championship. BMW saw it as an opportunity to get back into off-road sport and Peres was released by BMW management from all his other duties for three months so he could focus on building a prototype.

When Peres rode the bike to the runner-up position in the 1978 championships, it was enough to encourage BMW to develop the bike further for the following year. The result was the GS800, sometimes referred to as the 'Six Days GS'; it was not only victorious in that year's German championship, but it also won two gold medals at that year's ISDT.

That bike was then used as the inspiration for the new R80G/S production machine, with Peres again among the team of engineers who developed it. He worked at BMW for a total of 37 years and is still a regular speaker at BMW events.

Peres was an enthusiastic enduro rider during the 1970s.

ABOVE: **BMW engineer Laszlo Peres is today regarded as the 'father of the G/S'.**

Peres' works racer, the GS800, became the template for the road-going R80G/S.

146

1980s: AN AGE OF ADVENTURE

BMW management was well aware of the impressive sales success of a new breed of larger-capacity, single-cylinder dual-purpose or 'trail' bikes that were being launched by other manufacturers, epitomized by Yamaha's new XT 500. They took this trend as inspiration, along with the continued success of their own factory racers, and commissioned a new development team in late 1978, led by Laszlo Peres. Their brief was to get an 'off-road' boxer, which also looked good and worked well on the road, up and running as soon as possible. Given its relatively small production figures – BMW's motorcycle output at the time was barely a third of what it is today – and with little money available, and even less time, it was clear that any new machine would have to come out of BMW's proven 'modular' approach. In other words, it would need to use as many existing components as possible, and there would be no new powertrain.

One of the first prototypes of the new R80G/S, pictured in 1979.

Before the G/S there had already been a tradition of BMW boxers in enduro riding.

147

■ 1980s: AN AGE OF ADVENTURE

After a development period of just one year and nine months, in late 1980, the R80G/S was presented to the international press in Avignon, France, on 1 September 1980. It was immediately clear that BMW had achieved just what it had hoped to achieve: a large-capacity touring motorcycle with off-road ability. It caused a sensation. Sceptics had wondered how an 800cc motorcycle with shaft drive and weighing almost 200kg could be suited to off-road riding, but the press event left the journalists jubilant. German biking magazine *Das Motorrad* called it 'the best road motorcycle BMW has ever built'.

On the road, the 800cc model producing 50bhp ticked every box, while off the beaten track it proved far more usable than the cynics had predicted. The genius of the G/S – 'Gelände/Straße' (for 'off-road/road') – was that it was never intended as a pure off-road machine. Instead, it was meant to combine the best of both worlds. To create it, Peres and his team had taken proven, existing components and put them together in a unique new recipe: the engine was the balanced 800cc boxer and the frame was from the smaller, lighter R65. Most importantly of all, however, the new combination of components, along with other weight-saving measures such as the extensive use of plastics and a single instrument dial, meant that the all-up weight of the G/S was just 186kg fully fuelled. Its agile handling certainly impressed the journalists in Avignon.

One of the most talked-about features was the new, specially developed single swing arm. Christened 'Monolever', it housed the integrated driveshaft and was supported by a single, central spring strut to the rear frame. This meant that the rear wheel was free-standing on the left-hand side and

ABOVE: **Essentially a 'parts-bin special', the R80G/S's engine was straight from the R80.**

The sales success of the R80G/S effectively secured the company's future.

148

1980s: AN AGE OF ADVENTURE

ABOVE: **Key to the design of the R80G/S was a modular 'parts bin' approach. Some items, however, such as the headlamp cowling, were new.**

LEFT: **One of the most identifiable and successful BMW boxers of all time: the 1980 R80G/S.**

The clever Monolever rear end allowed easy removal of the rear wheel and eased exhaust routing.

■ 1980s: AN AGE OF ADVENTURE

ABOVE LEFT: **The first G/S featured a three-stud rear-wheel coupling. This was updated to four in 1987.**

ABOVE RIGHT: **Instrumentation on the G/S was kept deliberately simple, to save both weight and costs.**

LEFT: **A bright colour scheme in BMW's M-sport livery emphasized the R80G/S's sporting ability.**

fixed to the axle drive with just three nuts, so it could be removed very quickly, like a car wheel. It brought numerous benefits. Monolever was not only 2kg lighter than a conventional solution (which was important in an off-road context), it also had greater torsional rigidity, was cheaper to manufacture and made maintenance and repairs much easier, too. What is more, there was now nothing on the left-hand side of the bike to obstruct its new two-into-one exhaust.

Elsewhere, much of the G/S was familiar. Apart from the swing arm pivot, some small brackets and the positioning of the footrests, the frame was identical to that of the R45 and R65. But the R80-derived engine, although appearing similar, was actually significantly updated. Strengthened engine housings with improved lubrication guaranteed greater thermal stability and a longer service life. The sump, meanwhile, was protected by a perforated bash plate. A new

1980s: AN AGE OF ADVENTURE

ABOVE: **At the press launch for the R80G/S, BMW's newcomer caused a sensation.**

Nobody expected that a machine as big as the R80G/S could perform so well off-road.

1980s: AN AGE OF ADVENTURE

low-profile air filter allowed easier assembly and reduced intake noise.

Lightweight cylinders with special Nikasil coated liners helped slice 3.4kg off the bike's weight, while the new, 40 per cent lighter clutch saved a further 4.7kg. This clutch, which also served as a flywheel, enhanced the smoothness of the five-speed transmission, too. Further weight was saved by the extensive adoption of plastic parts, such as the cover for the H4 headlamp (another enduro first), the high front mudguard, side panels, the base of the new seat and the rear mudguard.

On the modular theme, the G/S's cleverly arranged central electrics were sourced from the R45/ R65 and located under a new 19.5-litre fuel tank with enduro screw-on filler cap specially designed for the G/S. The telescopic front forks and front disc brake, meanwhile (another first on an enduro bike), were taken from the R100/7.

Making its debut on a BMW was the G/S's maintenance-free, contact-free electronic Bosch ignition system, which was lighter and occupied less space with its twin ignition coil. The G/S also broke new ground when it came to its tyres, using specially developed Metzelers with an off-road tread that was capable of withstanding a top speed of 180km/h.

Perhaps understandably, the reaction the R80G/S received when it was unveiled to the public at the IFMA show in Cologne in 1980 was to be expected. Slightly more suprising, perhaps, was the large number of orders that were placed there and then. By the end of 1981 a total of 6,631 machines – more than twice the number originally planned – had left Berlin. Overall, one in five BMWs sold in 1981 was a G/S; it was a motorcycle that played a critical role in reviving BMW's fortunes. With the benefit of hindsight, however, the first G/S had also done far more than that. Its continued success and reinvention over the years led the way to the creation of a whole new market segment that no only endures today, but remains the cornerstone of modern BMW. Without that original boxer-powered G/S, BMW simply would not be the same.

1980–87 R80G/S

Engine		Tyres	21-3.00in cross-ply front, 18-4.00 cross-ply rear
Type	BMW air-cooled boxer twin		
Internal code	N/A	Wheels	Wire spoke
Block material	Cast iron	Rim width	N/A
Head material	Aluminium		
Bore and stroke	84.8 × 70.6mm	*Brakes*	
Capacity	797.5cc	Type	Front. single 260mm disc, rear 200mm drum
Valves	ohv, 2 valves per cylinder		
Compression ratio	8.2:1		
Carburettor	2 × Bing CV 64/32/305	*Dimensions*	
Max. power (DIN)	50bhp @ 6,500rpm	Wheelbase	57.67in 1465mm
Max. torque	41lb ft @ 5,000rpm	Overall length	87.79in 2230mm
Fuel capacity	4.28gall (19.5ltr)	Overall width	32.28in 820mm
		Overall height	45.27in 1150mm
Transmission		Unladen weight	409lb 186kg
Gearbox	5-speed, manual		
Clutch	Single dry plate	*Performance*	
Final drive	Shaft	Top speed	104mph 168km/h
		0–60mph	5.6secs
Chassis			
Frame	Tubular steel double loop	Price	DM 8920
Front suspension	Telescopic fork		
Rear suspension	Swing arm, Monolever single shock	No. built	21,864

1980s: AN AGE OF ADVENTURE

MORE BOXER VARIATIONS

The immediate success of the R80G/S may have ensured the future of BMW Motorrad, but it did not instantly change the direction of the company. The long-term plan in place: to phase out the larger boxers, to be replaced by the all-new K series. In the meantime, however, some updates were due.

First, from January 1980, the /7 models were fitted with revised crankcases incorporating a modified oil circuit. Another engine revision was carried out for 1981, with new lightweight alloy cylinders with hard-chrome plated bores to increase wear resistance. Also starting that year, all /7 models were fitted with a new airbox with a plate air filter plus new Brembo brake calipers.

The first new model designation also came that year, when the ageing, unloved R100T had its 'T' removed, along with other revisions, which saw the new R100 generate an additional 2bhp. In addition, there were numerous modifications made to the chassis, including wider cast-alloy wheels and an improved front brake. The irony was that, despite still being pitched as a tourer, the new R100, now with 67bhp and a relatively light unladen weight of 218kg (with a full tank), meant that boxer aficionados actually regarded it as the true sports model in the BMW line-up.

Another new model in 1981 was the R100CS (with 'CS' standing for 'Classic Sport'). Essentially, this was the existing R100S complete with sporty, cockpit fairing but with the slightly more powerful 70bhp boxer twin engine from the RS and RT. It was all finished off with classic wire wheels and subtle colour schemes. The idea was to appeal more to the traditional BMW rider than the futuristic RS did. One by-product of that specification was that, with its marginally lower weight but the same power output as the RS, the CS was the fastest BMW of its time, capable of a top speed of 200km/h. Although the CS did not achieve anything like the popularity of the RS, it was quite successful, with sales of 4,038 units at the respectable price tag of DM 11,260.

The most striking new model of all in 1981 represented a last roll of the dice for BMW's smaller air-cooled boxer. The R65LS (with 'LS' standing for 'Luxury Sport) came with an engine and chassis that were essentially the same as on the standard R65, but had a twin-disc front brake set-up, enlarged drum brake at the rear and innovative composite wheels. Most remarkable was its appearance, which came courtesy of a futuristic cockpit fairing, new seat and tail fairing, and some brazen colour schemes. It had all been created by designer Hans A. Muth.

More was to come in 1982, when, reinvigorated by the success of its G/S, BMW presented yet more variations of its venerable boxer twin while awaiting the arrival of the all-new K series.

The radically styled R65LS followed the G/S in 1981.

■ 1980s: AN AGE OF ADVENTURE

1982's R80ST was intended to be a pure road version of the R80G/S.

The first was inspired directly by the success of the R80G/S two years earlier, but this time it was to be a pure road version. The new R80ST (with 'ST' standing for *Straße* or 'road') retained the core concept of the G/S, with its 800cc boxer engine, and the small frame of the R65, including innovative single-sided swing arm and raised exhaust system, but it had been retuned for riding on the street. As such, it had been given slightly shorter travel suspension, a smaller 19-inch front wheel and road-going tyres. It was also equipped with a low front mudguard and the cockpit and

Despite decent manners and clean styling, the ST was not a success.

154

1980s: AN AGE OF ADVENTURE

round headlamp from the small series R45/R65, in order to create a visual profile that was distinct from that of the G/S. A number of testers believed that the ST outclassed the G/S, with its nimble performance and cornering agility, but ST sales were sluggish. This was possibly because it had a number of the disadvantages of the G/S, namely the short bench seat and raised exhaust, but did not benefit from that bike's style and versatility.

The R65LS and R80ST may have been too radical for some, but 1982 also brought a new air-cooled boxer for traditionalists. The new R80RT differed from the R100RT (which had been around since 1978) only by virtue of its 800cc engine. However, although it had been eagerly anticipated, it was also quickly realized that the 50bhp engine mounted in the chassis of the R100RT struggled with the extra weight of its touring fairing, resulting in fairly muted performance. As a result, potential customers who were accustomed to the 100RT's robust performance were largely underwhelmed, and this reaction was reflected in disappointing public sales figures. On the up side, however, the R80RT did prove popular with the police and other government agencies, as it was significantly more keenly priced than the R100RT.

The all-new K100 finally took centre stage in 1983. That year was unsurprisingly a quiet one for BMW's boxers, but there were still new models to come in the following year. Production of the 1000cc boxer models was stopped temporarily in 1984, in favour of the new K series, and the future of the boxer was carefully considered. Even the extensive modifications made in 1981 were unable to conceal the fact that the design of the bigger bikes was now conspicuously outdated in comparison with the latest four-cylinder models. Furthermore, extensive investment would be required if the large-capacity, air-cooled boxer engines were going to conform with increasingly stringent regulations governing exhaust gas and noise.

The plan, therefore, was to use the advanced, 1000cc four-cylinder motorcycles of the K series, as launched in 1983, to replace the 1000cc boxers in BMW's line-up over a transitionary period.

The later 1980s also saw the introduction of the new K series on the BMW production lines.

155

■ 1980s: AN AGE OF ADVENTURE

KRAUSER MKM1000: THE ULTIMATE BOXER?

The Krauser MKM1000 of 1982, one of the most desirable airhead boxers of all, was not actually built by BMW, but by luggage and parts specialists Krauser. which had ties with the BMW factory going back to the 1950s. It featured an all-new, computer-designed sports frame, uprated 1000cc boxer engine (complete, if optioned, with Krauser's special four-valve cylinder heads) and racy full sports bodywork at a time before the term 'racer replica' had been invented. Produced in limited numbers, it was not just the most exotic and exclusive BMW boxer on the market; it was one of the world's most desirable sportsters, full stop.

The driving force and catalyst behind the motorcycle was Michael 'Mike' Krauser, who had won the German sidecar racing championship from 1955 to 1958 with the works BMW team. In the 1960s, he ran his own team of Rennsport outfits and in the 1970s managed BMW's factory sidecar racing teams. At around the same time, Krauser also developed his first removable, injection-moulded plastic side cases, or panniers. The product quickly became a leader in the field and would subsequently become synonymous with BMW's touring motorcycles. From this initial success, Krauser's company produced an ever-increasing range of BMW accessories, including performance parts.

Having developed such a close connection with BMW, Krauser decided to produce a complete, luxury performance BMW motorcycle – the MKM. First, he built a racer using a 1000cc boxer engine and his own frame. Then, after that had proved competitive, he turned to producing a road version, seeking assistance from Alfred Halbfeld, Klaus Pepperl and Michael Neher of tuning firm HPN, who had also been involved in BMW's Paris–Dakar bikes.

Krauser's close relationship with BMW led to the factory agreeing to supply components, including complete R100RS engines, transmissions, forks, handlebars, switchgear and brakes. Even the exhaust and mufflers were BMW, but mounted in such a way that they swept up more sharply than on the donor R100RS. What is more, BMW even agreed, as long as the drivetrain components remained stock, to give them a warranty.

Krauser also offered the option of fitting the engine with his own, painstakingly developed four-valve cylinder heads. These, along with a pair of 40mm Dell'Orto PHM carburettors, a BMW 336Rs sport cam and Ducati-Conti-style stainless steel silencers, bumped peak power up from the standard 60bhp to 72bhp.

The factory-endorsed Krauser MKM 1000 was probably the sportiest of all boxers.

1980s: AN AGE OF ADVENTURE

Yet it was not really the engine that set the MKM apart. It was the computer-designed space frame. Assembled from a mass of thin-wall steel tubes, including 52 straight tubes and four curved ones welded together at 150 points, the entire unit weighed just 11.6kg, 6kg less than the original. It gave the MKM both a longer wheelbase than the RS and sharper steering geometry. The RS fork stanchions were also shortened. The unique fairing, meanwhile, plus one-piece tank cover and single seat cowling, were all fibreglass with a livery reflecting Krauser's racing colours.

Production began in 1980 and ended in 1982 and there were a number of changes made over that time. Early bikes had ATE single-piston brake calipers, aluminium fuel tank with a Monza-style filler, black frame, steel cylinders and a contact-breaker ignition. Later examples had Brembo twin-piston calipers, a steel fuel tank with stock BMW locking fuel cap, Nikasil cylinder liners and electronic ignition.

Just over 200 were built in total, making today's survivors, especially in four-valve trim, some of the rarest and most desirable BMW boxers of all. The most recent to come up for auction sold for around £30,000.

The Krauser's optional four-valve heads also boosted peak power to 72bhp.

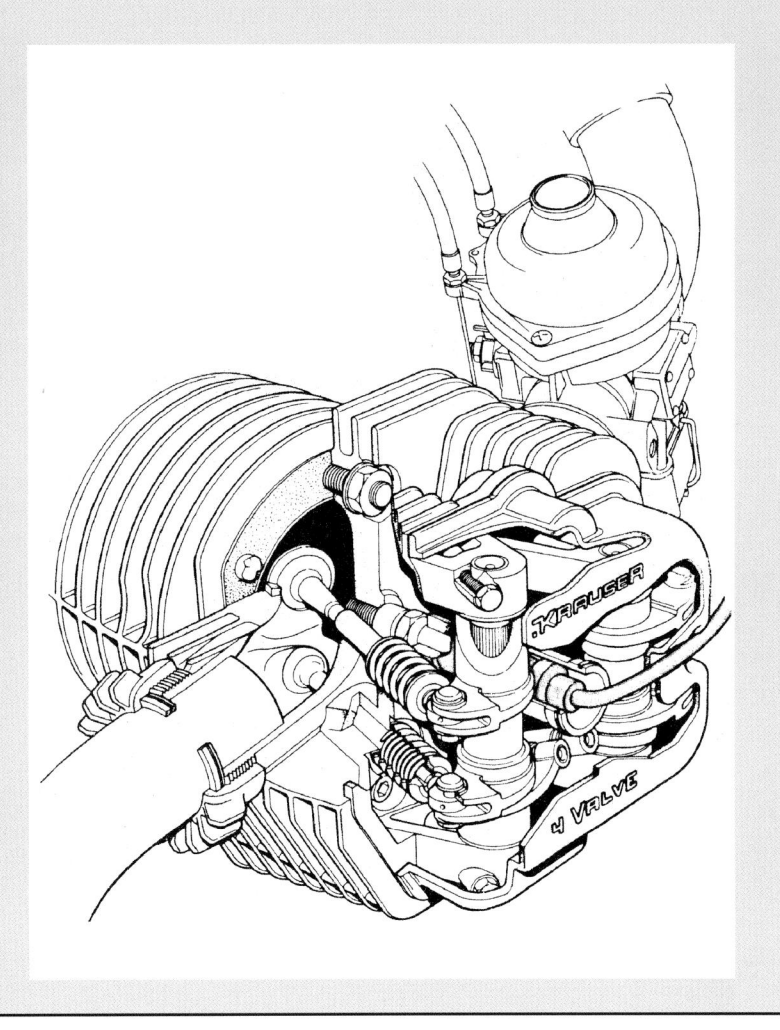

However, BMW could not contemplate the complete demise of the boxer at this stage. They would still need some more keenly priced alternatives in the mid-range below the K models. The R80ST was agile, but its styling was not popular and it had not been particularly well received by traditionally conservative boxer buyers. BMW decided to come up with a new, basic 800cc boxer with a design that harked back more to the last big boxer bikes – 1984's new R80.

The new boxer's main feature was the frame concept derived from the G/S with a single swing arm known as Monolever. Significantly, however, the R80's central spring strut was connected directly to the axle and not the swing arm, as it had been on the G/S. The frame itself was now made of reinforced round tubing rather than the conical oval tubing, and the modernizing theme was continued in the front end, which was essentially that of the new K series, including its updated telescopic forks, Brembo disc brake and 18-inch cast-alloy wheels. The instruments and headlamp, meanwhile, were carried over from the R80/7, as were the handlebars and controls. The new bike's fuel tank, complete with recessed cap lid, resembled that of the /7 series, but its base was remodelled to suit the new frame, while the front mudguard, side cover, seat and exhaust were also new. Overall, the R80 presented a familiar yet more dynamic profile.

Meanwhile, following criticisms of the original, a new version of the R80RT tourer was also presented using the same frame, single-sided swing arm, wheels, brakes and other upgrades already familiar from the R80. To distinguish

1980s: AN AGE OF ADVENTURE

1980–1982 Krauser MKM1000

Engine

Type	BMW air-cooled boxer twin
Internal code	N/A
Block material	Cast iron
Head material	Aluminium
Bore and stroke	94 × 70.6.5mm
Capacity	980cc
Valves	ohv, 2 valves per cylinder
Compression ratio	8.2:1
Carburettor	2 × Bing 40mm
Max. power (DIN)	70bhp @ 7,500rpm
Max. torque	55.7lb ft @ 5,500rpm
Fuel capacity	4.6gall (17.5ltr)

Transmission

Gearbox	5-speed, manual
Clutch	Single dry plate
Final drive	Shaft

Chassis

Frame	Tubular steel trellis
Front suspension	Telescopic fork
Rear suspension	Swing arm, Boge dual shock
Tyres	19-3.50in cross-ply front, 130/80 V18 cross-ply rear
Wheels	Cast alloy
Rim width	N/A

Brakes

Type	Front. twin 260mm disc, rear single 260mm disc

Dimensions

Wheelbase	N/A
Overall length	N/A
Overall width	N/A
Overall height	N/A
Unladen weight	N/A

Performance

Top speed	138mph 222km/h
0–60mph	N/A

Price	$11.995
No. built	237

The G/S's clever Monolever eventually found its way on to the R80RT and R80.

it, this version is commonly referred to as the R80RT Monolever.

In fact, the new RT had an even greater impact than the unfaired R80. The reduced unladen weight, combined with the mildly revised engine and new exhaust, gave the new RT a higher-revving and more lively character. The new bike was significantly more responsive than the previous model. Visual modifications, ranging from the new front mudguard, side cover and new bench seat, also gave the upgraded RT a more dynamic and youthful appearance.

Together, the new pair were warmly received. As a result, when the 1000cc boxers were discontinued, company management reviewed their original plan and came to the conclusion that the air-cooled boxers were not ready to be consigned to the history books just yet.

In 1985, meanwhile, yet another new 'small' BMW boxer made an appearance. Although that year saw the unsuccessful R45, R65 and R65LS discontinued from BMW's range, as they were relatively expensive to manufacture and failed to achieve significant sales success, BMW had no intention of relinquishing the 'entry-level' sector completely. From 1 April 1986, Germany had introduced restrictions on all new motorcycle riders. They were to be limited for two years to machines generating a maximum of 27bhp, with a minimum weight of 140kg.

To capitalize on the revised regulations, BMW came up with a new R65 based heavily on the new R80. The basic principle was to combine the latest Monolever frame of the 800cc model with the 650cc short stroke engine of the old R65/R65LS. The resulting bike was then supplied in two power levels – 27bhp and 48bhp. The slightly reduced power of the 48bhp version compared with the 50bhp of the previous R65/R65LS was due, incidentally, to the engine's reduced compression ratio. This, in turn, was due to BMW redesigning it to run on the new lead-free petrol. The 27bhp version, meanwhile, was created by having not just smaller valves but also smaller carburettors and a different camshaft. A by-product of this was a significantly improved peak torque compared with the previous R45, which also made it much easier to ride, particularly for the novice rider.

Of the two, the 27bhp R65 was far more successful, as the 48bhp R65 compared unfavourably with the older 50bhp R80; as a result, the 48bhp R65 was dropped from BMW's range in 1989. By contrast, the 27bhp version lived on as the starter model in BMW's line-up right up until 1993.

RETURN OF THE BIG AIR-COOLED BOXERS

Surprisingly, the big air-cooled boxers were about to make a comeback, too. By 1986 the clamour for the return of the bigger machines was steadily increasing, especially in the USA and Japan. For fans of the big twins, the new K75 and K100, with their three and four-cylinder engines, were simply not authentic BMWs. And although the smaller 800cc boxers continued in production, a significant number of customers did not consider them adequate replacements for the more flamboyant 1000cc machines that had been discontinued.

As a result, at the International Bicycle and Motorcycle Show (IFMA) in Cologne in 1986, BMW reintroduced a new version of the R100RS. At first glance, it looked identical to its predecessor, which had been last manufactured in 1984. However, on closer inspection it became clear that BMW's engineers had been hard at work, combining the familiar RS fairing with the latest Monolever chassis and cycle parts from the 800.

The reactivated 1000cc boxer engine had undergone a number of changes in order to comply with new regulations relating to noise emissions, which had become much stricter. The new RS no longer generated the prestigious 70bhp as before. Now, it made just 60bhp. However, the revised boxer engine compensated for this with a much more torquey delivery, which enhanced riding pleasure. This, combined with the more agile Monolever chassis, made the revamped RS so popular that it was quickly in unexpectedly high demand. Originally planned as a special limited edition of just 1,000 examples, BMW instead reinstated the RS into its motorcycle range and it continued to be manufactured until 1992.

As a response to the demand for the revived R100RS, which turned out to be far stronger than expected, BMW also decided, one year later, to revive its R100RT tourer, using the same approach. The performance of the 'new' RT benefited from a combination of proven wind and weather protection provided by the RT fairing, a revised boxer engine and its lighter, more nimble Monolever chassis, in the same way as the RS had done. The power loss of 10bhp from the old RT was even less important in the tourer than it had been in the sportier RS. Indeed, the revised engine's reduced unladen weight, extra torque and more cultured, smoother-running engine were effective in persuading touring riders of the new bike's merits and more than amply compensated for the slight lowering, by 5km/h, of the bike's top speed. It was also now supplied as standard with a luggage rack and pannier racks, together with the new streamlined cases from the K series.

■ 1980s: AN AGE OF ADVENTURE

1986 also saw the surprise reintroduction of the flagship R100RS, albeit slightly updated.

UPDATING THE GS

That same year, 1987, also saw the next generation of the R80G/S. This time there was not just one new version, but two: the new R80GS and new R100GS as first presented in the late summer of 1987. Both promised greater comfort, improved performance and better brakes.

Apart from the additional, larger model, the key upgrade was the adoption of a new driveshaft system in place of the old Monolever. This was dubbed Paralever by BMW and intended to eradicate the undesirable 'rearing up' of the shaft drive, which had traditionally been experienced during hard acceleration. In truth, BMW had known about this 'torque reaction' phenomenon for decades. Indeed, engineer Alex von Falkenhausen had fitted the factory racing machines with a double-joint swing arm as early as 1955 in order to improve handling. However, this technology – for which BMW secured a patent – was not initially carried over to series production and BMW motorcycles retained the standard rear swing arm with universal joint until 1987. Paralever's principle of using a parallelogram-type suspension system to decouple the rear-wheel swing arm from the drive and deceleration forces meant the 'torque reaction' of the shaft drive was almost completely removed.

By 1987, however, BMW was finally keen to use the system on its road bikes and to make it a stand-out sales feature. With a sound set of test results in their possession, they soon decided to adopt the Paralever single-sided swing arm for the successor to the R80G/S, the R80GS. In fact, the system worked so well that it was later adopted for all BMW motorcycles.

Innovation could also be found at the front of the new GS. In order to introduce progressive damping into its larger, telescopic front forks, which were now supplied by Italian firm Marzocchi, a conventional left-hand leg was combined with a conical bushing working in conjunction with a valve in the right-hand leg. As a result, the compression stage in the fork through the first stage of travel barely had any effect. However, when the fork more fully compressed, the cone caused the annular gap to shrink, stiffening up the damping and ensuring that the fork could even withstand landings after jumps. Added to which, the fork now suffered barely any contortion thanks to the installation of a hollow, and therefore lightweight, 25mm diameter axle. The result was much-improved overall ride comfort.

1980s: AN AGE OF ADVENTURE

1987 saw the first big updates to the successful G/S, including a new R80GS.

BELOW: **One key difference on the R80GS and the R100GS was the new torque-reducing Paralever in place of the old Monolever.**

Paralever BMW R80 GS/R100 GS

BMW Motorrad GmbH + Co.
Kundendienst

1 Doppelgelenkwelle mit Torsionsdämpfer
2 Doppelgelenkschwinge
3 Schubstange
4 Kegelrad
5 Aluminiumglocke
6 Tellerrad
7 Bremsschlüssel

1980s: AN AGE OF ADVENTURE

The Paralever system had been experimented with since the 1950s but was now put into production for the first time.

The GS innovations did not end there. The two bikes' new 'cross-spoke' wheels were another world first. Locating the spokes on the outer edge of the wheel rim allowed the use of the latest tubeless tyres, and individual spokes could be replaced without having to take off the wheel or tyre. An additional benefit was that the flatter spoke angle enhanced the wheel's elasticity, giving it extra strength to deal with impacts and overloading. There was also more space available for the brake calipers to operate on the larger brake discs.

Both the individual chassis components and the GS chassis as a whole were newly thought out and developed, as was the frame. The cross tubes above and below the revised swing arm mounting point were stronger than those of the R80G/S. The pivot point of the right rear spring strut on the main frame had also been modified. Another new element was the stiffer, longer and heavier rear subframe, which was bolted to the main frame, as before.

There was more. In response to requests from customers, BMW upped the capacity of the GS's fuel tank to 26 litres, offering a good compromise between its predecessor's standard 19.5 litres and the Dakar kit version from 1983,

which could hold 32 litres. A larger and more comfortable seat had also long been on the wish list of many a G/S owner. Refinements were also made to a range of smaller details. The new, longer rear subframe allowed the fitment of a more powerful battery; four wheel bolts (in place of the old G/S's three) ensured the rear wheel was more safely secured; and the fuel cap was now lockable and easier to refuel from a can (as often needed when riding off-road). A new front mudguard, meanwhile, was developed in the wind tunnel to make it less prone to distortion at motorway speeds, while a new, large, light-alloy bash plate was mounted in front of the centre stand to protect not only the sump, but also the exhaust headers.

The new bike weighed 15kg more than the old R80G/S – a third was made up of to its larger tank, while the remaining 10kg were accounted for by the various improvements above.

The 800cc version was powered by the same boxer engine as before and so continued to generate 50bhp. It also did without the 100's headlamp fairing, something which helped distinguish it from its new bigger brother and justified it being a more keenly priced alternative to the larger R100GS, which was DM 2000 more expensive.

All of these updates combined, plus the improved performance both on- and off-road, were the reason for the bike's subtle name change. The removal of the backslash between the G (for *Gelände* or 'off-road') and S (for *Straße* or 'road') allowed for its re-interpretation as *Geländesport* (or 'off-road sport').

Inevitably, it was the new bigger version, the R100GS, which grabbed the most attention. Following the emergence of new rivals such as the Suzuki DR750 and the upcoming Yamaha XTZ750, BMW's newcomer was once again emphatically the biggest displacement enduro of its time thanks to its 1000cc engine, which was familiar from the previous year's R100RS. Delivering a full 60bhp from its 980cc at 6,500rpm, in experienced hands it was also significantly faster, even off-road.

Apart from the new headlamp cowling, the new R100GS also came with an oil cooler mounted on the engine crash bars, which helped distinguish it from the R80GS. In Germany, despite being more expensive, it shot straight to the top of the sales charts, fully vindicating BMW's decision to increase the engine output.

There was one further new GS launched in 1987 that, outside of Germany at least, is less well remembered. Coinciding with the launch of the new R80GS and R100GS in

1980s: AN AGE OF ADVENTURE

Alongside the new **R80GS**, 1987 also saw the introduction of a bigger brother – the **R100GS**.

BELOW: **With 60bhp from its larger engine, plus a larger handlebar fairing, the R100GS proved a decent touring machine in its own right.**

163

1980s: AN AGE OF ADVENTURE

Although it was larger, the new R100GS was also an impressive performer off-road.

1987, BMW presented the R65GS as an entry-level version. Intended purely for the domestic German market, where new riders were restricted to machines producing only 27bhp, the new bike looked very similar to the old R80G/S, which had only just been discontinued. The main difference was that, instead of a capacity of 800cc generating 50bhp, it had a capacity of 650cc generating 27bhp.

Sadly, the R65GS was not a sales success. With a relatively high (for novices) price, combined with the engineering of the old Monolever chassis and the rather dated appearance of the old R80G/S, it was less appealing than the new GSs that had just come out. Indeed, it was completely overshadowed by its newer, bigger siblings. Disappointing sales figures forced BMW to remove the model from the range as early as 1992. This version of the boxer GS therefore remains one of the rarest BMWs of the modern era and an interesting collector's item.

R100GS PARIS–DAKAR

Another GS variant, introduced the following year, 1988, proved far more successful and laid the foundations for the modern interpretation of the BMW adventure bike, which remains so successful to this day.

Following its success in the Paris–Dakar desert race, BMW had offered a Paris–Dakar kit for the original R80G/S in 1983, but sales had failed to meet expectations. The company decided to try again in 1988, presenting a new kit at the International Bicycle and Motorcycle Show (IFMA), intended as a touring conversion for its new R80GS and R100GS. The kit comprised a plastic tank with a capacity of 35 litres incorporating a small luggage compartment, a front fairing complete with tubular crash bars, an integrated rectangular headlamp and a larger windshield. The kit also included a single seat and a luggage rack, while additional elements included an engine spoiler and a headlamp grille made of strong plastic to provide protection against flying stones.

Although public reaction was strong, sales of the kit were relatively slow again, at least to begin with. However, this began to change in the spring of 1989 when BMW added a R100GS Paris–Dakar model to its line-up, with the complete kit already factory installed. Later simply designated as the R100GS PD, this version became hugely popular among long-distance touring motorcyclists due to its versatility, and contributed a substantial proportion of GS sales.

1980s: AN AGE OF ADVENTURE

BMW first introduced a Paris–Dakar version of its original R80G/S as an accessories kit back in 1983.

For 1988, BMW offered a Paris–Dakar version of its new R100GS.

It is no overstatement to say the emergence and popularity of the Paris–Dakar Rally desert race, begun at around the same time as the launch of the original R80G/S, had been a significant factor in the success of BMW's radical enduro. It was a natural, if not perfect, fit for the rigours of the long-distance, off-road endurance race – the world's toughest and most-publicized off-road event. And the race was an ideal promotional tool for the new BMW. As a 50bhp, large-capacity twin when most rivals were 500cc singles or similar, the G/S was also a favourite for winning it.

Originally open to cars and motorcycles, the first Paris–Dakar Rally was held in 1979, covering 9,500 kilometres, with just 30 per cent on surfaced roads and much of the rest over the Sahara desert. The first year's motorcycle race

165

■ 1980s: AN AGE OF ADVENTURE

Comprising a larger, 35-litre plastic tank, rugged crash bars and more, the Paris–Dakar version set the template for adventure bikes to come.

First offered as a kit, the Paris–Dakar version became a stand-alone model during 1989.

was won by Cyril Neveu aboard a modified Yamaha XT500. Neveu repeated the feat in 1980, but it was already becoming clear that a new force was arriving on the scene. In that year, BMW entered two modified R80G/Ss via its French importer, ridden by local hero Jean-Claude 'Fenouil' Morellet and Hubert Auriol. Despite showing clear performance potential, Auriol failed to finish, while 'Fenouil' ultimately claimed fifth. But that was just the start.

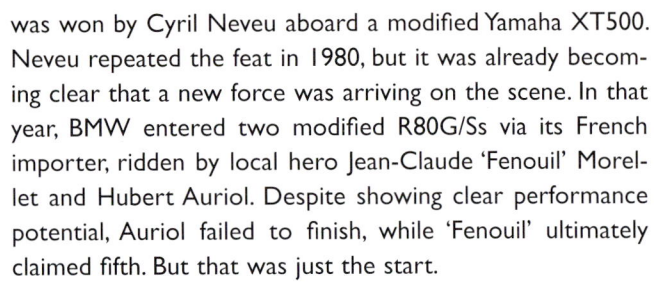

The following year, BMW motorsports director Dietmar Beinhauer commissioned specialists HPN, based in Seibersdorf in Bavaria, to convert three more G/Ss, in close cooperation with BMW Motorsport. This time, Auriol went on to win, while 'Fenouil' came fourth. A privately entered G/S, meanwhile, ridden by French policeman Bernard Neimer, crossed the line in seventh place. These achievements highlighted the potential of the G/S, with only minimal modifications, and G/S sales unsurprisingly rose around the world.

In 1982, the BMW team were beset with mechanical gremlins but in 1983 they returned, with BMW tuner and off-road rider Herbert Scheck having boosted engine capacity to 980cc and output to 70bhp. It was enough to power Auriol to his second victory. In 1984, with the team now racing in Penthouse colours and the bikes sporting massive 45-litre fuel tanks, Auriol was joined by the diminutive Belgian Gaston Rahier. Rahier pipped Auriol in a G/S 1-2, inspiring BMW to produce a special-edition R80G/S bearing the Dakar name.

In 1985, with the team now sponsored by Marlboro-Playboy, Rahier repeated his success, leaving former teammate Auriol, now riding for Cagiva, trailing second.

1980s: AN AGE OF ADVENTURE

Paris–Dakar legend Hubert Auriol first entered the race aboard the new R80G/S in 1980.

In 1984, Auriol took part in the Paris–Dakar aboard a much-improved G/S, a works entry with *Penthouse* magazine livery.

■ 1980s: AN AGE OF ADVENTURE

ABOVE LEFT: **The big G/S proved itself not only adept off-road, but also fast and durable.**

ABOVE RIGHT: **For 1984, Auriol was partnered by diminutive Belgian rider Gaston Rahier, who went on to win.**

In the 1980 Paris–Dakar, Auriol failed to finish, but his G/S teammate 'Fenouil' came fifth.

1980s: AN AGE OF ADVENTURE

KEY MODELS

1981–85 R65LS

The R65LS is probably one of the most left-field BMW air-cooled boxers of all. It was not a commercial success, but its style, ride and rarity make it one of the most significant of all 1980s machines.

In the spring of 1981, BMW expanded its so-called *kleine Baureihe*, or 'small series' boxer family, as exemplified by the existing R45, by adding a more sporting, luxury and premium-priced R65. It was dubbed the R65LS where 'LS' stood for Luxus Sport or 'luxury sport'.

Although its engine and chassis were little changed from the standard R65, it had been upgraded with a number of modifications, the most striking of which was undoubtedly its revised styling. The company had turned to ex-BMW employee Hans A. Muth, whose own design studio Target Design had recently gained fame by being responsible for Suzuki's radical Katana family. Muth's futuristic cockpit fairing for the LS, along with a new bench seat and tail fairing to match, were intended to create a unique visual profile, to set the R65LS apart from its predecessor. While it was not as radical or extreme as the Katana, for a BMW boxer it certainly looked like something from the twenty-first century. The new lines were then emphasized further by the use of just two bold colour schemes: Henna Red and Polaris Silver Metallic, each with a contrasting black tank base, black side covers and a black anodized exhaust system.

On top of the restyle, the LS's sporting pretensions were given added credibility by the use of a twin-disc front brake (in place of the stock R65's single), plus a drum brake enlarged to 220mm at the rear. One final technical gem was provided by the LS's use of innovative composite wheels, which featured an aluminium rim cast together with a lightweight alloy, die-cast hub in a patented process. This was claimed to improve elasticity of the wheel while also making a significant saving in weight.

These sophisticated alterations unfortunately also helped make the LS a full DM 2000 more expensive than its standard R65 brother, without any tangible improvement in performance. Its styling was also seen as controversial, and as a result the LS's appeal was limited. Only just over 6,000 were sold before it was pulled from production in 1985.

In 1984, the two machines of Auriol and Rahier dominated the Paris–Dakar.

With the G/S's reputation assured, BMW wound down its works involvement in the Dakar from late 1986, and it was left to privateers Eddy Hau, Richard Schalber and Jutta Kleinschmidt to provide the fireworks. Particularly worthy of note were Hau's victory on his privately entered HPN GS in the Marathon class of the 1988 Dakar, and Jutta Kleinschmidt's fifth place in the Marathon section of the 1992 Paris–Cape Town Rally. A BMW engineer at the time, Kleinschmidt reeled off over 12,700 kilometres to cross the finishing line on what was – apart from the suspension and exhaust – a standard-issue R100GS Paris–Dakar.

The oddball R65LS was styled by Hans A. Muth, who had also styled the 1973 R90S.

1981–85 R65LS

Engine
Type	BMW air-cooled boxer twin
Internal code	N/A
Block material	Cast iron
Head material	Aluminium
Bore and stroke	82 × 61.5mm
Capacity	649.6cc
Valves	ohv, 2 valves per cylinder
Compression ratio	9.2:1
Carburettor	2 × Bing CV 64/32/307
Max. power (DIN)	50bhp @ 7,250rpm
Max. torque	38lb ft @ 6,500rpm
Fuel capacity	4.83gall (22ltr)

Transmission
Gearbox	5-speed, manual
Clutch	Single dry plate
Final drive	Shaft

Chassis
Frame	Tubular steel double loop
Front suspension	Telescopic fork
Rear suspension	Swing arm, twin shock

Tyres	18-3.25in cross-ply front, 18-4.00 cross-ply rear
Wheels	Cast alloy
Rim width	N/A

Brakes
Type	Front. twin 260mm disc, rear 200mm drum

Dimensions
Wheelbase	54.7in 1390mm
Overall length	83.07in 2110mm
Overall width	27.08in 688mm
Overall height	42.51in 1080mm
Unladen weight	455lb 207kg

Performance
Top speed	108mph 175km/h
0–60mph	5.8secs

Price	DM 8955
No. built	6,389

1980s: AN AGE OF ADVENTURE

1983 K100: The Bike Conceived to Kill the Boxer

After 60 years of air-cooled boxer twins, BMW introduced its all-new, liquid-cooled, longitudinally mounted K series, initially with the 1000cc K100, in 1983.

Conceived as the successor and replacement for BMW's signature twins, its limited success and the furore it created from loyal boxer fans actually directly led to the reinstatement of the big twins, following a brief period in 1986 when they had gone out of production. Subsequent to that, the K series was also a factor in the creation of the airheads' ultimate successor, the all-new oil-cooled boxer twin, starting in 1993.

The core idea for the K – to mount a longitudinally positioned in-line engine horizontally – came from BMW development engineer Josef Fritzenwenger. However, there was far more to the innovative 987cc machine than just engine layout. The K100 was also the first four-cylinder BMW motorcycle, the first with electronic fuel injection and the first engine to be used as a stressed member in the new BMW K100's steel space frame. The K100 was also the world's first series-produced motorcycle available with anti-lock brakes.

A full model series soon took shape, in the form of the K100RS, K100RT and K100LT, and by the end of 1984 more than 30,000 units had already been sold. It had been conceived from the outset to form the basis of an additional three-cylinder machine, and in 1986 it was joined by the 740cc K75 triples as well.

However, although it was certainly not a failure, the K series never did succeed in replacing BMW's signature boxer twins. Although there were successive updates and reconfigurations, the only surviving K bikes today are variants of the stupendous six-cylinder version. BMW's latest incarnation of the boxer R, meanwhile, goes from strength to strength, with six different models in its latest line-up and with a new air-cooled cruiser version on the way…

The 1980s were supposed to be all about the all-new K100. It did not work out that way.

1980s: AN AGE OF ADVENTURE

Boxer fans were not convinced by the new liquid-cooled, four-cylinder, fuel-injected K series engine.

1983–1990 K100

Engine
Type	BMW liquid-cooled in-line four
Internal code	N/A
Block material	Aluminium
Head material	Aluminium
Bore and stroke	67 × 70mm
Capacity	987cc
Valves	DOHC, 2 valves per cylinder
Compression ratio	10.2:1
Carburettor	Bosch fuel injection
Max. power (DIN)	90bhp @ 8,000rpm
Max. torque	63lb ft @ 6,000rpm
Fuel capacity	4.62gall (21ltr)

Transmission
Gearbox	5-speed, manual
Clutch	Single dry plate
Final drive	Shaft

Chassis
Frame	Tubular steel trellis
Front suspension	Telescopic fork
Rear suspension	Swing arm, Monolever single shock

Tyres	100/80 V18 front, 130/90 V17 rear
Wheels	Cast alloy
Rim width	N/A

Brakes
Type	Front. twin 285mm disc, rear single 285mm disc

Dimensions
Wheelbase	59.6in 1516mm
Overall length	87.4in 2220mm
Overall width	37.8in 960mm
Overall height	45.5in 1155mm
Unladen weight	526lb 239kg

Performance
Top speed	133mph 215km/h
0–60mph	N/A

Price	DM 12,490
No. built	12,871

CHAPTER NINE

1990s: THE END OF THE AIRHEADS?

The 1980s had, surprisingly, given the air-cooled BMW boxers a reprieve, when the success of the new G/S and clamour for the return of big twins such as the R100RS forced the reversal of BMW's plan to phase them out in favour of the new K series. However, it was also clear that, going into the 1990s, it was a situation that could not last for ever.

Ever-tightening emissions and noise regulations, along with ever-increasing performance demands from the marketplace, meant that the days of the airheads were truly numbered. Plans for an all-new, high-tech replacement – this time following the traditional boxer/shaft drive layout but with oil-cooling, four-valve heads and fuel injection – were, by 1990, already well developed. A strategy to create a new 'entry-level' single-cylinder model – BMW's first since the mid-1960s – would be the final death knell for the smaller boxer twins. And the K series of three- and four-cylinder superbikes would be refreshed and reinvigorated, first and most conspicuously by the firm's new K100RS, complete with the world's first ABS system, in 1990.

Another prophet of doom for the air-cooled line came in 1991. On 18 March, the 1,000,000th BMW motorcycle was produced at Spandau. Tellingly, however, it was not a boxer but a K75RT, which was ceremoniously handed over to the Berlin Senator for Trade and Technology and subsequently used to raise money for the Red Cross. Clearly, a new era in BMW motorcycling was about to begin.

THE LAST HURRAH

Revisions to the 'Enduros'

Until all that came to pass, however, the air-cooled boxers, in a variety of guises, from GS adventure bike to R roadster and RT tourer, would have one last 'hurrah'. The successful R80 and R100GS 'enduros' were the first of these to benefit when both underwent a comprehensive model update for the model year 1991.

The extra touring comfort offered by the Paris–Dakar variant of the R100GS in 1988 had proved very popular with the majority of GS buyers, who did most of their riding on road. It was therefore no surprise that the extensive update package introduced for the model year 1991 R80GS and R100GS reflected these preferences. The most obvious difference was to the visual appearance of the two bikes. Both now as standard were protected by a half fairing bolted directly to the frame via external tubular brackets in place of the small, handlebar-mounted 'cockpit' fairing of before.

The fairing itself was fairly familiar, being derived from that of the R100GS Paris–Dakar special edition launched in 1989. In addition, in place of the former small, round headlamp, a new, more modern-looking rectangular unit was fitted, as also featured in the earlier Paris–Dakar fairing. This had been originally sourced from the K75S triple.

The instrument panel now integrated inside the new fairing was also updated, comprising two 100mm diameter round dials of equal size. The new R80GS immediately benefited from having a tachometer as standard, where it had only previously been available as an extra price option. The new fairing's screen, however, was a different shape from that of the Paris–Dakar version and was also now tinted.

Less conspicuous changes included the oil sump being modified and the oil volume increased by 0.25 litre. The Boge shock absorber at the rear, which had previously been criticized for being too hard, was replaced by a higher-quality Marzocchi component that had several different adjustment options. A new, semi-floating brake disc was now fitted at the front, with the aim of preventing any distortion; the steering-

173

1990s: THE END OF THE AIRHEADS?

For 1991, the popular GS was updated again. It had come a long way from the 1980 original.

head bearings were updated with a new roller type so that bearing play could be adjusted for off-road use; the handlebar switchgear was also replaced by the new design, which had debuted on BMW's new K series machines, complete with revised indicator switch design.

The GS's fuel tank filler cap was now recessed with the safety flap cover, as first introduced on the /7 series machines, while the tank's volume was reduced by 2 litres to 24 litres. A Paris–Dakar version of the GS, meanwhile, was also revised, with a new cockpit and new windshield.

Like all other boxer models, the latest GS models could now also be specified – as an extra-cost option – with a pollutant-reducing catalytic converter. This technology, as already tried and tested in the USA, worked according to the principle of exhaust afterburning, and cut carbon monoxide emissions by 40 per cent and hydrocarbon emissions by 30 per cent.

A New Classic R

That year, 1991, BMW had another surprise ready for its boxer fans alongside the revision of the GS models. The overwhelming success of the Paralever GS launched in 1987 had encouraged the company to make a renewed attempt to produce a spin-off road motorcycle. Their reasoning was that, as most GS customers never actually rode their bikes on the dirt, and enjoyed them purely on the road, why could the concept not be transferred successfully to a pure road-going machine? This time, though, they decided to take a different route.

BMW had learnt lessons from the failure of the earlier R80ST, as conceived as a road spin-off of the original R80G/S. This time, they would take no risks with the bike's design; instead, the new R100R 'Roadster' was given a pure-blooded, naked profile with classic styling elements. Although the main frame and Paralever swing arm were incorporated from the GS, together with its 17-inch wheel including drum brake, and while the 24-litre tank with recessed tank cover and the two large instruments in the cockpit also originated from the GS, the new R's rear subframe, suspension and smaller 18-inch front wheel were new. Those elements, together with road-going tyres, formed the basis for the new machine.

The new, classic, R, was further set apart by reviving the classic round head covers last used in the /6 series while its brakes were upgraded with the latest four-piston calipers from K series along with the GS's semi-floating disc. Handlebar controls and instruments also came from the K series, including the new, controversial, separated indicator switches. Other detail changes, meanwhile, included, cross-spoke

1990s: THE END OF THE AIRHEADS?

The new R100R roadster used GS running gear but avoided the mistakes of the R80ST.

The R's boxer twin was essentially unchanged, but it was restyled to mimic classic airheads of the past.

wheel rims, a two-in-one exhaust system with low-slung, chromed silencers and chromed, round, 200mm headlamp.

This time, the result was so warmly received that, in the following year, 1992, at the request of a number of European export markets, a second and smaller version of the R100R roadster was launched. This was the R80R. By using the 800cc engine, the R80R produced lower emissions and therefore succeeded in overcoming registration barriers in countries such as Switzerland, where the 1000cc twin-valve air-cooled boxer could not.

In order to achieve reasonable production volumes, this new boxer roadster was also marketed in Germany, in not

175

■ 1990s: THE END OF THE AIRHEADS?

The R's wire wheels and other cosmetic touches were intended to commemorate the heritage of the airhead boxers.

BELOW: **By the mid-1990s, plans were well developed to replace the airheads with an all-new machine – the oilhead boxer twin.**

just one, but two versions. The first produced 50bhp, while the other was retuned to just 27bhp, with the aim of appealing to beginners and motorcycle schools. Two years later, as unveiled in the autumn of 1993 to go on sale for the model year of 1994, this lower-power version was retuned again to 34bhp, to conform to the latest, revised novice licence regulations.

The R80R was only distinguishable from the R100R by its smaller engine, the absence of an oil cooler (as fitted as standard on the 1000cc model) and by different ratios for the speedometer and rear-wheel drive. Otherwise, the frame, chassis, brakes and styling were identical to those of its sister model. The new R80R had also been intended to replace the existing Monolever-equipped R80, although this did not actually happen. The conventional R80 remained in production primarily for government agencies such as the police right through to the beginning of 1995, when production of both models was finally discontinued.

AN OIL-COOLED BOXER AND A SINGLE-CYLINDER

As the upgrades were hinting, the old boxer engine was now reaching the end of its life. BMW's Motorrad range was overdue a significant, fundamental update, but the challenge would be coming up with something that would continue to satisfy BMW's faithful followers. After all, sales of the R80GS/R100GS models alone would reach over 45,000 by the time the last example rolled off the Berlin production line in 1996. Whatever BMW came up with had a tough act to follow.

Appropriately, the new bike came in 1993, 70 years after the introduction of the R32, and it was new in not just one,

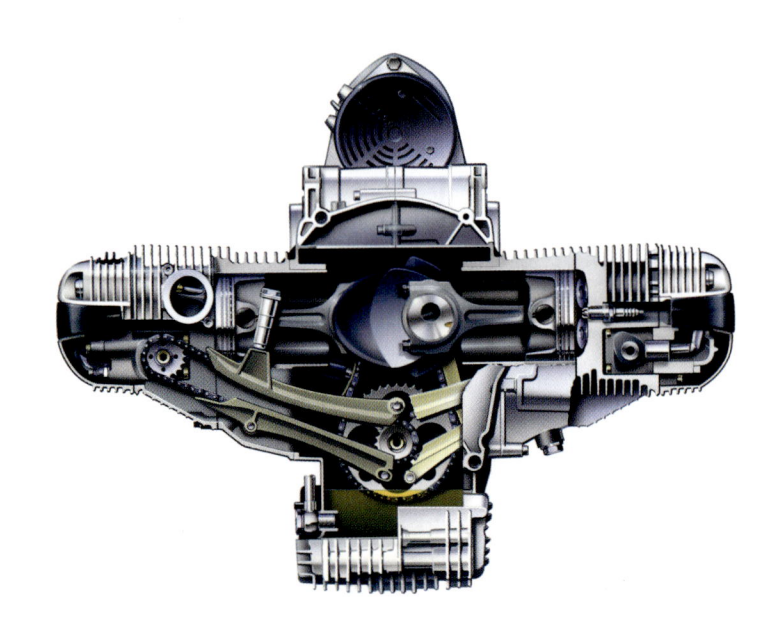

1990s: THE END OF THE AIRHEADS?

but two massively important ways. First, and most significantly, the powerplant that would sound the final death knell for the long-lived and much-loved airhead would be an all-new boxer – an oil-cooled, four-valve, fuel-injected one. Having learnt from the disappointments of the K series in 1983, BMW this time successfully produced a fully modernized unit, complete with the latest technologies and performance expectations. Crucially, it also retained many of the traditions and appeal of the shaft-driven boxer twin.

The first bike to use the new Type R259 power unit was 1993's R1100RS. The following year came a new enduro, the R1100GS, and, in autumn of the same year, the R850/1100 R roadsters. In 1995, the all-new R1100RT arrived as a replacement for the touring R100RT. All were radical in their own way and all also lifted BMW technology to new heights. In addition to BMW's second-generation anti-lock braking system, ABS II, the new family of boxers also introduced an innovative new front suspension system, called Telelever.

The first bike to use the new oilhead motor was the R1100RS, which was intended as a successor to the old R100RS.

In 1994, the R1100RS was followed by an all-new oilhead GS – the R1100GS

177

1990s: THE END OF THE AIRHEADS?

The oil-cooled boxer was not the only all-new BMW in 1993. That year, after more than 25 years away, BMW also staged a return to the single-cylinder class. The new series was granted a fresh model designation, not to mention a water-cooled single-cylinder engine producing 35 kW/48bhp, co-developed with Rotax. The BMW F650 was a lightweight and agile enduro-style motorcycle built by Aprilia in Italy and aimed at entry-level riders, although it was more than capable off-road, too: French rider Richard Sainct rode the rally version of the bike to victory in the Paris–Dakar Rally in 1999 and 2000.

CELEBRATING THE AIRHEADS

Even though the airhead boxers now seemed obsolete, they were not done quite yet. From 1993 until 1996, when the last Type 247-engined machine rolled off the Spandau production lines, a number of final, celebratory models were to be introduced.

The first of these was the R100R Mystic, produced from 1993 to 1995. A special model intended for riders who were attracted by the R100R but wanted a more vintage design, it used essentially the same mechanicals and 'platform' of the R100R, but was given a more streamlined look, with a few revised details.

Accordingly, the plastic trim on the R's instrument panel had been replaced by a slender strip of polished aluminium with integrated round indicator lamps; the speedometer and rev counter were also finished with classic, round chrome surrounds. The high, touring handlebars of the R100R were replaced by lower and differently angled, sportier handlebars, which helped give a more forward-angled riding position. However, the biggest difference was the completely redesigned bench seat, which was significantly shorter and narrower than that of the R100R. The low contours of the Mystic's seat also meant that it required different side trims.

Finally, the Mystic's round exhaust was positioned slightly closer to the rear frame and its rear tyre was also a wider 140mm, although the same size of wheel rim was retained.

Initially, Mystic Red Metallic was the only colour option. However, by the time production came to an end, at the beginning of 1996, two alternatives in red/black and yellow/black were being supplied, with 300 examples of each built.

An initiative for another special model came from the head of the BMW Motorrad Centre in Munich, after he discovered the special Mystic upgrade kit produced by Doken in Japan in 1993. This led to the idea of creating a special edition that was assembled by hand, with customers being able to select their own paint finish. Approximately 50 examples of the 'Pre-Series Mystic' machine were manufactured and, in 1994, BMW included it as a special model in the standard

In 1993, BMW also came up with another commemorative model to mark the end of the airhead line – the R100R Mystic.

178

1990s: THE END OF THE AIRHEADS?

product range. Furthermore, a run of 90 machines powered by the 800cc engine was produced exclusively for the Swiss market, on account of local regulations that could not be overcome by the 1000cc version.

While production of the R80R was discontinued in 1994, the R100R soldiered on. This time, from the end of 1994, it was produced as the R100R Classic – a 'farewell model' that remained in BMW's product range until the beginning of 1996.

In that same year, 1994, BMW launched an additional Classic version of its revived RT to commemorate the unavoidable, imminent departure of the twin-valve boxers. The visual profile of the R100RT Classic was quite distinct from that of the standard RT, thanks to its exclusive, two-tone paint finish in elegant Arctic Grey/Graphite Metallic, including hand pinstriping and colour-matched pannier lids. Special lettering on the fairing was another feature while the RT Classic also came with a top box, special 'comfort' seat, cylinder protectors and hazard warning lights. In this form, the last twin-valve boxer RT finally rolled off the production line at the beginning of 1996.

However, it was the hugely popular boxer enduros, the GSs and their spin-off Paris–Dakar variants, which, having done so much to reinvigorate and revitalize BMW in the early 1980s, were, fittingly, the ones that marked the real end of the air-cooled, two-valve boxers.

After the updates of 1991, the R100GS Paris–Dakar remained largely unchanged until it finally went out of production, along with the remaining GSs, in 1996. However, it did receive a few embellishments along the way.

Following BMW's established pattern, its departure was heralded by a special model, launched in 1995. The R100GS PD Classic was supplied only in black, with chrome tubular brackets and cylinder protectors and the classic round valve covers that had been seen on the other Classic models. However, with a short production run of only one year, it is a rare beast today and the most sought after of twin-valve boxer GS motorcycles, after the R80GS Basic. It was that model, the R80GS Basic, introduced in 1996 as a limited-run homage to the original 1980 R80G/S, that would ultimately be the very last air-cooled, twin-valve boxer.

The main frame, 800cc twin-valve boxer engine and chassis components including brakes of the Basic were lifted straight from the last R80GS, complete with Paralever rear suspension and cross-spoke wire wheels. In addition, the Basic benefited from upgrades including a high-quality White Power shock absorber at the rear, along with a cartridge system for the front forks. The colour scheme comprised a blue finish for the frame with white bodywork, intended to recall the precursor to the original G/S – the GS800 racer from the 1970s.

The 1994 R100RT Classic was also intended as a 'last-of-the-line' airhead model.

The popular R100GS Paris–Dakar remained in production right up to 1996.

RIGHT: The big, plastic-tanked and super-rugged all-rounder remains one of the best airheads to this day.

Anyone who finds a decent example of the R100GS Paris–Dakar, complete with luggage and accessories, will have the chance to enjoy one of the best world traveller machines.

Styled as a limited-edition collector's piece – from its headlamp/speedometer unit, through to its tank, bench seat and tail – evoking memories of the original 80G/S, the Basic was never truly intended as a serious competitor for BMW's new, four-valve R1100GS. Although it was welcomed enthusiastically by airhead fans and offered decent performance both on- and off-road, the Basic suffered initially from sluggish sales. This, however, was transformed when the final example rolled off the assembly line in Berlin in December 1996 and everyone became aware of its significance. Today, the R80GS Basic is the most sought after and valuable model from the last twin-valve boxer generation.

On 19 December 1996, a great chapter in German motor-cycling history came to a close, after over 70 years of air-cooled boxer production and 27 of the final 247 type engine as introduced on the /5 series. At the final tally, BMW had sold 685,850 examples of the classic boxer series worldwide since 1923, 467,000 of which had been built at the Spandau plant since 1969.

1990s: THE END OF THE AIRHEADS?

The 1996 R80G/S Basic was inspired by the 1980 original and built in limited numbers to mark the end of airhead production.

KEY MODELS

1996 R80GS Basic: The Last Airhead

When the time came in 1996 to end the airhead line, BMW decided to produce one final commemorative model. The R80GS Basic, as its name suggests, was a evocation of the original 1980 R80G/S, which had done so much at a crucial time to revive BMW's fortunes. It was based on the engine and chassis of the then current R80GS, including its Paralever rear end, but given bodywork, including clocks and console, that mimicked those of its illustrious forbear (the tank actually came from the R80ST road version). It also wore the rounded valve covers from the other Classic Rs of that era.

Although it was styled very closely to the 1980 original, detail changes on the R80G/S Basic included rocker covers and a four-stud real wheel.

181

1996 BMW R80GS Basic

Engine
Type	BMW air-cooled boxer twin
Internal code	N/A
Block material	Cast iron
Head material	Aluminium
Bore and stroke	84.8 × 70.6mm
Capacity	797.5cc
Valves	ohv, 2 valves per cylinder
Compression ratio	8.2:1
Carburettor	2 × Bing CV 64/32/305
Max. power (DIN)	50bhp @ 6,500rpm
Max. torque	41lb ft @ 5,000rpm
Fuel capacity	4.28gall (19.5ltr)

Transmission
Gearbox	5-speed, manual
Clutch	Single dry plate
Final drive	Shaft

Chassis
Frame	Tubular steel double loop
Front suspension	Telescopic fork
Rear suspension	Swing arm, Paralever single shock
Tyres	21-3.00in cross-ply front, 18-4.00 cross-ply rear
Wheels	Wire spoke
Rim width	N/A

Brakes
Type	Front. single 285mm disc, rear 225mm disc

Dimensions
Wheelbase	59.84in 1520mm
Overall length	90.16in 2290mm
Overall width	32.28in 820mm
Overall height	45.86in 1165mm
Unladen weight	460lb 209kg

Performance
Top speed	N/A
0–60mph	N/A
Price	DM 15,500
No. built	3,003

Suspension was uprated with a White Power shock at the rear and improved Marzocchi forks; wire wheels were of the later, cross-spoke design and its livery, a blue frame along with white bodywork, was a nod to the GS800 racers of Lazslo Peres in the late 1970s, which had been the original inspiration for the G/S itself. A very limited number of 'Kalahari' large-tanked versions with a 35-litre Paris–Dakar fuel tank, were also made and sold exclusively in South Africa.

Although a capable performer both off- and on-road, the Basic was initially a sales flop due to it effectively being obsolete by then, thanks to BMW's own new oilhead R1100GS. However, when it became the last airhead to roll out of the Spandau plant, in December 1996, its significance was suddenly apparent and examples became hugely prized. Today, with only around 3,000 having been built, it is the most desirable and collectable of all late-era BMW airheads.

1993–2001 R1100RS: The 'Oilhead' Revolution Begins

The sports tourer R1100RS was the first of the new BMW four-valve boxer generation that spelled the end for the airheads. The all-new, oil- and air-cooled R259 engine, or 'oilhead' as it became known, was not merely a revision of the old engine but a completely new design. It had been conceived not only to compete with the large-capacity, multi-cylinder Japanese bikes in terms of performance, but also to show the world that BMW still believed in the boxer engine design, and that there was life in its signature unit yet.

The new engine had a capacity increase and the chain-driven camshafts were moved to the mid-head to allow the use of short rockers to actuate the valves and extend the power range. Fuel injection now featured, along with the latest digital engine electronics to ensure the new boxer also complied with ever-tightening emissions restrictions. An oil-cooler regulated the temperature of the four-valve heads, while the cylinders remained air-cooled. Its 1085cc capacity yielded output of 66kW or 90bhp.

There were plenty of advances elsewhere, too. One special feature was the ergonomic package, which enabled the motorcycle to be adapted individually to the rider. The fairing and handlebars were adjustable and the split seat could be raised or lowered, too – features that have remained on virtually every new BMW since. Even more revolutionary was the R1100RS's new Telelever front suspension system, which

1993's R1100RS oilhead spelled the end of the road for the old airhead series.

With 90bhp from its 1085cc, more regulated temperatures and fuel injection, the new engine became the basis for a whole new dynasty of BMW boxers.

dispensed with the traditional forks used since the late 1960s to again separate suspension and damping from the steering.

Over the years that followed, this new engine and motorcycle concept was carried over to all of BMW's boxer models, including new 850cc variants. The R1100GS and R1100R came in 1994, the smaller R850R in 1995, the R1100RT in 1996, along with the R850GS and sporty R1100S in 1998. In 1997, the BMW R1200C took to the road – and to the silver screen, when the brand's first cruiser was ridden by Pierce Brosnan in the James Bond film *Tomorrow Never Dies*. The derivatives of these bikes remain at the heart of BMW's line-up to this day.

1993–2001 BMW R1100RS

Price	DM 19,250
Engine	oil/air-cooled 4v dohc boxer twin
Capacity	1085cc
Output	90bhp @ 7,250rpm
Kerb weight	239kg
Top speed	215km/h
No. built	26,403

183

CHAPTER TEN

EPILOGUE

Did the 1990s see the definitive end of the airhead? Not quite... Although BMW's original two-valve boxer twin finally went out of production with the last R100GS Basic in December 1996, the airhead story is not over.

It is true that, for the next decade or so after production of the R100GS ended, BMW forged a different, more modern path. Its new F series singles, as introduced with the F650 'Funduro' in 1993, established themselves as BMW's affordable, entry-level machines. Today, now expanded into parallel twins, they live on as the Bavarian marque's mid-range offerings. The K multi-cylinder series, first launched as the K100 four in 1983, also survives, albeit in a very different form. Although its high-tech features proved controversial initially and it conspicuously failed to usurp BMW's big boxers as planned, the bikes evolved through the 1980s, 90s and noughties and ultimately achieved significant success. The series encompasses models as diverse as the K100RS sports tourer, K1300R roadster and K1300GT tourer. The latest and greatest today is the stupendous, six-cylinder K1600GTL full-dress tourer. There is simply nothing else like it.

BMW shocked the world again in the noughties by entering the superbike category, a class that the Japanese had come to call their own. BMW's first S1000RR, in 2009, revolutionized the sports-bike world. It was remarkable for its class-redefining power, producing 190bhp+ from an all-new transverse four-cylinder at a time when the best the Japanese could muster was 170–175. It was also distinguished by its class-leading electronic rider aids. It has been updated repeatedly since to become not just a true superbike class leader, but also a winner in world superbikes and at the TT. Not bad for a brand which had been so closely associated with somewhat 'old-fashioned' boxer twins...

Through all the changes, BMW Motorrad has continued by be characterized by boxer twins – but by a new generation of modernized four-valve models. First, there was the oilhead 259 powerplant as introduced in 1993, expanded to 1150cc form in 1999, then to 1200 in 2004. The latter was, in turn, usurped by an-all new, liquid-cooled 125bhp boxer engine from 2013. Today, the updated version of this engine powers five different models, including the best-selling GS and RT. The older, oil-cooled version, meanwhile, lives on, powering the whole family of R nineT 'heritage' machines.

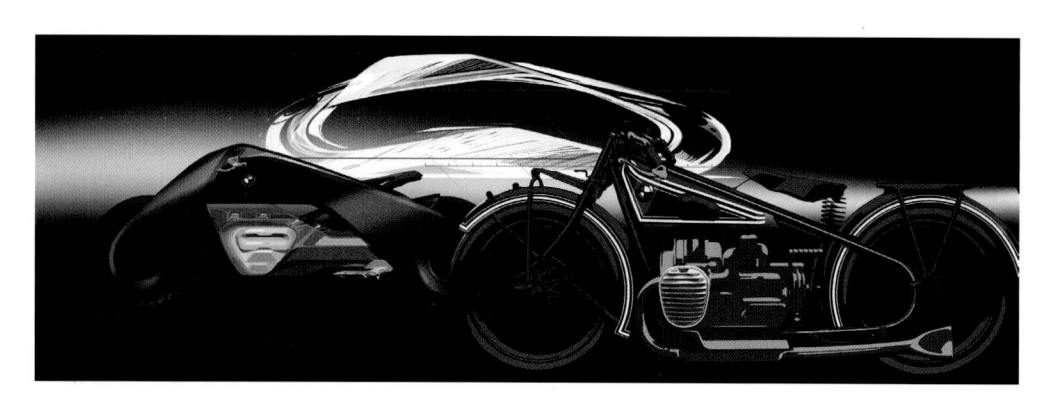

BMW has asserted repeatedly that the boxer layout will remain a key part of the marque's identity.

BMW has recognized more than most manufacturers the importance of its heritage, particularly in its Munich museum.

The participation of BMW's heritage machines at events such as the Goodwood Revival keeps them in the public eye.

Reg Pridmore's AMA-winning R90S has been seen taking part in the Goodwood Festival of Speed.

Ex-BMW racers such as Troy Corser help keep BMW's classic airheads on show.

REINTERPRETING THE BOXER HERITAGE

It is that growth of – and appreciation for – BMW's boxer heritage that helps retain the popularity of the airheads and makes it such an important influence over BMW's future. After the 'blip' of the initial K series in 1983, no one now knows that better – and exploits it more successfully – than BMW itself. Its extremely impressive museum in Munich presents the whole of the marque's boxer heritage, right back to the original R32. BMW is also one of motorcycling's most active manufacturers when it comes to heritage events. Its historic airheads, such as the R51/3, are regular attractions at major events such as the Goodwood Festival of Speed in the UK, where former racers such as Troy Corser can be seen demonstrating the bike up the famous Goodwood hill. At the late-summer sister event, the Goodwood Revival, some of BMW's great old airhead racers regularly take part in the Barry Sheene Memorial races.

Last but by no means least, BMW, alone among the leading motorcycle manufacturers, has an annual, free-to-enter rally for all things boxer. BMW's Motorrad Days, usually held over the first weekend in July in the picturesque Alpine town of Garmisch-Partenkirchen near the Austrian border, is a joyous, factory-sponsored festival that celebrates the past, present and future of the brand. It attracts airhead boxer fans in their thousands. There are historic and special bikes, visits and talks by BMW's greats (including, for example, the likes of the 'father of the GS' Laszlo Peres and Dakar racer Hubert Auriol), custom bikes, ride-outs, trade stalls galore, the opportunity to try out the latest boxers and, in true Bavarian style, a vast 'Oktoberfest-style' beer tent in which to eat, drink and sing the evening away.

The airhead continues to make its presence felt elsewhere, too. The rise, in recent years, of the retro scrambler and café racer customizing scene, as exemplified by the popularity of The Bike Shed in London's Shoreditch and of new magazines such as *Built*, has seen one bike more than any other become hugely popular with customizers: the BMW airhead. Once-unloved old /6 and /7 series machines from the 1970s and 80s have been snapped up, made over and given a whole new lease of life (although some 'reinterpretations' may make BMW purists squirm!). Custom shops such as Kevil's in the UK's West Country have made a name for themselves by creating virtually all-new airheads, which are bang on trend for the twenty-first century. And, inspired by customizer Roland Sands' 'R90' modern reinterpretation of the 1973 R90S built to mark 90 years of BMW Motorrad, the BMW factory has decided to get in on the act. Its current R nineT family, although strictly speaking based on the oilhead R1200R for practical reasons, is, in spirit at least, every inch a modern airhead custom.

The R nineT was originally intended as a limited edition commemorative machine, but proved so successful that it not only went into extended production, but has also spun off a whole family of heritage boxer variants. Its success in 2013 even encouraged BMW to build a special version, the

ABOVE: **BMW's Motorrad Days annual festival in Garmisch is an important event where classic BMWs are regularly seen.**

Some airhead owners modify or customize their bikes to suit the current retro fashion.

R nineT /5, in commemoration of one of the celebrated airhead boxers of all, the 1969 R75/5. In other words, today, if a customer wants the look of the classic /5 series airhead, but with the mechanicals and performance of a contemporary machine, they can have it.

BMW's modern re-creation of the airhead aura does not end there. It started in 2013 and has been gaining pace ever since, and an all-new, air-cooled boxer is once again on the cards. First came a special custom re-creation of the historic 1930s R5 – a hint that BMW were taking its boxer heritage seriously and that the idea of a new, classically styled boxer might be coming in the future. That bike was the R5 Hommage.

Then, even more excitingly, came the first whispers of an all-new, 1800cc flat twin set to be the heart of a

EPILOGUE

BMW has capitalized on the retro 'scrambler' scene by introducing its airhead-influenced R nineT model.

new BMW cruiser family, and built to take on the likes of Harley-Davidson in the lucrative US market. A series of three special custom machines, each using the new engine and each suggesting additional details about the forthcoming production machine, were revealed one by one. All had been commissioned by BMW themselves, who also supplied prototype examples of the new powerplant, built by specially selected custom houses in Japan, the USA and by BMW themselves.

If all that is not enough to confirm that the boxer layout has a bright future, even if the airhead specifically does not, the news in 2016 that BMW was developing an all-new, electric boxer for the motorcycling future beyond internal combustion engines, certainly does. The airhead BMW boxer is dead? Not by a long way…

2013 BMW CONCEPT NINETY: THE CATALYST FOR THE RETRO BOXER

In May 2013, to mark not just 90 years of BMW Motorrad but also 40 years since the iconic R90S, BMW unveiled a very special model at the Concorso d'Eleganza Villa d'Este 2013. This was the BMW Concept Ninety.

Back in 1973, the R90S was unveiled by BMW as the flagship model of its new /6 series range. Boasting a top speed of just over 200km/h (124mph), the R90S was one of the fastest production bikes of its day and went on to claim numerous prizes in a variety of race series.

But it was much more than that. It was the world's first production motorcycle to feature a front fairing as standard. This, together with a sporty tail end and striking Daytona Orange paintwork, meant that, even when parked, the R90S exuded a powerful aura like no other. The 'poster bike' was born, and it was not long before other manufacturers were gracing their own motorcycles with aerodynamically honed front and rear fairings. Today, this erstwhile trendsetter is one of BMW's true motorcycling icons.

According to Edgar Heinrich, head of design at BMW Motorrad, at the Concept Ninety's, 'The BMW R90S hails from an era in which bikers were regarded as outlaws. There was something rebellious about it – it was fast, loud and wild. Pure emotion. And it has retained its fascination to this day.'

In partnership with American custom bike company Roland Sands Design, headed by former motorcycle racer Roland Sands, the Concept Ninety was built as a one-off

EPILOGUE

ABOVE LEFT: **The Concept Ninety was a one-off custom commissioned by BMW and built by Roland Sands.**

ABOVE RIGHT: **The inspiration for the Concept Ninety was the R90S of 1973, but the newer bike was based around a modern BMW powertrain and chassis.**

The Daytona Orange livery mimicked that of the 1973 bike.

homage to the R90S. The intention, according to BMW, was to 'resurrect that spirit of the emotionally charged superbike, translating the emotionality and inspiration of the earlier model into a contemporary guise', but the Concept Ninety did much more.

'Today, BMW motorcycles stand for perfection and function,' explained Ola Stenegard, head of vehicle design at BMW Motorrad, at the Concept Ninety's unveiling. 'That is what we have worked hard to achieve and something we are very proud of. But we want more than that. With the BMW Concept Ninety we want to show how reduced and pure an emotional BMW motorcycle can be.'

The Concept Ninety's bodywork was in hand-crafted aluminium. Its rich orange colour was a nod to the legendary

189

■ EPILOGUE

Daytona Orange of the R90S. Where halogen lighting had been cutting-edge on the R90S, the Concept Ninety featured the latest LED, yet it still honoured its ancestor with a round headlamp design. Below the bodywork sat the historic air-cooled flat twin boxer engine, actually that from the R1200R of the time, entirely in black with contrasting details.

At the end of that year, the production interpretation, the R nineT was unveiled. It did without the radical fairing and overt R90S references, presenting a more generic, retro airhead roadster look. It went on sale initially as a limited edition in early 2014, but its success was such that volume production took over and a whole R nineT family, later including a similarly faired Racer version, was created.

Concept Ninety creator Roland Sands later admitted that the base bike from which his machine was created was a pre-production R nineT prototype. But if the whole exercise, with hindsight, was something of a marketing ploy for the upcoming, airhead-reminiscent R nineT, even BMW could not have predicted how successful their 'airhead revival' would be. Today, the popularity of the R nineT series is second only to that of the GS enduro family.

2016 R5 HOMMAGE

On 20 May 2016, at the prestigious Concorso d'Eleganza Villa d'Este, BMW once again reminded the press and public how significant its historic airhead twins remained – and how significant an influence they were on its future direction – with the unveiling of the special R5 Hommage.

Eighty years earlier, the firm had first unveiled the original R5, a machine so advanced that it would influence motorcycle construction right through to the 1950s. Inspired by the 500cc factory racer of 1935, the R5 was one of the most ground-breaking sports bikes of the late 1930s, thanks to its lightweight construction. The R5 Hommage would be a special, factory-commissioned one-off, custom-built to mark the anniversary and honour the original. The intention was to take the essence of the original R5 airhead and to bring it into the modern era. The signs of BMW reinventing its airhead boxer twin legacy were evident again.

Edgar Heinrich, head of design at BMW Motorrad, spoke at the unveiling of the R5 Hommage: 'At its debut, the R5 was not only a masterpiece of engineering; the clarity of its lines and the elegance of its proportions also made it stand out clearly from the masses. To this day, the R5 remains one of the most aesthetically appealing motorcycles in BMW history in my view.'

'In my opinion, its fascinating and unique beauty lies in its sheer simplicity,' added Ola Stenegard, head of vehicle design and creative director of heritage at BMW Motorrad. 'In today's world it is very simple to keep it complicated, but very complicated to keep it simple. And the BMW R5 captures the very essence of a motorcycle. Our aim was to

The R5 Hommage was a custom specially commissioned by **BMW** to commemorate the original 1930s R5.

EPILOGUE

The R5 Hommage was powered by an original R5 engine that had been recommissioned and repaired.

Modern brakes and wheels were used to encourage the public to ponder what a modern custom airhead boxer might look like...

transport its clarity and elegant aesthetic appeal to the modern era – creating a respectful combination of old-school and high-tech with a dash of high performance.'

At the core of the R5 Hommage was an original 500cc two-cylinder R5 engine, provided by motorcycle enthusiast Sebastian Gutsch. The rest of the bike was elaborately hand-crafted from scratch. Specialist custom-builders Ronny and Benny Noren were called upon to produce the parts according to specifications set out by BMW Motorrad's own design team. Having built custom machines, including boxers,

191

EPILOGUE

for more than 30 years the two brothers were the perfect choice.

The original R5's twin-cylinder four-stroke boxer engine was a completely clean-sheet design at the time, resulting in a peak power output of 24bhp at 5,500rpm. The valve drive was taken care of by two camshafts driven by a timing chain. Thanks in part to a similarly all-new frame made of electrically welded oval-section steel tubing, the lightweight R5 reached a top speed of 135km/h, making it almost as fast as BMW's 750cc, 33bhp R17 of the time. Maybe that is why the R5 quickly became so popular with racers.

As the donor engine for the Hommage bike had been slightly damaged by racing, a number of components, such as the valve cover and the breastplate of the boxer engine, had to be newly machined from billet aluminium. This also helped give the historic engine a dash of modern flair. Ronny and Benny Noren proved the perfect partners for the project, especially when it came to creating a fitting external appearance for the new bike and producing the missing parts required for the engine and gearbox. The new parts gradually took shape in the Noren brothers' workshop, based again on sketches by the BMW Motorrad design team. As such, the Hommage was a genuine custom bike, with a frame, fuel tank and rear mudguard that are unique, bespoke, hand-crafted components. Most important of all, the newly fashioned parts were a successful translation of the original R5 to the modern day.

The overall result was impressive. Even from a distance the proportions conveyed the timeless beauty of the pure, minimalist, original R5 and reinterpreted them for the modern age. The frame and fuel tank echoed the elegant teardrop shape of the original, although in a more modern, streamlined interpretation. One example was the steering head angle, which was more extreme, to give the R5 Hommage a longer, more substantial profile, while at the same time underlining the fact that this machine was aimed at the custom world. On the frame, the focus was on the oval-shaped tubes, which had been such a striking feature of the original. Together, the frame and fuel tank drew a continuous line from the steering head to the rear wheel hub, giving the bike's profile a touch of elegance, while the hand-formed steel rear mudguard perpetuated the minimalistic look.

One particular defining feature relating to the appearance of the original R5 was the telescopic fork – new at the time – which had characteristic covers that were aerodynamically shaped at headlamp level. The R5 Hommage reinterpreted this element in a modern style based on a production fork.

The leading edge of the fork covers echoed the 'crease' on the breastplate and valve covers with an interpretation of the 'R5 rib'. Meanwhile, its brake and clutch levers were operated from the bar-ends, as on the original – again, old and new were blended.

The essence of the original R5 was also evoked by the minimalist proportions of the Hommage – but again with significant changes. Although based on that of an original R5, the engine was substantially updated, with a specially developed supercharger, which in turn hinted at BMW's world-beating 255 Kompressor of the same era, and which significantly boosted the 26bhp output of the original R5 to more acceptable modern levels. In addition, a completely new, stainless steel exhaust ensured this increase in power was appropriately reflected in terms of noise. Modern motorcycle engineering also made its presence felt in the rear suspension system, in the latest disc brakes and in the intricately fabricated wheel hubs front and rear, with the one at the back also combing the rear brake and spoke housing in a single unit. It was a clever detail that again reflected the minimalistic approach of the original R5.

Finally, the R5 Hommage's livery was carefully chosen to reflect its classic, airhead roots. The basic theme, of course, was classic, old-school BMW black with white pinstripes, slightly tweaked of course to suit the Hommage bike's more contemporary style. In addition to the opaquely finished surfaces, the 'smoke' finish on the fuel tank and rear mudguard was designed to allow the steel underneath to show through. In addition to the white pinstripes, the black finish on the fuel tank and rear mudguard also came into its own, in true custom style, thanks to a metallic finish with a slight flake effect.

Meanwhile, the engine cases and gearbox, finished in bead-blasted aluminium, provided the perfect background for the new polished aluminium components such as the machined breastplate and valve covers with their R5-style 'crease'. The soft lustre of the polished aluminium was especially reminiscent of the original R5, while the overall image was rounded off with a hand-stitched leather seat with high-quality embossing.

2016: A VISION OF A BOXER FUTURE

If 2016 was marked by BMW Motorrad looking back into its past to create a contemporary interpretation of one of the

EPILOGUE

ABOVE: **As part of its centenary celebrations, BMW's Vision Next 100 project examined what future BMW boxers might look like.**

This concept motorcycle may be an advanced electric-powered machine but its air-cooled boxer influence is clear.

classic airhead boxers, it was also significant for the 100th anniversary of the foundation of BMW, as the company looked at what a BMW boxer bike might be in the future.

Nor was it all about bikes. Modern BMW is, of course, much, much more than 'just' an aero engine and motorcycle company.

To mark its centenary year, the firm presented the first fruit of an ambitious project to explore its future across all its brands: BMW cars, Rolls-Royce, MINI and, of course, BMW Motorrad.

Called 'Vision Next 100', the culmination of the motor-cycle project was presented to the world's press in Los

193

■ EPILOGUE

'Look, no hands' (or stands). Clever gyroscopes kept the concept machine upright.

Angeles on 11 October 2016. Not only was it a startling vision of the future, but it was also a striking reinterpretation of BMW Motorrad's past. It was the boxer reborn.

Edgar Heinrich, head of design at BMW Motorrad, outlined the core principles underlying his brand's Vision Vehicle: 'The BMW Motorrad Vision Next 100 embodies the BMW Group's vision of biking in a connected world – an analogue experience in a digital age. Motorcycling is about escaping from the everyday: the moment you straddle your bike, you are absolutely free. Your bike is The Great Escape.'

Vision Next 100 stood for the ultimate riding experience, Heinrich continued. Liberated from the need to wear a helmet and protective clothing, as the motorcycle was effectively uncrashable, the rider would be able to enjoy to the full the sensations of motorcycling – acceleration, and the effects of the elements – and to savour every moment.

Inevitably, the technical details and concepts required to deliver that experience were vague, but two things stood out: First, once the futuristic and silent concept machine, no doubt electric-powered, had been ridden into the auditorium and then parked by its helmetless, female rider, it stood up unaided. It seemed to confound the laws of physics by needing no side or centre stand. Sophisticated gyroscopes are thought to have been behind it.

The second aspect was perhaps even more striking. While the 'future bike' revealed no specifics, no details about its powertrain, no hint of what technology may be being used or considered, one aspect was unmissable: its silhouette was that of a traditional BMW boxer.

AN ALL-NEW AIR-COOLED BOXER?

Clearly, the likes of the Concept Ninety, R5 Hommage and Vision Next 100 machines tipped more than a nod at the significance and themes of the historic BMW airhead boxers of the past. However, there was no tangible sign from BMW that a genuine, new, production airhead boxer might ever be built again – at least not until late 2018.

On 6 December of that year, Japanese motorcycle customizer Custom Works Zon unveiled an all-new custom bike. There was nothing much new in that, one might think, except that the announcement was made by BMW themselves and the bike was powered by a prototype of an all-new, air-cooled BMW boxer engine. The airhead was back – or at least, as onlookers soon found out, it was on its way fairly soon.

Founded by Yuichi Yoshizawa and Yoshikazu Ueda in Shiga, Japan in 2003, Custom Works Zon has gained a reputation for its exceptional creations. It is a small workshop, but it has won innumerable prizes and awards over the years, clearly reflecting its skill, craftsmanship and distinctive style.

ABOVE: **Rumours that an all-new, air-cooled boxer was in the works were first confirmed by this specially commissioned custom.**

Built by Japanese specialists Custom Works Zon, 'The Departed' was based around a prototype of the new 1800cc boxer engine supplied by BMW themselves.

EPILOGUE

The new custom bike, called 'The Departed', was presented at the 2018 Hot Rod Custom Show in Yokohama, Japan. Commissioned by BMW Motorrad, it had at its core a prototype of a completely new boxer engine, supplied by BMW themselves. Yoshizawa was thrilled to collaborate with BMW Motorrad: 'It was a great honour and a challenge to be able to build a motorcycle around the prototype of such a spectacular new boxer engine for one of the most tradition-steeped manufacturers.'

Naturally, the appearance of the new BMW prototype boxer led to a huge amount of speculation about its exact form, layout, performance and ultimate likely use. The external geometry and visible elements, such as the push-rods running above the cylinders in chrome-plated protection ducts, harked back to BMW boxer engines that were built until the late 1960s – but with an obviously larger capacity and a modern air/oil cooling system. BMW, however, refused to comment, saying only that further details about the engine and its possible future use would be communicated at a later point in time.

The design of Zon's bike, meanwhile, was also of great interest. It offered classic styling, modern production techniques and a wealth of craftsmanship, and it was produced to the highest Japanese standards. The low silhouette of the bike was reminiscent of Ernst Henne's record-breaking machines of the late 1920s and 30s. The large, 21-inch front and 26-inch rear wheels were milled from solid aluminium and fitted with relatively narrow tyres, while the girder fork was also made of solid aluminium.

Elsewhere, the rear swing arm was made of steel tubing and attached to the tubular space frame by means of a hidden suspension unit. Meanwhile, the fuel tank, seat unit and front trim were all crafted by hand from sheet metal.

Perhaps unsurprisingly, the bike, and the reaction it created, led to 'The Departed' earning the prestigious 'Best of Show Motorcycle' at the Hot Rod Custom Show. But that was only the start of the rumours about BMW's upcoming new airhead…

THE 'REVIVAL BIRDCAGE'

The rumours of an all-new BMW airhead boxer were given further fuel less than six months after the unveiling of 'The Departed' when, in April the following year, another specially commissioned custom bike using the all-new prototype BMW boxer engine was unveiled – this time in the USA.

On 11 April 2019, American customizers Revival Cycles unveiled their latest creation in a move reminiscent of the previous unveiling. It was simultaneously announced by BMW themselves, at an exclusive Revival Party on the eve of the annual Handbuilt Show in Austin, Texas, immediately prior to the MotoGP at the nearby Circuit of the Americas.

This bike was name the 'Revival Birdcage' and, as before, was based on the prototype of a completely new type of BMW boxer engine.

'The "Revival Birdcage" turned out great and really showcases our Big Boxer perfectly,' said Timo Resch, Vice President Sales and Marketing BMW Motorrad. 'Following "The Departed" from Custom Works Zon, this is the second fascinating custom bike built around the prototype of the BMW Motorrad Big Boxer. We will also be showing a BMW Motorrad developed concept bike featuring this engine in the first half-year of 2019. BMW Motorrad will present a series production motorcycle with the Big Boxer for the Cruiser segment in the course of 2020.'

To say it was exciting news for boxer fans is an understatement. In addition, BMW had now formally confirmed that a new big 'air-cooled' boxer (strictly speaking, it is both air- and oil-cooled) was on the way, would be used in an all-new cruiser and would be presented in 2020.

'We admire the work done by Revival, who have developed into one of the most noteworthy US customizers in the custom scene over the last years,' continued Timo Resch at the show. 'Naturally we want to keep growing. One step we will take to do so, certainly in the US market, is to enter the cruiser segment. BMW Motorrad is consistently pursuing its growth strategy with the clear aim of becoming the number one in the Premium Big Bike Segment.'

The frame of the 'Revival Birdcage' was made of titanium and developed by Revival Cycles. 'This was our first time to build a frame with titanium, that alone was already a significant challenge,' said Alan Stulberg, head of Revival Cycles. 'Regardless, the frame came together very well in the end and we are very pleased with the result as it accomplished the goal of being nearly transparent. We wanted to focus attention on the engine and that is precisely what we achieved with this completely unique frame we designed. You can easily view the engine and the drivetrain from all angles.'

Almost every single other part on the bike, such as handlebars, footrests, shift lever, seat and unique carbon suspension components, was individually crafted, too.

Again, as with 'The Departed', Stulberg's team was inspired by Ernst Hennes' record-setting machines from the late

Another, similar custom machine was also built around the prototype engine by US customizers Revival Cycles.

BELOW: **Called the 'Revival Birdcage', Revival Cycles' one-off bike gave the best views yet of the forthcoming new airhead.**

1920s and early 30s. It took around six months to develop the result. 'We had already dreamed about this bike for years and in December 2018 we received the engine and could finally get to work,' he said. 'I've always been a fan of the boxer engine, but the pure physical size and aesthetic appeal of this prototype really inspired us.'

The finished bike was completed in just five months. But once again, more was still to come…

'CONCEPT 18'

BMW used the opportunity of the prestigious Concorso d'Eleganza Villa d'Este on 24 May 2018, on the banks of Lake Como in Italy, to unveil the most striking manifestation yet of its forthcoming, all-new, air-/oil-cooled boxer twin airhead.

Called 'Concept R18', it was another all-new one-off, following in the footsteps of Custom Works Zon's 'The Departed' and Revival Cycles' 'Birdcage', to be powered by BMW's much-discussed all-new engine. The difference this time was that it was designed by BMW themselves and was clearly nearer to any upcoming production model than ever before. The idea, according to BMW, was to 'transport the essence of the big BMW Motorrad classics into the modern age', or in other words, to take a historical motorcycle design and give it a modern, custom attitude.

But the best glimpse of the new 1800cc airhead cruiser came from BMW themselves in mid-2019.

The Concept R18 was a finished one-off styled by **BMW** themselves, with influences from the past…

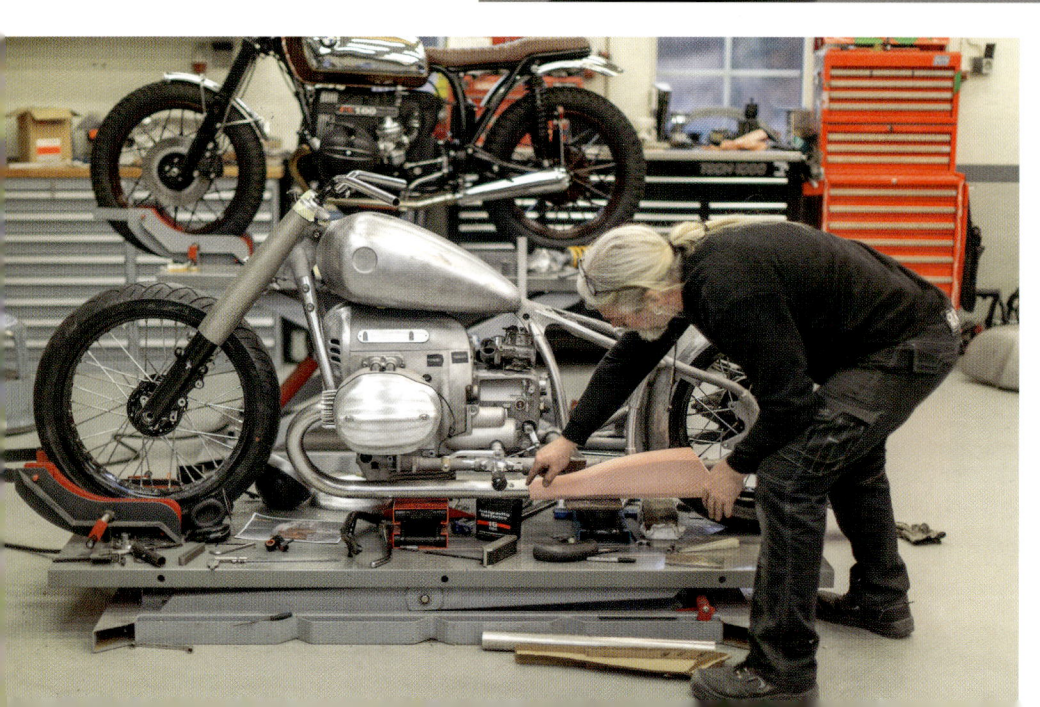

… and built by **BMW**, too. As for the final production bike, everyone is currently still waiting to see…

Dr Markus Schramm, head of BMW Motorrad, introduced the concept: 'With this dream bike, BMW Motorrad presents its own version of an emotional and authentic offer for the large cruiser segment.'

Edgar Heinrich, head of BMW Motorrad Design, added: 'With its clear aesthetics openly on display, the Concept R18 embodies for me what motorcycling, at its core, is really about. It is all about feeling instead of thinking, and not using technology for self-staging, instead giving space for imagination. This concept bike appeals to something deep down – you just want to just get on it and ride off. But when you get off it again, you don't just put it in the garage and walk away – you turn around again and give it a final parting glance.'

As before, the heart of the concept machine was a large, newly designed, two-cylinder 1800cc boxer engine – but this time it seemed to be in an even more finished state than before. According to BMW, its outward appearance was designed to be reminiscent of the flat twin engines that BMW Motorrad had built until the end of the 1960s, but with a considerably bigger displacement and modern air/oil cooling.

The overall bike was also obviously designed down to the last detail: the engine block and transmission were made of bead-blasted aluminium, providing an ideal stage on which to present the hand-polished aluminium components, as well as the belt guard and valve covers. The engine badge bore the name of the concept bike and emphasized its overall quality. In addition, Solex dual carburettors – similar to those used in the BMW 2002 car – harked back to the brand's history and added an extra touch of authenticity.

'The biggest challenge in the design is to render everything visible. Every part has a functional purpose. There are not many who would dare to take such an absolutely honest approach,' said Bart Janssen Groesbeek, designer of the Concept bike.

Another highlight was the exposed, chrome-plated universal shaft that connected the rear wheel to its drive. There were no further covers anywhere on the bike, so that its engineering remained clearly visible. Similarly, the electronics were reduced to no more than a starter and lights, underlining the purity of its design.

As for its colour scheme, like the earlier R5 Hommage, the Concept R18 used the typical, classic BMW colour scheme of white, with hand-applied pinstripes on the forks and fuel tank, in combination with a black base colour. A discreet yellow-gold varnish effect gave the bright twin lines an exclusive touch, and the black effect paintwork on the tank and fork rods revealed, in the best custom style, an unusual depth when the sunlight struck the large metallic particles in the various layers of the paintwork.

Similarly, the design of the embossed leather seat was borrowed from the classics of the 1950s. Reinterpreted and somewhat more comfortable, its style sat perfectly within the overall design. The cantilever monoshock, meanwhile, was integrated beneath the seat. The graphics of the headlamp were also reminiscent of the 1950s, with the classic U shape of the original glass cover interpreted as LED lamp elements.

Every one of these details hinted at the possible style and look of the upcoming new 1800cc airhead, in merging traditional and historic design into a newly coherent whole.

'For me, motorcycles like the Concept R18 are a response to a growing need among the motorcycling community,' continued Edgar Heinrich. 'Instead of technology, the focus here is on simplification, authenticity and transparency. I observe an almost romantic yearning for real mechanical engineering. Our aim with this concept bike is to address this need and turn it into an analogue statement in a digital age. We have a rich history of iconic motorcycles, and they all bear the same design characteristics. We believe that this can still work well together today with the current technology.'

Roll on the new 1800…

WHAT NEXT?

While the impending arrival of an all-new airhead boxer in 2020 is great news for boxer fans, there is also a growing realization that conventional, internal combustion boxer twins cannot go on for ever, and that electric-powered motorcycles are the future. BMW seems to have this covered, too. In 2016, BMW had presented its mysterious Vision Next 100 electric concept machine, complete with boxer profile. Three years later, in June 2019, BMW reaffirmed in a press statement how important the boxer layout was for any future BMW motorcycle – electric or otherwise: 'As we consistently pursue electrification, the question arises as to what a BMW motorcycle might look like that is electrically powered? And how would it reveal itself at first sight to be a BMW? One possible answer to these questions is provided by the BMW Motorrad Vision DC Roadster, a highly emotional naked bike with electric drive.'

Even if the future is electric, BMW seems determined to retain the style and architecture of its classic airhead twins.

ABOVE: **Another recent concept, the 'Vision DC Roadster' is an electric concept machine that explores how BMW might retain its heritage airhead style.**

Yes, it is modern and futuristic, but it is also a classic **BMW** airhead boxer...

EPILOGUE

Edgar Heinrich, head of design at BMW Motorrad, explained the thinking behind the project: 'The boxer engine is the heart of BMW Motorrad – an absolute stalwart of its character. But BMW Motorrad stands for visionary zero-emissions vehicle concepts, too. In view of this, one question that arises is: what would happen if we were to replace the boxer engine with an electric motor and the required battery? The Vision Bike shows how we're able to retain the identity and iconic appearance of BMW Motorrad in distinctive form while at the same time presenting an exciting new type of riding pleasure. After all, anyone who's ever tried it out in practice knows very well that riding on two wheels is just as exciting when it's electrically powered! The high level of torque right at set-off makes for breath-taking acceleration. This almost brutal power delivery creates a whole new experience of dynamic performance. And the BMW Motorrad Vision DC Roadster puts a face to this experience.'

Everyone knows that, on a motorcycle, more than on any other vehicle, the engine is the centrepiece. It is the fundamental element that provides the basis for the entire architecture. When it comes to electric motors and drivetrains, the components and therefore packaging are completely different. Where a conventional internal combustion engine is characterized by its swept capacity and the number and arrangement of its cylinders, with an electrically powered vehicle it is the battery that dictates most of the drivetrain's shape and size. The electric motor itself is comparatively small.

The solution to this was at the heart of the BMW's Vision DC Roadster – retaining the iconic appearance of a boxer while filling it with a new function. As a result, the Vision is still instantly recognizable as a BMW motorcycle, only revealing its electric nature on closer inspection. In place of what previously would have been the engine, there is now a vertically fitted, longitudinally orientated battery. Protruding from each side of this are two elements, which mimic the profile of the old boxer twin and, in serving a cooling function, are designed with cooling ribs and integrated ventilators. As in the boxer engine of the original R32, the cooling elements are placed in the air stream.

The electric motor itself, meanwhile, is cylinder-shaped and located underneath the battery unit to form a direct connection with the shaft drive, again in the style of the airhead boxer. In this way, the Vision DC roadster adheres to the signature engine architecture that was largely maintained throughout the history of BMW Motorrad, while at the same time taking it a step further.

On top of that, in side view, the Vision DC Roadster presents a dramatic profile with a low front section and short, high rear, intended to convey a sense of agility. In place of the fuel tank, a flat, finely wrought tubular structure now spans the bike's top, then integrates the seat.

The large battery with its laterally protruding cooling systems is positioned at the centre of a frame, which is milled from aluminium. And the protruding cooling elements are also given a slight forward tilt, to echo that of the battery. When starting the electric motor, these cooling elements apparently move out slightly, indicating that the bike is ready to go.

Overall, according to BMW, the appearance of the Vision DC is designed to convey a sense of lightness so as to emphasize driving dynamics. Elements such as the seat and cooling system appear to hover around the battery. On the frame, milled grooves reduce the perceived bulk and highlight the bike's longitudinal dynamics. Materials such as carbon fibre and aluminium reduce overall weight and give the Vision DC roadster a technical appeal.

Ultimately, the Vision DC Roadster is a fantasy, a concept that may never become a reality, but it is reassuring to see that, even when it begins to explore alternative drive forms, BMW still chooses to create a new, distinctive aesthetic that is firmly rooted in its airhead past.

KEY MODEL: 2019 R NINET /5

A classic, remembered

For fans of the airhead who needed a truly modern machine, BMW came to the rescue in 2019, with a new addition to its classic, heritage R nineT family, the R nineT /5. It was a model created to mark the 50th anniversary of the /5 series and 50 years of BMW Motorrad production in Berlin Spandau.

Many of those who got their first taste of two wheels in the late 1960s and early 1970s have vivid memories of the innovative /5 series, which was first launched in 1969 – especially the top-of-the-range R75/5. For others, the R75/5 was a dream bike from their youth. For BMW, the new R nineT /5 was intended to bring that era back to life, drawing on some of the stylistic elements of the historic model to create a distinctive modern machine with plenty of nostalgic flair.

One of BMW's latest production roadsters, the R nineT /5 has also been styled to resemble the old airheads.

An R nineT with extra styling touches, the R nineT /5 was inspired by the classic 1969 R75/5 and built as a limited edition to mark its 50th anniversary.

ABOVE: **Those extra styling touches include blue paint, wire wheels, fork gaiters and rubber knee pads…**

… **and a special '50 Years of /5 Series' badge affixed to the tank.**

EPILOGUE

The new bike featured period knee pads, as well as a body finish in Lupine Blue metallic with smoke effect and double pinstripes on the fuel tank, which bore a special anniversary emblem. Its chromed mirrors and exhaust manifold harked back to the historic /5 series, as did its double seat, which was contoured in the style of the /5 with cross-embossing applied to the seat cover itself and the pillion grab strap. The white piping and rubber gaiters on the telescopic forks were also a nod to the original. Meanwhile, the finish of the engine, gearbox, fork slider tubes, wheel hubs and spokes in Aluminium Silver evoked the legendary /5, as did the black-finished components such as the frame and the shaft drive housing. An appropriate nod to the past was provided by the steel shell of the headlamp, which was also finished in black, just like that of its historic forebear.

It might not be a true airhead but, until the arrival of the eagerly anticipated all-new R18 in 2020, it is the closest brand-new version that is available to buy.

2019 R nineT /5

Engine
Type	BMW oil/air-cooled boxer twin
Internal code	N/A
Block material	Aluminium
Head material	Aluminium
Bore and stroke	101 × 73mm
Capacity	1170cc
Valves	DOHC, 4 valves per cylinder
Compression ratio	12.0:1
Carburettor	Bosch fuel injection
Max. power (DIN)	110hp @ 7,550rpm
Max. torque	85.6lb ft @ 6,000rpm
Fuel capacity	3.7gall (18ltr)

Transmission
Gearbox	6-speed, manual
Clutch	Single dry plate
Final drive	Shaft

Chassis
Frame	Tubular steel space frame
Front suspension	46mm inverted telescopic forks
Rear suspension	Swing arm, Paralever single shock

Tyres	120/70 ZR17 front, 18055 ZR17 rear
Wheels	Cross spoke
Rim width	N/A

Brakes
Type	Front. twin 320mm disc, rear 265mm disc

Dimensions
Wheelbase	59.9in 1520mm
Overall length	83.1in 2110mm
Overall width	35.4in 900mm
Overall height	48.8in 1240mm
Unladen weight	485lb 220kg

Performance
Top speed	N/A
0–60mph	N/A

Price	N/A
No. built	N/A

APPENDIX

AIRHEAD PRODUCTION NUMBERS

Model	Period	Units made	Model	Period	Units made
R32	1923–1926	3,090	R60/5	1969–1973	22,721
R37	1925–1926	152	R75/5	1969–1973	38,370
R39	1925–1927	855	R60/6	1973–1976	13,511
R42	1926–1928	6,502	R75/6	1973–1976	17,587
R47	1927–1928	1,720	R90/6	1973–1976	21,097
R52	1928–1929	4,377	R90S	1973–1976	17,465
R57	1928–1930	1,005	R60/7	1976–1982	11,163
R62	1928–1929	4,355	R75/7	1976–1979	6,264
R63	1928–1929	794	R100/7	1976–1980	12,056
R11	1929–1934	7,500	R100S	1976–1980	11,762
R16	1929–1934	1,006	R100RS	1976–1984	33,648
R12	1935–1942	36,008	R80/7	1977–1984	18,522
R17	1935–1937	434	R65	1978–1985	57,612
R7	1935	1	R100RT	1978–1984	18,015
R5	1936–1937	2,652	R100T	1978–1980	5,463
R6	1937–1937	1,850	R100	1980–1984	10,111
R51	1938–1940	3,775	R100CS	1980–1984	4,038
R61	1938–1941	3,747	R80G/S	1980–1987	21,864
R66	1938–1941	1,669	R65LS	1981–1985	6,389
R71	1938–1941	3,458	R80ST	1982–1984	5,963
R51/2	1950–1951	5,000	R80RT	1982–1984	7,315
R51/3	1951–1954	18,420	R80	1984–1995	13,815
R67	1951	1,470	R80RT Mono	1984–1995	22,069
R67/2	1952–1954	4,234	R65 Mono	1985–1993	8,260
R68	1952–1954	1,452	R100RS Mono	1986–1992	6,081
R67/3	1955–1956	700	R65GS	1987–1992	1,727
R50	1955–1960	13,510	R80GS	1987–1996	11,375
R60	1956–1960	3,530	R100GS	1987–1996	34,007
R69	1955–1960	2,956	R100RT Mono	1987–1995	9,738
R50/2	1960–1969	19,036	R80R	1991–1994	3,593
R50S	1960–1962	1,634	R100R	1991–1995	20,589
R60/2	1960–1969	17,306	R100R Mystic	1993–1995	3,700
R69S	1960–1969	11,317	R80GS Basic	1996	3,003
R50/5	1969–1973	7,865			

Index

AMA superbikes 128
Adler 96
Auriol, Hubert 166–169, 186
Auspitzer, Julius 12, 14
Austin Seven 36, 37

BMW
  /5 series 110–112
  /6 series 122, 124–125
  /7 series 129, 136
  Concept Ninety 188–190
  F650 178
  K series 145, 155, 173, 174, 184
  K100 171–172
  Kompressor 9, 48, 49, 57, 63, 64, 65, 66, 67, 70, 91, 102
  R nineT 186, 188
  R nineT /5 201–204
  R100CS 153
  R100GS 160–163, 173, 184
  R100GS Paris–Dakar 164, 173
  R100R 174–175
  R100R Classic 179
  R100R Mystic 178
  R100RS 126, 129–132, 134–136, 142, 144, 159, 160, 173
  R100RS 9
  R100RT 138, 142, 159
  R100RT Classic 179
  R100T 138–139
  R11 30, 36, 45, 46, 47, 48, 53, 54
  R1100GS 177, 180
  R1100RS 177, 182–183
  R1100RT 177
  R12 53, 54, 56, 58, 59, 60, 71, 73, 74, 76
  R16 30, 34, 36, 45, 46, 47, 48, 53, 74
  R17 53, 54, 56, 71, 74
  R2 48

R23 71, 81, 88
R24 81–83, 84–86, 88
R26 95, 106
R27 106
R32 9, 14, 19, 20, 23, 24, 25, 26, 27, 28, 29, 30, 37, 39, 40, 48, 53, 122, 186
R35 81
R37 30, 31, 35, 37, 38, 40, 41
R39 36, 37
R39 72
R4 48, 76
R42 30, 31, 32, 39, 40
R45 136–137, 143, 144, 152, 159
R47 32, 35, 40, 42
R5 48, 53, 55, 56, 60, 61, 62, 64, 71, 88, 187
R5 Hommage 190–192
R50 95, 96, 104–105
R50/2 105, 106
R50/60/69US 110
R50S 106
R51 9, 55, 56, 61, 70, 76, 88
R51 SS & RS 55, 57
R51/2 88, 89
R51/3 88, 89, 97–100, 186
R52 30, 31, 33, 35, 41, 43
R57 35, 42, 44
R6 55, 71, 75
R60 95
R60/2 106–107
R60/5 117–119
R61 55, 71
R61 71
R62 35, 43, 45
R63 33, 34
R63 35, 44
R65 136–137, 143, 152, 159
R65GS 164

206

INDEX

R65LS 153, 155, 159, 169–170
R66 55, 71, 72, 75
R67 88, 89, 90, 97
R67/2 90
R67/3 95
R68 54, 74
R68 90, 98–102
R69 9, 95
R69S 10
R69S 106, 108, 110, 114–116
R7 48, 49, 50, 51, 52, 53, 56
R71 55, 71, 76
R75 9, 54, 76–77, 78–80, 81
R75/5 119–121, 187
R80/7 133
R80G/S 144–152, 154, 157
R80G/S 9, 10
R80GS 160–162, 173
R80GS Basic 179–180, 181–182, 184
R80R 175–176
R80RT 155, 157
R80RT Monolever 158–159
R80ST 154, 155, 157, 174
R90S 9, 10, 122, 124–126, 127–129, 139–141, 144, 188, 190
RS54 91, 92–94, 102–104
Vision DC Roadster 199–201
WR750 35, 65
Barter, Joseph 8
Bayerische Flugzeugwerke 13, 15, 19, 20, 22
Benz, Karl 7, 8
Bleriot, Louis 12
Boning, Alfred 49, 50, 51, 52, 53, 102

Castiglioni, Camillo 15, 19, 20, 21, 22
Concept 18 197–199
Corser, Troy 186
Cron, Fritz 92
Custom Works Zon 194–195
Cycle World 109

DKW 96
Dahne, Helmut 127, 129
Dale, Dickie 91
Diemer, Franz-Zeno 18
Douglas motorcycles 8, 19, 23
Ducati 7

Eisenach 22, 36, 37, 81, 84
Enders, Klaus 91

Falkenhausen, Alexander von 55, 71, 78, 111, 118
Flugwerk Deutschland 12
Friz, Max 7, 8, 9, 14, 15, 16, 18, 19, 20, 23, 27, 28, 30

Gerlinger, Karl Heinz 145
Goodwood Revival 185, 186

Harley-Davidson 7
Heinrich, Edgar 188, 190, 199
Helios motorcycles 19, 20, 23, 28
Henne, Ernst 30, 35, 65, 126
Horex 96

Isle of Man TT 65, 67–69
Ischinger, Leonard 52, 102

Kawasaki Z1 122
Knorr-Bemse 15, 19, 22
Krauser MKM1000 156–158

M2B15 engine 7, 9, 19, 20, 21, 23, 30
M2B33 engine 9, 24, 27
M2B36 engine 30
M43a engine 39
Marwitz, Hans-Gunther von der 118
Meier, Georg 57, 65, 67–69, 70, 71, 91
Messerschmitt 11, 80
Mini 11
Moto Guzzi 7
  V7 7
Motorrad magazine 148
Muth, Hans 153, 169–170

Nazi party 15, 63, 77
Noll, Wilhelm 92–94, 104

Oliver, Eric 92
Otto-Flugzeugwerke 13, 23
Otto, Gustav 12, 13, 15

Paris–Dakar Rally 164–169
Peres, Laszlo 145, 146, 186
Pininfarina 126, 134
Popp, Franz Josef 12, 14, 15, 17, 19, 23
Porsche, Ferdinand 52
Pridmore, Reg 128, 185

Quandt, Herbert 37, 96, 97, 106

Rahier, Gaston 166, 168–169

207

INDEX

Rapp, Karl Friedrich 12, 14, 15
Rapp Motorenwerke 12, 14, 15, 17
Revival Cycles 196–197
Rolls-Royce 11

Sands, Roland 188–190
Schek, Herbert 145, 166
Schleicher, Rudolf 23, 53, 63, 102, 118
Second World War 48, 49, 54, 73, 76–83, 87
Spandau factory 11, 112, 113, 173, 180
Stenegard, Ola 189–190
Stolle, Martin 7, 8, 19, 20

Treaty of Versailles 15, 18, 19

Triumph 7
  Speed Twin 7
  Bonneville 7
Type III/IIIa aero engine 18, 19, 30

Victoria motorcycles 19, 20, 22
Vision Next 100 193–194

West, Jock 65, 67, 68–69, 70
Wirth, Joseph 12
Wright brothers 12

Zeller, Walter 91
Zündapp 76, 80